SAINTS ALIVE!

BY THE SAME AUTHOR

Hodder & Stoughton Ltd

The Practice of Evangelism
Being and Believing

SAINTS ALIVE!

BRYAN GREEN

Rector of Birmingham
Canon of Birmingham Cathedral

LONDON
EPWORTH PRESS

FIRST PUBLISHED IN 1959
REPRINTED 1959

© THE EPWORTH PRESS 1959

Book Steward
FRANK H. CUMBERS

SET IN MONOTYPE IMPRINT AND PRINTED IN
GREAT BRITAIN BY BUTLER AND TANNER LTD
FROME AND LONDON

To
my daughter
JILL

Preface

THIS BOOK is intended for the ordinary man who wants to know something of what it means to be a Christian and to lead the Christian life. Thoughtful people have a right to be told what is implied in the demands of Christian discipleship before they are asked to make their surrender to Christ; not that anyone can possibly know all that it will mean before experiencing the new life that He gives. Young people in love, if they are wise, think out some of the implications of marriage before their wedding day, but they find, as many others have done, that afterwards they learn gradually how far-reaching are the full demands of love. Part of the tragedy of some broken marriages finds its origin precisely in this fact, that the couple never realized on what they were embarking. The all too common slackening off of zeal and loyalty of many Christians is frequently due to the same cause, that they did not understand enough about Christian discipleship before they entered into it.

The purpose of this book is in a modest fashion to seek to outline what it means to be a Christian in the world of today.

I do not know what is the experience of other writers on this subject. Mine has been an interesting one. To write about the Gospel and the glorious doctrine of justification by faith is a humbling experience; but it is humbling in quite a different way when one tries to write of Christian discipleship.

To speak of the Gospel, and to make plain the wonder of God's love which in Christ makes us sure that He takes us just as we are, accepts us sinners though we are, and unites us with Himself by His Spirit, is exhilarating. One is indeed humbled by the sense of one's own worthlessness, and the complete inadequacy of one's faith and gratitude in response to all that

He has done, and all that He is. Certainly it convicts of sin; yet there is also an undertone of confidence and of sharing in the triumph of the Gospel. We glory in Christ and the wonder of His redemption. Strangely we feel that in spite of what we are, we have a right, nay, an inescapable duty, to declare what we know, and to proclaim from the house-tops what Christ has done for us.

Writing about Christian discipleship and something of the meaning of Christian living also humbles us and convicts us of sin. We know how far short we fall of the ideals of the new life in Christ of which we write. There is, too, gratitude in our hearts that in any measure at all we have been able to live this life, but—and here is the difference—there is little sense that we must stand on the house-tops and proclaim the Christian life as we know it, or shout it aloud. We feel we represent our Master so poorly that we have little right to say anything very much about Christian living. It is a salutary experience, and I can only hope that what I have felt in this way comes out in what I have written.

My first thanks must be to my publishers, the Epworth Press. When they first approached me, an Anglican clergyman, with the invitation to write the Methodist Lent Book for 1959 I regarded this as a great privilege which I could not easily refuse. I am glad to say that from the time of my conversion fellowship with those of other Christian Churches has always been my happy experience. It would be invidious to make comparisons, but perhaps I may be permitted to say that I always find myself in a particularly congenial relationship with the Church of Scotland and with the Methodists. In the case of the latter is it because of the 'enthusiasm' against which Monsignor Ronald Knox warns us? Anyhow, I hope the form of this book will enable Methodists and others to find it suitable for devotional reading through the six weeks of Lent.

Another word of explanation is necessary. Having accepted the invitation to write this book I cast my material in the form of lectures. These have been delivered to members of the Parish Church at Gerrards Cross. I wish to thank them and their Vicar for their kindly hospitality, their thoughtful listening, and their all too generous appreciation. To me it was an inspiration to speak in the setting of a live, flourishing and spiritual Christian community.

Finally, I owe a debt of gratitude to friends of mine who have helped me in the writing of this book. To Bishop Stephen Neill, and to the late Canon B. K. Cunningham I am indebted for putting into my mind, more than twenty-five years ago, fruitful ideas which eventually have resulted in this book.

I am most grateful to three friends of mine who in the middle of their busy lives consented to read the manuscript, and whose suggestions and criticisms were most helpful and in many cases adopted. They are the Rev. Dr James Stewart, Professor of New College, Edinburgh; the Dean of Liverpool, the Very Rev. F. W. Dillistone; and Canon G. H. Hewitt, Education Secretary in the Diocese of Sheffield.

I wish also to thank the Community of St Julian's, near Horsham, for the truly holy and yet utterly joyful peace of their house in which, as with my first book, I had the privilege of staying while writing these chapters.

I close with an expression of thanks to my publishers for their help and courtesy, and as with my earlier book to my Secretary, Margery Northcott, for typing the book and preparing it for the Press.

BRYAN GREEN

The Rectory
Birmingham

Contents

CHAPTER I

Where real Christianity begins

IT WAS once said of a bishop: 'He is so heavenly minded that he is no earthly use.' Now, if our religion is so heavenly minded that it makes us no earthly use then one thing is quite clear; whatever it is, it is not the true religion of Jesus Christ, because the first thing that a careful reader notices when he picks up the New Testament is that Christianity is a religion for this world as well as for the next. If we are going to be Christians we have to be Christians in our own day and in our own generation. Christianity, therefore, cannot be just an other-worldly religion.

One of the happy changes that has come over the Churches during the last fifty years is a much more definite acceptance and a clearer understanding of what is implied by the social Gospel. It is a commonplace today to which we all pay at least lip service, that religion has something to do with *this* life and *this* world, as well as to do with *that* life and *that* world. Yet it is important to make the point, because there is still far too much emasculated and weak Christianity—a pietism which seems to suggest that we turn to Christ mainly in order to be right for heaven. True though it is that we need to be prepared to die and to face the hereafter, for the world after death, if real, most certainly matters, we must see that it is even more urgent to be right with God in the present in order to live our life today.

It is true that the Bible continually emphasizes—and many modern Christians continually forget—ideas such as 'your citizenship is in heaven'. Of course it does, and rightly, for here we are being pointed forward to our final goal, the goal to which the true Christian genuinely looks forward, not simply living for this life with its short three score years and ten, but to the fuller life beyond time and space. That is our final goal, that is where we really belong as Christians, because that is where God most fully is, and where Christ reigns. 'Where your treasure is, there will your heart be also.' If we really love God then this life with God should be the place where our treasure is, and on which our heart's desire is focused.

When, however, we accept the fact that true Christianity has much to do with this life here and now we are not accepting anything easy. It is not possible, though some people try to do it, to turn to the New Testament, examine the example and teaching of Christ, and then transfer what we see there straight from first-century Palestine to twentieth-century England. We cannot say: 'It was right and fitting then, so it is right and fitting now.' First-century Palestine was quite different from our twentieth-century world, and therefore it is not very easy to make our Christianity relevant to this day and age.

On the one hand, I always think it is a little naïve when anybody says: 'There is no argument. I can tell you how we ought to deal with the H-bomb (which is a twentieth-century phenomenon). Jesus said: "If anybody hits you on one cheek, turn the other." You can apply that straight away to the H-bomb. If anybody wants to drop an H-bomb on me, then I must take it, and if he wants to he can drop another one. I am not going to do anything to protect myself.'

Christian pacifism may or may not be right; but it cannot be rightly supported by this kind of argument. We cannot treat the New Testament and the teaching of Jesus in this fashion, and apply it to life today just like that.

On the other hand, there is an even greater danger, and that is to dismiss or water down the teaching of Jesus, and say it has nothing to do with life today. The basic principles of living that Jesus gave us, the spirit with which He lived, are as applicable today as they ever were. Our task, in order to make our Christianity relevant, is so to grasp with our own minds the spirit and mind of Jesus that we are able to bring them to bear on our life today. To try and see how that spirit and mind should work out in our own situations, that is the task before every real, thoughtful Christian.

I do not intend in these chapters to describe and analyse our twentieth-century situation; of such analyses we have far too many. There are, however, one or two aspects of our life today which need to be emphasized and recognized clearly before we can attempt to see how to live a positive Christian life. As the late William Temple said: 'Modern man does not suffer, generally speaking, from much sense of guilt and shame; he does, however, suffer tremendously from a sense of frustration and powerlessness.'

This is due, quite obviously, to the contradiction in which we find ourselves. On the one hand, the outstanding characteristic of our age is our scientific control of life, our amazing 'know-how' in the managing of material forces and in the direction of our mental powers. We have never been so clever.

Against this fact we do not seem to have discovered the 'know-how' for living together. As a President of the Royal Society for the Advancement of Science said a few years ago: 'We are not good enough to be so clever.' Of course this makes us frustrated and perplexed as soon as we stop to think sensibly about life today. On the one hand there are our scientific resources which would enable us to live amazingly well; did not Mr Butler say our standards of living could be doubled in twenty years? On the other hand, we are living with a 'cold war'. Racial discrimination and segregation rear their ugly heads. Reasonable and true patriotism has given place to fierce and stupid nationalisms. The future certainly does not make a bright and happy prospect, if we are honest. We do not seem to be making any real progress in the art of personal relationships and of living together.

Where does our failure lie? The reasons, no doubt, are many and complex. Those who are not Christians will give different reasons from those who are; but I believe that at heart the real reason for our failure to live together as a human family is because we have forgotten our heavenly Father. Most certainly this is a godless age. Christendom, which once had some regard for the spiritual and the supernatural, has become already largely godless, while under the impact of our modern western civilization Africa and Asia seem to be losing their sense of the spiritual, and becoming in their turn godless.

This is the kind of world, this is the kind of thinking, in which we have to be Christians. We have to live amongst a mass of people who are, to all intents and purposes, practical atheists. This ungodliness, and this irreligion, create the situation we have to face. When General Omar Bradley said 'What we need is not more men of science, but more men of God' he was speaking the truth. But the men of God have got to be men of God in a world in which God has largely been forgotten. That quite precisely is the problem—how to live as a man of God in a world and in a society in which the majority deny the importance of God, and some even the existence of God.

This, from the Christian point of view, reveals the basic sin of our age, the sin of godlessness, and at the same time exposes the real source of our troubles and the cause of our bad personal relationships; and it is in this kind of godless and irreligious atmosphere that we must, if we are Christians, live as men and women of God.

The real challenge to us is to live as those in whose lives God really counts, to be men of faith and obedience to Him in a world that simply does not bother about Him at all. This is a supremely difficult life to live, because all the influences around us are saying to us, to use a modern colloquialism: 'Fix it yourself; there is no need to call in God.' But before we can live in this world as men of God we must first become for ourselves men of God, and this demands a radical and personal experience.

A man of God is a very definite kind of person. He cannot be easily defined or neatly identified, although he can be and ought to be clearly recognized as being a man of God. He is a man to whom God is real, in whose life God is the central force and the most important fact. He has had in some way a personal encounter with the Beyond, and in that encounter he has surrendered his will.

The nearest human analogy is that of a man in love. Many definitions have been attempted to explain what love is, and none is satisfactory. Those who observe others who love cannot neatly catalogue what constitutes that experience of loving. Those who are in love are certain that they are, but cannot adequately explain what they know and have experienced. Yet we can recognize, and what is more important, believe we should be able to recognize, a man in love. He too should know it, because if the experience is a valid one it should alter his behaviour, lead to radical decisions, and shape his future life.

So it is with the man of God. In varying ways, as with the love experience, God has become real to him: to put it another way, he has experienced God in a vivid personal encounter. He knows it, and it has altered his life; or rather, he knows that it will alter his life, for the change may be sudden or it may be gradual. No one must seek to stereotype or dogmatize about the way of this experience, by what means it comes, or how it happens. If it is an authentic Christian experience of God a man will have encountered God in and through Jesus Christ. His awareness of God will be a discovery of a God who at one and the same time meets him with an absolute moral challenge as seen in the humanity of Jesus, and yet at the same moment offers him the forgiveness and help of a Saviour-God who utterly loves him. From then on he will become a real Christian, or Christ's man.

Nicodemus, a churchman, once posed this question to Jesus Himself. 'Lord, how do I become a man of God?'—that is partly what he meant in his discussion with Jesus about seeing the kingdom of God. Jesus' reply was strange and searching: 'You have got to be born all over again. You know the facts of life—that which is born of the flesh is flesh.

Nicodemus, you had a straightforward, honest-to-goodness human birth—that's how you arrived into this world.' 'Yes, indeed,' replied Nicodemus; 'I know that all right, but how can I possibly be born all over again.' Jesus continued: 'You will have to be if you want to become a man of God. Even if you can't grasp it with your mind it is an experience you must receive. Just as you had to be born physically to become a man, so you must be born of the Spirit to become a man of God. You need to have a real new life. As you had to begin your human life, so you have to begin your spiritual life. You must be born again.'

This emphasis appears often in the teaching of Jesus. He was always making the point that the spiritual life, the life of the man of God, must have a beginning. He used metaphors like these: 'Without God your life is as if you were dead—dead to God, God means nothing. When you have had the new birth you are alive to God—God now means something. Before this spiritual birth a man is lost, he is wandering away from God as the prodigal son wandered away. After the new birth he knows he has been found, found by the Father, and now he is at home, really at home, with God. Before that he was perishing, missing the mark; now he is saved, an integrated and real person.' Paul, making the same point of the Christian Gospel, used other metaphors. Before our new birth, he tells us, we are enemies of God, self-willed and self-centred; afterwards we have become friends, reconciled.

I am not concerned to press the metaphors too far, but I am concerned to make perfectly plain the New Testament presupposition that somewhere there must be in my experience a personal encounter with God in Christ if I am to be a man of God as the New Testament understands a man of God. After all, it was to 'save sinners' that Jesus Christ came. This new birth, this new life from God, is inseparably linked with the coming of Christ. He came to die upon the Cross under the impact of our sin, to show God's love in face of our sin, God's hatred of our sin, and to suffer for our sin. On the first Easter Day He rose again victorious to show here on the stage of history that God's love and goodness are the real spiritual power behind the world.

Yet all this is not enough. These are only the historic facts. Christ did come on the first Christmas Day; He did die on the first Good Friday; He did rise on the first Easter Sunday; but it was not until Pentecost, the first Whit Sunday, that the Spirit of God, who is just like Jesus, entered men's and women's hearts, making Christ real to them, and giving them the new birth, the new life in Christ, so that they became in the Christian sense men and women of God.

In every discussion about the new birth it cannot be said too often or too plainly that is is the *fact* of the new birth that matters, and not the date nor the method. In spite of the clearest teaching about this there is still much misunderstanding. We must walk carefully between Scylla and Charybdis. We must not make the Christian experience so vague and shadowy and ill-defined that we distort it into a general religiosity; nor, on the other hand, must we define it so clearly that it seems that only with certain emotional accompaniments can it happen. The deepest human personal relationship is the only adequate analogy here. Consider the experience of falling in love. There is what may be called, somewhat inexactly, love at first sight—a dramatic and definite encounter between two persons who discover that they were meant for each other, discover it with some emotion, at a definite time, in a definite place.

To others the love experience comes differently. They have many attempts on several occasions, they fancy it is true love, then discover it was a passing fancy or a temporary infatuation. After some time of despair and disillusionment they try again, until finally true love enters their lives.

Thirdly, there are those who met in childhood as family friends; the friendship deepened, until later on they almost slipped into the experience of love, discovering that what began as friendship had passed beyond; friends for years, they were now lovers.

These illustrations are always inexact, but the three ways

cover, roughly speaking, how men and women fall in love. It does not matter in which way it happens. It is essentially a definite experience: 'We are in love.' It is a conscious experience: 'We know we are in love.' It is a life-changing experience: 'We want to be married.'

So it is with the new birth. It may come with a dramatic, sudden crisis at a point of time and in a certain place, with conviction of sin, and with an emotional struggle. I am met by the Living Christ, and I have to say yes or no to Him. Such are often the converts at mass evangelistic rallies.

Again, for others there is a long intellectual and moral struggle. Such a man often thinks he has become a real Christian, that he really can now believe the Christian Faith. Then he finds that he has not yet arrived. At length, after years of striving, he finds Christ and is found by Him.

Again, there is a third group who are fortunate enough to be brought up in a true Christian home, perhaps baptized in infancy, later received into full Church membership, living after the pattern of Christian ethics. Such people often slip almost imperceptibly into the new life. Their spiritual re-birth is almost unconscious, for there is little or no emotional or moral struggle.

What needs to be said, and said quite plainly, is that it is of no importance whatever in which of the three ways I enter into the new life in Christ. It is certainly a definite experience: 'I am a man in Christ.' It is conscious: 'I know I am His.' It is life-changing: 'I desire to be led by His Spirit day by day.'

Keeping this analogy in mind we see that just as the love experience ushers in the married life, so the new birth is only the beginning; after this beginning there must be a continuing. Those who rightly emphasize conversion to Christ must also emphasize continuance in Christ. After the new birth we are meant to grow in grace, and in the knowledge of Jesus Christ our Lord and Saviour; and it is this Christian life which is the real witness to the truth and relevance of the Gospel.

None the less in Church circles today, in spite of all the

evangelism in the last decades, it is still necessary to assert that a man cannot live the Christian life until he has first become a real Christian. It is still quite possible to be a churchgoer without ever being truly born again. It is still possible to try to follow the code of Christian behaviour without God being the living, central fact of life. It is still possible to receive the Sacrament without knowing the Saviour, and to come to the Communion without coming to Christ. It is still possible to make a regular practice of worshipping in church without the opening of the heart and the submission of the will to the God whom we profess to worship.

CHAPTER II

The Basis of Certainty

THE CHRISTIAN life is meant to have a certain quality or temper inherent within it. The Christian disciple should have certain marks which bear witness that he is indeed a man of God. J. B. Phillips in his preface to the Acts of the Apostles remarks that one fact stood out in his mind in the course of his translation work: and that was the vitality of New Testament Christian living, and the amazing contrast between it and that of much modern Christian discipleship. The Christian Church in the New Testament, in spite of many faults and failures, in spite of human imperfections and sins, throbs with vitality. Here there is enthusiasm, initiative, drive, creativeness; it is indeed a new phenomenon in human history. G. K. Chesterton notices the same fact, and describes the New Testament Christian as a person who feels himself to be 'carrying about a key to life', and the Christian Church as a 'winged thunderbolt of everlasting enthusiasm, as new as it is old'.

One reason for this vitality was, and still should be, that the Christian life is *a life of certainty*. The Christian is meant to know that he is a real Christian; he is not meant to be a prey to doubts, fears and anxieties about the reality of his religion. In the New Testament again and again we find emphasis laid upon the word 'know'. 'We *know* that we have passed from death unto life, because we love the brethren.'[1] 'I *know* whom I have believed, and am persuaded that he is able to keep that which I have committed unto him against that

[1] 1 John 3:14.

day.'[2] 'Hereby we know that he abideth in us.'[3] 'This is life eternal, that they might know thee the only true God, and Jesus Christ, whom thou hast sent.'[4] So the quotations could be multiplied. The whole climate of the New Testament religion is the climate of certainty, of certainty about God and a personal experience of Him. Paul perhaps sums it up most beautifully in the grand passage in Philippians where he says: 'I count all things but loss for the excellency of the knowledge of Christ Jesus my Lord . . . that I may win Christ, and be found in him . . . that I may know him, and the power of his resurrection.'[5]

From this certainly two characteristic emotions of the New Testament emerge. The early Christians were a joyful community. Paul, writing to his friends from prison, talked a great deal about joy, and urged them continually to 'rejoice in the Lord'. Here was no superficial happiness nor freedom from a measure of sorrow; for many Christians they were dark days of persecution, misunderstanding, of loneliness and fear; but so certain were they of God that their inner joy remained.

The other emotion was hope. At first glance they had little for which to hope; for were they not a motley crowd, most of them of the poorer, less educated classes, despised and harried? Yet they were full of hope, not in the least because they were certain of themselves, of their faith, of the success of their efforts, but because they were certain of God and of what He could do through them. Such Christians, if they were here today, would have been, in face of militant communism and secular atheism, full of hope and joy, because they were not only certain of their own personal knowledge of God in Christ, but because they were certain that this God whom they knew was the Lord of all life, and that the kingdoms of this world in the end would become the kingdoms of their God and of His Christ. That is a fair description of the New Testament Christian. Is it not lamentably true that amongst

[2] 2 Timothy 1[12].   [3] 1 John 3[24].
[4] John 17[3].   [5] Philippians 3[8].

modern Christians today this note of certainty is largely absent?

We must, however, understand what is meant by Christian certainty. In the strict philosophical sense it is not absolute certainty; it is better described as a probable certainty, but none the less it is such a probable certainty that our lives can be based upon it.

Here is a happily married man who is away from his wife across the seas. He does not wake up in the morning, immediately put through a transatlantic call and speak to his wife over the phone, anxiously asking her: 'Darling, do you love me?' He is certain of that, just as certain of that as he could be about anything in his life; and there is no presumption in this certainty. Doubtless in the strict philosophical sense he has no absolute certainty; he may be making a mistake; all these years he may have misinterpreted the meaning of all that his wife has said, has done, has been; but the absence of absolute certainty does not worry him; in his own mind he has a probable certainty that on all the evidence his wife does love him, and that their personal relationship is secure. He is, therefore, freed from all anxiety and worry about that fact, and he lives his life happily based on a probable certainty.

Moreover, it is important to observe that this probable certainty in his wife's love is not shaken by the fact that, as all sensible people are, he is fully aware of his own short-comings, his failures to be the perfect husband, to return adequately the love he is so freely given. This undoubtedly produces a sense of humility and gratitude, but it doesn't shake his certainty of his wife's love.

So it is with our knowledge of God in Christ. Our certainty of Him should take away all anxiety, doubt and fear, and enable us to say with St Paul, that 'we know Him in whom we have believed'.

Another point that must be made clear is that this certainty of our relationship with God in Christ does not free us from doubts about the Christian faith, nor about many aspects of Christian living. As a matter of fact, I am inclined to think that a measure of doubt is a necessary ingredient in Christian progress. The Christian life has its times of shadow. 'Lord, I believe, help Thou my unbelief' can be a truly Christian prayer. Further by way of a rough illustration we can divide Christians into two groups, both of whom enjoy a genuine Christian experience. There are those who have what is called 'a simple faith', and who never worry intellectually about their Christianity. My Mother is like that—a wonderful Christian both in her inner personal religion, and in the witness of her active living. She knows and loves her Saviour, and has never had any intellectual doubts or questioning about her faith. She was quite unable to understand my doubts and difficulties, and could not see why I should be worried: 'It's just a matter of faith.' Such Christians are people of great spiritual power; they are the salt of the earth. We cannot argue with them—in fact, we do not wish to. They know—and we know they know.

On the other hand, there is a second group of Christians who, because of their mental make-up must think things out, and who cannot have convictions unless these convictions make sense to them. In their own way they are trying to carry out their Lord's injunction. 'Thou shalt love the Lord thy God with all thy mind.' Having minds, they have to use them to think about their religion. It is not true to suggest that such Christians want to prove everything; they know there is much that never can be proved. It is not that they want to have a nice, watertight explanation for all God's ways with men; but it is that they must think about all that interests them, and therefore about God who interests them most of all. Such thinking inevitably brings to mind a series of doubts and question marks. I remember the late Canon Streeter once saying to me at a lunch: 'If you settle the answer before you start to think, you can't think.' That chance remark was a great help to me as a student, for I soon found that when you start to think without settling the answer beforehand you quite soon land yourself into doubts, and find mistaken answers which afterwards turn out to be wrong, and so forth.

25

But for many Christians this is a necessary element if they are to be real, live and thinking Christians. But deeper than these doubts and questions should be the certainty of Christ, though this certainty does not free us from a large measure of intellectual doubt.

Moreover, it is possible to be certain about God, and yet very uncertain from time to time about His guidance. Recall my analogy of husband and wife. It is true that in the early days of marriage, while certain of each other's love, they may often be uncertain about each other's wishes. The experience of living together will tend to correct this, so that after a long married life each may instinctively know the other's will, but even then there may still be some measure of uncertainty. So it is with our experience of God. In time, through coming to understand more truly the spirit and mind of Jesus, we can be fairly sure of the general will of God, but in matters of guidance day by day we are left often extremely uncertain as to how He wants us to act, or what He wishes us to do.

Furthermore, assured as we can be about our personal relationship with God, we can still be a prey to much anxiety and to much questioning about our own spiritual state and progress in discipleship. Most of us know what it is sadly to wonder whether we are making any progress in the Christian life, whether we are becoming deeper Christians, or whether perhaps we are slipping away from a spiritual level to which God has brought us. In all this there is plenty of room for doubts and uncertainties and questionings, but underneath them all we can have the privilege of a strong certainty of our standing with God as His forgiven, redeemed children.

On what can this certainty be based? It must not depend upon anything subjective in us, for we are fickle and change too easily. Therefore, neither my feelings nor my behaviour as I observe them can be the guarantee of my personal relationship with God.

The first ground of my assurance is fairly and squarely the character of God Himself. It is sometimes expressed in the words, 'We rest on the promises of God', but this is liable to misunderstanding. That is why it is better to state the doctrine of assurance as Paul himself does in the Epistle to the Romans, resting it upon the basis of what God is and eternally will be. Let me illustrate, by the use of a text much used in evangelism: 'Behold, I stand at the door and knock. If any man hear my voice and open the door, I will come in to him.' Countless thousands of men and women have found this text a focus point for their faith. Its simple picture language enables us to open the door and receive Christ as Saviour and Lord. Then it offers encouragement to believe Christ's promise, and to find assurance that He has entered. It may be put like this: 'You have heard His voice; you have known that God is calling you; you have been convicted of your need for Him; you want Him in your life—that is hearing His voice. You are willing by an act of will to change your mind, to repent, and in the simple trust of faith to ask Him to enter your life, to come as your forgiving Saviour, to take control as your Master—now you have opened the door. How do you know that He has entered? How do you know that He has brought you into a new relationship with Himself? Because He has promised: 'I will come in, and you believe His promise.'

This is perfectly true, and as I have said, thousands of true Christians throughout the world have found an assurance of God and His forgiveness through some such promise of scripture. But the ground of assurance should not really be allowed to rest just here. What lies behind those words, 'I will come in'? We cannot find a genuine certainty of God from a few words in printer's ink on India paper in a book called the Bible. Behind these words stands the whole fact of Christ, and all that God's act in history in Him has declared about the character of God who has so acted. Behind these words stands the Christ who died on the Cross for sinners; behind these words stands the Christ who as a living Saviour has entered and changed human lives ever since by His Spirit.

So then, my certainty rests not on a few Bible texts or promises, valuable though they are, nor even on any one particular event in history, splendid and revealing though that may be; it rests upon the eternal, unchanging God who in Christ has declared once and for all and unmistakably that He is righteous, but yet loves and forgives the sinner. That is our certainty. More than that faith cannot demand; and less than that would not satisfy.

Secondly, our certainty rests upon the covenant of God, especially His covenant as revealed in the Sacrament of Baptism. Here we are reminded again of the Old Testament covenant days, with the thought of 'covenant' initiating us into a new relationship. In our baptism we are baptized into the death of Christ. With Paul's words in Romans Chapter 6 in mind we can picture a flowing river, beside which a man stands awaiting baptism. The water represents the redeeming blood of Christ, that is to say, God's redeeming, forgiving love for the sinner. It is ever flowing, flowing even before the man goes down to be baptized in it; it flows ceaselessly, and it flows always, and it flows for everyone. Into that flood the man steps; it envelops him, cleanses him, redeems him. He is identified thus with the blood of Christ, united with Christ by the love of God, and comes out to live a new life in a new relationship with God through the power of the Risen Christ. That outward baptism of water is the sacrament, the outward and visible sign of the inward and spiritual reality of his new life, of his dying to sin and becoming alive to God in Christ.

In this way our certainty rests upon the covenant of God expressed in baptism. Because, however, many of us have been baptized as infants something else must be said. The Christian experience is a fully personal relationship between God and man. It can never, from one point of view, be a one-sided relationship. True, in infant baptism God's love takes the initiative; but it awaits a conscious response. God's offer calls for my acceptance. All that infant baptism stands for is completed, in the Anglican Church, at Confirmation, and in other Churches by some other form of outward avowal of faith. Our fully completed baptism, then, becomes part of the ground of our assurance. Luther found his certainty by looking back and saying: 'I have been baptized.' If God's covenant means anything, then we are in covenant relationship with Him through baptism; we are among those whom He has redeemed by his precious blood. This is the second ground of assurance.

The third is the conviction of the Spirit. 'The Spirit himself beareth witness with our spirits that we are the children of God.' We must remember that this conviction of the Spirit is not a kind of feeling, an inward sense that I am all right. It is, rather, a deep inner conviction based upon evidence that the Holy Spirit is working in my life. I believe that all real Christians should be able to look at themselves, and with humility see that the Holy Spirit is bearing witness to their relationship with God.

What is the evidence for which we should look? It is not primarily that our behaviour is becoming more Christlike, though indeed this should be so; it is, rather, evidence that Jesus Christ is coming to mean more and more to us. It was Jesus Himself who said that one of the signs that the Holy Spirit is working within us would be that Christ would be 'glorified'. What exactly does this mean?

The word 'glory' in the New Testament often suggests the real nature of a person as seen, or revealed. For instance, we read: 'God . . . hath shined in our hearts, to give the light of the knowledge of the glory of God in the face of Jesus Christ.'[6] Here the thought is surely that God reveals to a person, and gives to him, the knowledge of something of His own real nature, and this real nature is seen in Christ. When our Lord refers to the Holy Spirit glorifying Him I think He means that as the Holy Spirit works in our lives we shall come to understand more of the person of Christ, and He will come to have more meaning for us.

Everybody has his own experience, but my own is something like this. Travelling about the world, as I have had the privilege and opportunity of doing, I naturally meet hundreds

[6] 2 Corinthians 4[6].

of professing Christians. As I get to know some of them reasonably intimately and we talk about religion, they tend to fall into two groups. The first make me uncertain as to whether they are real Christians or not. It is not my business to judge them, and I refuse to allow my mind to say to me, 'These are not Christians', but a question mark which I cannot prevent is raised in my mind.

The other group leave me in no doubt. The underlying note in their religion, the deep undertone constantly sounding, is a Christ-centredness. Inevitably, just as the compass-needle swings to the magnetic North, so their point of reference is Jesus Christ Himself.

One of the points that troubles me about much religious talk today is the over-emphasis on the word 'Church'. As I hope to make clear in a later chapter, I do not believe that the real Christian life is possible outside the Church, and that the Church is not an extra, but a necessity. Nevertheless I am unhappy when I hear people talking about the Church when I feel that they should be talking about Christ. I think there is a danger of overworking Paul's metaphor of the Church as the Body of Christ. It is a good metaphor, especially as he makes it quite clear that Christ is the Head of the body; both head and body are important, but if you press the metaphor, then I should claim that the head controls the body, and it is the head that matters more than the body. Similarly, the Church is the Body and reflects the mind and spirit of Christ here on earth; it should be a tool and instrument for His Spirit. None the less Christ is the Head of His Church, and we should give Him His pre-eminence both in our thinking and in our speaking.

I realize that in life's actual experience we cannot separate God from His world, or Christ from His Church, but in explanation and in speaking there is a distinction here, and if we do not make it we tend to blur the essential reality of Christ. It is particularly dangerous, because there is no doubt that it is all too possible to be a 'churchy' Christian, one to whom the Church is the centre, and not Christ. This is the kind of Christian of whom Karl Barth wrote: 'They are dangerous by-products and regrettable misunderstandings.'

If, therefore, we find our minds naturally turning toward Christ when we think of our religion or when we think of God, then perhaps we can believe that in some measure the Holy Spirit is bearing witness within us that we are true children of God.

These, then, are the grounds of the Christian's assurance and happy certainty—the character of God, the covenant of God, and a deep conviction about Christ.

CHAPTER III

A Life of Tension

THESE DAYS we are told we are living a life of tension, and that our great need is to relax. For many people tranquillizing pills seem a necessity, or, if we can afford it, the psychiatrist's couch. To a large extent this is true, for the pace and pressure of modern life does indeed produce much nervous tension, and to learn how to relax, and then how to find refreshment of mind and spirit, is a lesson that all of us must learn. It will, therefore, sound surprising when I suggest that the second mark of the true Christian life is that it is *a life of tension*. Here I am not using the word in the sense of nervous tension, but rather in the sense of a life strung taut between two opposite truths. It is something like a piece of elastic stretched taut between two points, and in that tautness is the real way of life. Let me explain.

The first focus-point is the peace of God, the serenity of which the Bible so often speaks. One of the first fruits of the work of the Holy Spirit in our hearts is that we are given the peace that passes all understanding. Jesus Himself promised it to us when He said: 'My peace I leave with you; my peace I give unto you.' Christian hymns are full of the idea, so are other Christian writings. When a man is right with God, then he is possessed by a deep inner serenity of heart and conscience. It is the hall-mark of the true Christian. If I were forced to choose one characteristic of a real saint it would be this serenity of mind, grounded in a deep, inner and abiding relationship with God.

When I was a boy one of my aunts made a great impression

on me, and as I grew into maturity she made an even greater impression. I often think she was one of the very few real and special saints I have ever met. She was a remarkable woman, educated and cultured, and violently evangelical. Her ordinary conversation and phraseology were strongly biblical. If she had not been a real saint no one for one moment would have tolerated what I can only describe as her overweening pietism, but because of this deep inner serenity and sincerity one could take from her phrases and ideas which would have been nauseating if anyone else had used them.

Before the first World War she had a Bible-class for London policemen. They hung on every word as she taught them Sunday by Sunday. As a schoolboy during the first World War I saw her manage a canteen full of soldiers; she talked to them about religion; they listened spell-bound, though her phrases and words were completely biblical.

Between the wars I introduced her once to a group of sophisticated young society women, smartly dressed and thoroughly worldly. My aunt was drab and dowdy. Within five minutes she had them eating out of her hand. She spoke to them of Christ.

On one occasion she was hurrying to catch a train at Paddington Station. Arriving dead on time she found the barrier gate slammed in her face. Out aloud she ejaculated, beaming all over her face: 'Never mind. Praise the Lord.' Then she went off to get a cup of tea. On returning for the next train, the ticket collector said: 'Excuse me, Ma'am. What was that you said when I slammed the door in your face half an hour ago?' 'I don't remember,' she replied. 'It sounded strange to me. Did you say something like "Praise the Lord"?' My aunt paused a moment, and then answered: 'Yes, I expect I did. I do praise Him. I am sure it is quite all right that I missed the train, and God has some purpose for me through it.' To her surprise the ticket collector asked: 'Would you mind missing another train, because I should like to speak to you after this one has gone.' So she missed another train, and he told her his story, the story of a marriage breaking up, of his longing for help, and before she caught her train she had helped him to put his faith in Christ, and later to put his marriage right.

The idea I am trying to underline is that this natural—and I emphasize the word 'natural'—serenity of mind and spirit is the hall-mark of a genuine Christian experience. That must be one focus-point in our Christian life.

The second focus-point is equally important, and if we do not live like a piece of elastic stretched taut between these two points then serenity alone would lead us to pietism and escapism. Let me illustrate.

Some years ago I was the main speaker at a students' conference. It was organized by a remarkably fine group of students, full of evangelistic zeal, and thoroughly sensible. Because they were good mixers they had managed to bring to the conference with them a number of their friends who were agnostics, atheists, and a few Communists. During the open session, as I sat at the back listening, I realized we were in for a heated discussion. A delightful young medical student was in the chair, and he invited the Christians to stand up and say what Christ meant to them. This a number did, most sincerely, but not very convincingly. One after the other they got up and said that now that Christ had come into their lives they were so happy. I knew there would be an explosion. One of the Communists got up and shouted: 'You Christians make me sick. Here you are gloating about your wretched little happiness in a world of exploitation and evil,' and then he went on to expatiate on the social evils that needed putting right. The chairman hastily got up, and interrupting him, said: 'I think we had better move on to something more practical.'

This underlines the second focus-point. It is that along with an inner serenity there must come to us a divine discontent—discontent with evil, wherever it is in God's world. True Christian living consists in the tautness or tension between inner peace and divine discontent. If we are Christians we have no right to say: 'God's in His heaven, all's right with the world.' All is not right with the world, even though God's in His heaven—and that is what brings the tension.

Paul expounds this very clearly when he says: 'The love of God is shed abroad in our hearts by the Holy Ghost which is given unto us.' Here the love of God is a subjective genitive. It does not mean our love for God, but refers to God's own love. Something of God's own divine love is given to us by the Holy Spirit. When He takes hold of us then within us is born something of His own divine love, and this inevitably creates divine discontent.

In that wonderful chapter in Isaiah we read: 'He shall see of the travail of his soul and be satisfied'—but He is not satisfied here and now with the world as it is. Jesus wept over Jerusalem because of the evil and disobedience that He saw. So when we are united with Christ we, too, must share in the fellowship of His sufferings; we must accept a deep and real discontent of mind and heart—discontent with our own sin and our own weakness; discontent with the evil and follies of the world. We must learn to hate all that ruins and spoils God's world, and hurts His children. To be really concerned and to find the burden of the sin intolerable are part and parcel of being a real Christian.

Here, then, is the tension—on the one hand it is easy to try to forget the evils of the world, and to practise a pietistic escapism by rejoicing in our own happiness and in our own peace with God. On the other hand, it is all too easy to rush into the world moved by divine discontent to try to change things by humanitarian philanthropy, losing as we do it our inner serenity, and the power which comes from it. It is a mark of Christian maturity to maintain the tension, and to hold both truths vividly alive in our hearts at the same time.

Masefield in his *Everlasting Mercy* preserves this tension perfectly:

> *I did not think, I did not strive,*
> *The deep peace burnt my me alive;*
> *The bolted door had broken in,*
> *I knew that I had done with sin.*
> *I knew that Christ had given me birth*
> *To brother all the souls on earth,*

And every bird and every beast,
Should share the crumbs broke at the feast.

Dr Billy Graham in his preaching often says: 'It is easy to be a Christian.' I know what he means, and he is perfectly right. Because God's forgiveness in Christ is a gift it is simple to accept. To take the gift offered is what anyone can do. But we must not twist this perfectly true remark to mean what Dr Graham never meant it to suggest, namely that Christianity is easy. The Christian life is difficult; it is a very costly business to live it properly, and part of that cost is the willingness to live in a continual tension between serenity and discontent.

To put it rather differently: We are ambassadors for Christ in an alien world. To put it somewhat differently again: We are meant to share in God's redemptive purpose, and no one can redeem anyone else without strain and stress and struggle. It is possible to enter into life to redeem it possessed with a sense of peace and serenity, but in the very struggle our hands get dirty because we are identified with that which we are seeking to redeem. This very involvement with evil situations produces the discontent and the strain about which I am writing.

Some years ago in America a graduate of one of the Universities was converted to Christ. The next day she gave me a poem she had written. Whether as poetry the verses are good or bad is of no consequence, but the thought expresses exactly what I have been trying to say:

Yesterday I longed for something intangible,
For a way, an escape—
For the fulfilment of my longing.
I looked at the sky
And wished it would swallow me;
Wrap me in its myriad clouds
And give me peace.
I wanted only to sleep—
To be insensible
To love—to feel no more.

36

But today I have found reality.
My eyes have been opened
And I long no more.
Christ has come—
He has fulfilled His promise,
I am complete.
He knocked at my heart's threshold,
I answered—
He walked in.
Now I wish to live—
To serve Him—
Never to shut my eyes—
Never to escape—
I am caught in the light,
Darkness holds no fear.
But I do not want it.
The sky is a distant haven,
It is near and living,
It is comfort, solace, beauty.
I want to see life
To recognize its dirt
And help to clean it.
I want to speak
To let the living Saviour
Use my lips, my heart, my brain,
To bring others to his way.
He suffered mortal anguish—
He overcame it—
He bore the burden,
And now he offers
Forgiveness as His gift.
He has come—
I am complete—
The promise is fulfilled.

CHAPTER IV

A Life of Daily Communion

IF CHRISTIAN discipleship is a personal relationship with the living God, then one of its marks must be that of *a life of daily communion* with the One whom we claim to love. It is true that in one sense our relationship with God in Christ is a once-for-all relationship—that is my certainty; but it is also a developing relationship to be continually maintained, and continually deepened. This we will call the third mark of the Christian life.

This the Bible makes very plain. We have 'boldness to enter into the holy place by the blood of Jesus.'[1] It is our right and privilege every day, because of God's love to us in Christ, to go into the holy place of His presence with the same freedom and spontaneity with which a child communicates with his father. We can talk to God with confidence and with love, looking up and saying: 'Abba, Father.'

This emphasis on simple daily communion with God is necessary, because we can so easily depersonalize God. Consider that New Testament phrase, 'the grace of God'. Grace is never an impersonal thing, and yet one often hears grace spoken about as if it is a thing that can be stored up as if it were a kind of celestial electricity. I made this point once at a meeting, and afterwards one of my audience produced a book, *A Guide to the First Communion*, in which there was a reference to a 'reserve of grace', and readers were encouraged to go to the Holy Communion in order to store up grace for the rest of the week. I understand what the writer was trying to say,

[1] Hebrews 10[19].

38

but there is a danger in the way in which he said it. Grace, in the Bible, is not impersonal. It points to a God who acts graciously. It is the gracious activity of God Himself, and we cannot store up God in a reservoir and, as it were, turn Him on when we need Him. It sounds almost blasphemous when written down in black-and-white, but there are many Christians who unconsciously think like this. They seem to believe that if they practise certain religious acts at a certain time then they can store up enough spiritual help—this impersonal stuff called grace—in a kind of reservoir inside themselves, so that when, for instance, on Monday they meet a strong temptation at 40-lb pressure they can stand up to it because they have 80-lb pressure of grace stored up within them, and then they will still have another 40-lb stored up for another emergency. Then next Sunday, having exhausted their supply, they can replenish their store and start again.

No Christian would put it exactly like this, I know, but it is a very prevalent attitude, and a very dangerous one. Before we know where we are we shall find ourselves back again under law, and in bondage to legalism. We shall find ourselves trying to perform certain acts at certain times thinking that by so doing we shall earn or collect spiritual power and grace. This utterly distorts the glorious fact of our personal relationship with God. We are either daily in touch with Him, or we are not. If we are, then He is there to help us all the time and in everything. 'Jesus Christ is the same yesterday and today, yea and for ever.'[2] 'I will never leave thee, nor forsake thee. So that we may boldly say, The Lord is my helper, and I will not fear what man shall do unto me.'[3] That confident assertion of Paul's, 'My grace is sufficient for thee: for my strength is made perfect in weakness',[4] means, when we paraphrase it, that Christ is saying to Paul: 'I, the gracious One, will always be sufficient to meet your needs, so that when you feel utterly weak then my strength is fully at your disposal.' Here is a real personal dependence of man upon God, a dependence which rests upon a daily and continuing inner communion.

[2] Hebrews 13[8].   [3] Hebrews 13[5].   [4] 2 Corinthians 12[9].

The experience of Christians through the centuries has underlined some of the ways by which this daily communion is best maintained. In a human friendship the relationship is maintained and deepened by talking to each other, by listening to each other, by working with each other, and simply by being with each other. So man's communion with God is developed. Prayer becomes an essential part of Christian living. There is no rule or regulation that prayers must be said every day, and that if this rule is broken we sin. From the point of view of law there is no commandment about praying. Even the teaching of the Bible about saying prayers, and the encouragement of our Lord to 'ask and you shall receive', are not so much commandments laid down for us to obey as practical and wise advice which we shall ignore at our spiritual peril. It is plain from our Lord's own practice, as well as from His teaching, that if we do not pray regularly then we shall not maintain and deepen our daily communion with God, that is why daily prayer is a habit we learn to accept for ourselves through experience rather than a commandment laid down by authority. It is obvious that unless I consciously turn my mind and spirit toward God at regular intervals, then under the pressure of daily life I shall find myself out of touch with Him.

The reason that I am stressing this attitude to prayer is because some Christians find themselves in bondage to rules and regulations about praying. All of us need a habit or plan for daily prayer, because we are weak and feeble creatures of time and sense; we need, therefore, the discipline of setting apart a time and place for deliberately and consciously turning toward God in prayer. But it should be a spontaneous desire to keep in communion with our Lord that should prompt us to keep this time and place for praying rather than that we should feel bound by some rule or regulation.

One of the encouraging signs in Christian literature during the last thirty or forty years has been the publication either of books of prayers, or of helps in the art of prayer. The Christian who wants to learn to pray better will have no difficulty at all in finding a suitable guide to help him to attain his object.

Bible-reading is another way of maintaining our communion with God, and here again during recent decades much help has been given by books both on the Bible itself, and on Bible-reading. Every serious student of the Bible should be able to find something that will give him just what he requires. There are, however, a few general principles that I wish to underline.

First, we must remember that we do not read the Bible primarily to seek from it rules of conduct, though indeed it contains admirable rules of conduct. Nor do we read it primarily to inform our minds about the Christian faith, although it is obvious that no one can discover the Christian faith except through the Bible. We read the Bible first and foremost in order that through the Bible God may speak to us. When Peter was telling Cornelius of the Gospel, we are told: 'The Holy Spirit descended on them all as they heard the Word behind his words.'[5] As we read the Scriptures we seek to hear the Word of God behind the printed words.

I find the doctrine of the inspiration of the Bible a difficult one, and the question of the authority of the Bible is no easy intellectual problem. Throughout the history of the Christian Church Christians have differed not only in their interpretation of the Scriptures, but also about such matters as historicity, infallibility and authority. These are important points, and I do not wish in the least to suggest that they do not matter, or that they can be by-passed by the Christian Church and by Christian scholars. It is, however, true in the experience of all Christians everywhere and always that when we go sincerely to the Bible wanting to hear the word of God, He does speak to us in the Scriptures as He seems to speak to us in no other way. The authoritative word of God comes to us through the Bible. Because of this fact Christians have always found that if they want to deepen their communion with God, and to progress in the Christian life, the reading of the Scriptures is essential. That is why both in public worship in the various liturgies a generous place is given to the reading of the Scriptures, and

[5] Acts 10[44] (Rieu's translation).

also in private, individual Christians are encouraged regularly to read the Bible.

In my experience both of evangelistic and of pastoral work I have become convinced that nothing is more important for the new convert and the young Christian beginner than to learn to know the Scriptures. By this I do not mean reading books about the Bible, or books on Christian doctrine based on the Bible; I mean reading the Bible itself. While I regard each book of the Bible as having its own special place in the volume of the Scriptures, and therefore in a sense necessary to the understanding of the whole, there are clearly some books more urgently important than others.

For the new convert the Epistles—letters specially written for new converts—are perhaps the part that should be read first. Yet we must remember that the Gospels are equally important, for here and here alone is the authentic record of the person and life of Christ.

This conviction as to the need for Bible-reading within the Anglican Church has nothing to do with churchmanship. The late Fr Algy Robertson, a Franciscan monk, and I often met at conferences for young people. It always caused us a certain amount of amusement to see which of us would be the first to recommend regular Bible study-groups as an essential for Christian growth. This emphasis may appear unnecessary, but it is surprising and distressing to notice in how many local churches of all denominations there seems to be an almost complete absence of regular Bible study-groups. This is a matter which urgently needs to be remedied.

When I was first ordained I had the privilege of starting and leading a Sunday afternoon meeting for secondary-school boys and girls between the ages of fourteen and nineteen. The attendance ranged between 250 and 300 each week. Perhaps the most significant activity was on a Wednesday morning at 7 o'clock, winter and summer alike, when anything up to eighty would gather before school for half an hour that we might read our Bibles together. There was nothing elaborate in our study; we just read the Bible from the point where we left off the week before, and let the Word of God speak to us. What is required? A Bible, with nice large print; a pencil, to mark passages that specially grip; and then let the Bible speak. It is almost as simple as that. There is room for the use from time to time of a good commentary, and of real, pains-taking study of the Bible to supplement the work in a Bible study-group, and to enrich daily private devotional reading of Bible passages; but I am sure from my experience there is need to grasp this basic principle of turning to the Bible to allow God to speak to us.

I owe this insight to my father in law—a former Keswick speaker. When I was engaged we used to have some hours together frequently during my vacations, and then we turned to the Bible. He read it, and without bothering about commentaries, or spending undue time on difficult words and phrases, he let the Word speak to us. We tried to understand what the Bible was saying to us, and then we listened for God's word.

Once we can grasp this attitude to the Bible, and use it as we read, then it does not matter very much what pattern or plan we have for our daily Bible-reading, or for our deeper study. We shall be in the attitude when the Bible will help us to maintain our daily communion with our Lord.

The third way of deepening our personal relationship with God is the Holy Communion. If one seriously surveys the experience of the Christian Church from its birth until now it is impossible to escape the conviction that of all the ways by which Christian people have deepened their communion with their Lord the way above all others has been the sacramental feeding upon the Body and Blood of Christ at the Lord's Supper. This is true not only when we look at the experience of the Roman Catholic and the Eastern Orthodox Churches, but also when we turn to the Reformed Communions. Think of the place given, on the one hand, to this Sacrament by the Lutherans, by the Anglicans and by the Church of Scotland; and also, for instance, by the Brethren, whose main service each Sunday morning is the Breaking of Bread.

I am not concerned either with the form of service in which

the Sacrament is taken, nor with the frequency of the taking, but rather with the fact that Christians of all the Churches recognize that here, and here pre-eminently, is an act by which our communion with God is maintained. It is a pity that this great Sacrament, which is meant to bind us together in fellowship as one body in Christ, and which, as experience shows, was given to us by our Lord to deepen and strenghten our communion with Him, should be the cause of so much division among His followers, and that barriers should be erected round the Table of the Lord to prevent us all meeting together, all of us who name His Name as that of our Lord and Saviour.

As I remarked about Bible-reading and prayer, so it is with the Holy Communion. There are many books written and easily available to suit every taste which will aid us in understanding this sacramental act, and in helping us the more worthily to partake. I want to stress three points only.

First, I think those of us who belong to one of the Reformed Churches should learn a lesson at this point from the Roman Church. There it is taught that to be absent wilfully from Mass on a Sunday morning is a mortal sin, that is, a sin which can produce deadly peril to the soul. I believe there is a genuine piece of spiritual truth being emphasized here, although I do not wish to press the point about *every* Sunday morning. In passing, however, I must refer to the New Testament suggestion that it was the practice of the early Christians to meet on each first day of the week for the breaking of bread. The point that matters, it seems to me, is the stress on the *regularity* of coming to the Holy Communion. We must not come just when we feel like it, or when we think we need some particular help. The great value of sacramental Communion is that it should be independent of our own subjective feelings, or our own personal needs. We come, in fellowship with others, to deepen our fellowship with our Lord by an outward and visible act—the receiving of the Sacrament. Experience shows that such a regular act does in fact maintain our communion with God, irrespective of our moods and feelings, of our ups and downs, of our sins and successes.

Another point worth making is this. The manner of the receiving of the Sacrament seems to me non-essential. In different communions we both celebrate and receive the Holy Communion in different ways. This is true; yet I myself find particular help in the fashion of the Anglican Church. Here we come up to the Table, kneel down in a line, and hold up our empty hands to receive the Sacrament of the Body and Blood of Christ. Notice the spirit of drama here. We are all levelled down as a whole group of sinners on our knees before Almighty God. This is an admirable reminder, always necessary when we seek to deepen our relationship with Him. There is no question of race or colour, of intellect or understanding, of position or privilege, of goodness or badness; we are all needy, utterly needy sinners. We hold up our empty hands, so that if the bread and wine are not placed into them we go away empty-handed. This is another great reminder that we are utterly dependent in our relationship with God upon His love and upon His forgiveness. 'Nothing in my hand I bring, Simply to thy cross I cling.' 'Unless thou save me I must die; O take me as I am.' Here is a constant reminder of the great truth of justification by faith. I know that I am accepted, though wholly unacceptable. I know He receives me, not because of what I am, but because of what He is. My communion with Him does not rest upon my effort, nor upon what I do, but upon His grace, and upon what He has done in Christ.

This is an authentic note of the Christian Gospel. It proclaims from the house-tops the essence of the Christian Faith, and makes clear beyond all shadow of doubt that the essential Christian experience of God is that of being accepted and forgiven by Him just as we are.

The third point to emphasize is the taking of the bread and eating it, the receiving of the wine and drinking it. Here is an act of identification, of appropriation, of making my own what is offered to me. What could stress more clearly the essential fact that unless Christ by His Spirit abides in me and I in Him, the fruits of the Christian life will never grow and develop? I am utterly dependent upon Him for the power to live for Him.

Absolutely clearly it focuses upon my attention, and for that matter upon the attention of the world, that utter dependence upon God Himself is the essence of being a Christian.

There are, I fully recognize, many other facets that devout Christians see in the Eucharistic service, and devotional literature abounds with these insights. Yet these three simple points are quite sufficient to make it clear that together with Bible-reading and prayer this Sacrament is essential in the life of a Christian is to have within it the quality of genuine daily communion with his Master.

CHAPTER V

Christlikeness

I—EFFICIENCY

THE FOURTH mark or quality of Christian discipleship is that it is *a life of growth in Christlikeness*. We must 'grow in grace, and in the knowledge of our Lord and Saviour Jesus Christ'.[1] 'Christ . . . leaving us an example, that ye should follow his steps.'[2] And as Paul puts it: 'Be imitators of me, as I am of Christ.'[3] John makes it crystal clear when he writes: 'He who says he abides in him ought to walk in the same way in which he [Jesus] walked.'[4]

What do we mean when we talk about Christlikeness? We make a mistake if we concentrate our meaning upon a literal imitation of Jesus. It is, of course, a very proper and sensible thing for a Christian to try to imitate the example of Jesus. It is an excellent challenge to ask ourselves from time to time, 'What would Jesus do?'—yet at the same time we must bear in mind that from another point of view we cannot possibly literally imitate Jesus, for Jesus was unique. If the great Christian affirmation is true that the 'Word became flesh', and that He 'was made man', then the personality of Jesus is something and in some way different from ourselves. God has come and taken our human nature upon Him so that in that sense we can never imitate the unique God-Man that Christ was and is. Moreover, quite apart from His uniqueness Jesus lived in a social environment utterly unlike that of the present

---

[1] 2 Peter 3[18].
[2] 1 Peter 2[21].
[3] 1 Corinthians 11[1] (*RSV*).
[4] 1 John 2[6] (*RSV*).

day. Habits, customs, religious sanctions and moral standards were very different. All these make a slavish imitation of Jesus impracticable.

On the other hand, there is the possibility of imitation much in the same way as we can say of a young man: 'He is the son of his father.' We do not mean simply that he is the child of his father, or that in his veins the same life blood courses; we are suggesting that he has his father's likenesses, some of his father's characteristics—he is 'a chip of the old block'. In the same way Christ can be to us, perfectly properly, a standard, a guide to follow, an example.

By Christlikeness I want, however, to emphasize a rather different idea, as suggested by Paul: 'And we all, with unveiled face, beholding the glory of the Lord, are being changed into his likeness from one degree of glory to another; for this comes from the Lord who is the Spirit.'[5] 'Unveiled face' refers to the fact that we can see God clearly in Christ, and can look upon Him without guilt and shame, because we are forgiven. Then Paul goes on to say that with this clear vision we can see something of the real nature and character of God—His 'glory'— and that the result of this insight will be that we ourselves will be changed, so that in our turn in some small degree we shall become like Him, and shall reflect something of His own character and nature. Paul concludes: 'This change is the work of the Holy Spirit.'

Here, then, is the secret of Christlikeness. As we focus our thinking on Christ so the Holy Spirit will begin to reproduce within us a little bit of the mind and temper of Jesus.[6] As the moon looks at the sun and so reflects the sun's likeness, I, if I look at Jesus, will find that by the Holy Spirit's help I shall be reflecting poorly but truly something of His likeness.[7]

Another analogy is worth considering. It is noticeable how sometimes two old people, a Darby and Joan, have grown to look like each other. As the years have passed during their married life they have been together so constantly, have looked

[5] 2 Corinthians 3[18] (*RSV*).   [6] Colossians 3[1,2].
[7] Hebrews 12[2].

48

at each other so frequently, that somehow they have grown very like each other, not only in ways and manners, but sometimes even in looks. If we have looked at Christ through the years, gradually perhaps some reflection of His ways and manners will be seen in us.

Yet here a warning note needs to be struck. We shall never notice this likeness in ourselves. The true Christian will never think that he is in the least Christlike, but if he is really allowing the Holy Spirit to work in his personality other people will occasionally notice in him a slight likeness to the Lord Jesus. That is really what Christlikeness means. It is not something that we can capture or achieve. We cannot make ourselves Christlike. If we possess it at all it is the Holy Spirit working out His ways in us; it is a fruit of the Spirit growing within us; it is the life of Christ reproducing within us something of His own character.[8]

What then are we endeavouring to do in our pursuit of Christian discipleship? Are we struggling to achieve this Christlikeness? Are we struggling to build a Christian character? Or are we letting the living Christ reproduce Himself in us? Are we, in the same way as we breathe the pure air into our lungs, allowing His Holy Spirit to fill us so as to bring forth His life in our lives? That is why, though from one point of view there is struggle and effort involved in being a Christian, there is, on the other hand, the need to emphasize this idea of 'letting go and letting God'. It is as I face my real self, and accept God to be to me what He really is, that I shall discover increasing wholeness and integration. If I am part of the body of Christ, then I must allow the thought and impulses of the Head to flow through me, and to control my actions and to supply me with life.

> *Channels only, blessed Master,*
> *Yet with all thy wondrous power*
> *Flowing through us, thou canst use us*
> *Every day and every hour.*

[8] Philippians 2³, Hebrews 13².

This is what I really mean by Christlikeness, and in this sense we can speak of 'the contemporary Christ'. It is the Spirit of Christ alive and vital revealing Himself through His followers in every day and generation. If we would share in offering this revelation to the world our daily prayer might well be:

> *Let the beauty of Jesus be seen in me,*
> *All His wonderful power and purity;*
> *O thou Spirit divine*
> *All my nature refine*
> *Till the beauty of Jesus be seen in me.*

Having established this premise as to the meaning of Christlikeness, what follows? In passing we must notice that it is obviously a growth. No one can arrive at Christian maturity suddenly or quickly, but growth in the right direction there should and must be. Yet as with all growth we should not worry about it. Jesus Himself told us that we must not be over-anxious, for after all, anxiety will never add a cubit to our stature. I once heard of a young child who was trying to grow a bulb. Every day she uprooted it to see how it was getting on—and it didn't. So there are many Christian people who are introspective, always fretting about their progress and their spiritual growth; can they expect to grow naturally and steadily?

This gradual development within us of the temper and spirit of Jesus raises a tremendous subject. In what way will the Spirit of Jesus be seen? What are some of the likenesses we may expect? It is a fascinating and vast subject, and in this and the following two chapters I can select only seven aspects for our consideration.

As I develop in Christlikeness it should mean a *rise in general personal efficiency*. It may seem surprising to headline this aspect, yet I think it is important to do so. In the Gospels it is clear that Jesus was efficient in His daily work. He did all things well. As the village carpenter, although there is no Bible evidence for this, tradition suggests that He made good ploughs, good tables, and so on. He was a craftsman. When He made the five thousand sit down for the outdoor meal He made them sit, according to the meaning of the New Testament Greek word, in rows like a flower garden. It was well organized, it was a good party. The arrangements for the Last Supper went smoothly; His plan for His triumphal ride into Jerusalem worked without a hitch. As a story-teller He was magnificent, because He had an orderly mind, and marshalled His facts clearly and with imagination. Christians, if Christlike, should be efficient people. Paul saw this when he exhorted the Romans: 'Don't be slothful in business'—in other words: Do your business properly.

This idea of efficiency reflecting the Spirit of Jesus must be applied not only to personal life, but also to the way in which Christians worship and conduct the business of the Church. I know it is possible to have an efficiently organized church which is not spiritual, but it should not be possible to have a spiritual church which is not efficient. Illustrations of what I mean abound.

The purpose of a hymn is to unite Christians in singing the praise of God—yet watch a congregation singing. So often there is little attempt to sing with enthusiasm and joy, so little attempt to bring out the meaning of the words, so little evidence that that united act of singing is an expression of united thoughts of praise and worship. This bad singing is plainly inefficient. Wesley's ideals for singing as expressed in the preface to the first collection of Methodist hymns strikes the right note: 'The words should be worthy and full of Christian doctrine, and the tune should be dignified and singable, so that all may join in.'

Two slight parentheses must be inserted here. Careless and casual hymn-singing is, of course, something much worse than inefficiency—inefficient though it is. It reveals a spiritual unreality in worship and ingratitude to God. Secondly, as an Anglican I must humbly acknowledge that Methodists as a general rule sing more enthusiastically than we do.

Another example is corporate prayer. The idea of saying

'Amen' at the end of a prayer is to link the individuals in the congregation with the minister who has just spoken the prayer. The people's 'Amen' is their agreement with what he has prayed. It is no sign of efficiency if at the end of a prayer instead of an audible and sincere 'Amen' there is nothing but silence. I could mention many other points, such as punctuality in starting a service, the orderly movement of the service, and so on. Efficiency is no substitute for the worship of the heart; but worship of heart and mind should express themselves in a well-ordered service.

This idea of efficiency should apply to the business administration of the Christian Church. It seems as if at last here in Britain we are beginning to recognize what our brethren in other parts of the Commonwealth and in America have long recognized, that we can honour God by the stewardship of our money. Business organizations such as the Wells, or the Fund Raising Directors, are seeking to help congregations to educate themselves in the needs for thoughtful and planned giving. What is surprising is the opposition encountered again and again by these organizations at meetings of church members. 'The giving of money to God is a spiritual matter,' it is objected. 'There is no need to have a business organization to teach us how to do it. We don't want commercialism in the churches', and so on. These criticisms to my mind are not only invalid, but seem to miss the major point which I am making in this chapter. It is true that we shall never give to God a right proportion of our resources unless our hearts are filled with love and gratitude toward Him; but on the other hand efficiency is a Christian virtue. It is altogether proper and right that we should learn from experience how to be efficient both in raising and in spending the money for God's work.

In this connexion it is distressing to hear on all sides how few members of most Christian congregations take the trouble to come to the business meetings of the church, and to be concerned with the management of its affairs. I write this with shame, for I suppose my own congregation at St Martin's has some fifteen hundred members, and for our Annual Business

Meeting we shall muster two hundred at the most. Here again I must admit that Methodist lay people take more interest in the business administration of their church than do Anglicans.

In personal life we shall never show the likeness of Christ as we should unless our daily lives are efficient. I remember once reading of a mother who attended the Keswick Convention. She was greatly stirred, and longed to receive the Second Blessing. This, according to the teaching she had heard, was the promise of a spiritual renewal, or the fullness of the Holy Spirit possessing her personality. Returning home, she spent extra time in studying her Bible, and prayed much longer each day than she had been doing. She was seeking for this Blessing. One day, after tea, she was reading her Bible and praying, looking for the coming of the Spirit, when her little girl of five ran up to her and said: 'Mummy, please play with me. This is when you always do.' 'No, run away, darling,' she replied; 'Can't you see I am reading my Bible? I am seeking for God's Second Blessing.' Disappointed and crestfallen the child answered: 'Mummy, you are always reading your Bible nowadays, and you never play with me.' That went straight to the mother's heart. Putting her Bible on one side, she played with her little girl, and as she played she found the Blessing, and felt a conviction that in some new way the power of God's Spirit was hers. As she sought to be an efficient mother so her Christian life deepened.

This is a very simple statement, but again and again it has been a tremendous help to those who have heard it. Busy housewives have been worried and anxious because they have so little time to read their Bibles, or to help in Church work. They feel they are being so little Christian in their witness and their work. Then they realize this great truth that being efficient in the house, making a real home of it, is in fact Christlike, and is a sign of genuine spiritual living. We must never try to separate the sacred from the secular. To the Christian everything is sacred, for everything is part of God's life, and is meant to be lived for Him. This world is God's world, and in seeking to make this world what it is meant to be we are doing God's business, and to do this efficiently is Christlike.

I am writing this chapter while staying in a Christian guest house, and it is a really Christian guest house, not because there is a great deal of corporate praying or other religious exercises—in fact, as a rule there are only fifteen minutes simple family prayers in the morning and evening in the homely little chapel with its straw-covered floor. It is Christian because of the way it is run. The meals are simple and well cooked, and always punctual. The rooms are tidy, artistically decorated, spotlessly clean. Without haste or fuss the organization runs smoothly, and an atmosphere of peace pervades everything. The efficiency is there without being bustling or obtrusive. It is in this very basic sense a Christian guest house—very different from some which advertise themselves as such in the Church papers.

To the Christian business man the challenge comes to be more efficient in business, to the secretary to be more efficient as a secretary, to the friend to be a better friend. And I will add, since this book may well be read by young people, a student should become a better student. Sometimes one finds sixth-formers or university students neglecting their studies in order to help with religious meetings or Church activities. In reality their true Christian work is to pass their examinations.

There is a naturalness and rightness here which is very Christlike, and utterly devoid of 'piousity'. I heard of a young fellow who was a member of his trade union and a regular churchgoer. One Tuesday evening he turned up at a Bible study-group. His minister noticed him and said: 'Tom, isn't tonight the night for the branch meeting of your trade union?' 'Yes,' he replied, 'but tonight I thought I would come to the Bible study.' 'Nonsense,' the minister retorted; 'Go off to your branch meeting. That's the place where tonight you can serve God—being what you ought to be, an efficient member of your trade union.'

That minister was quite right. One of the depressing facts of our modern industrial situation is that Christian men who work in our factories do not pull their weight in their branch activities. We owe a great deal in our Labour movement in Britain to the fact that many of its first leaders and pioneers were Methodist Local Preachers. Today things are very different, but it still is not too late for Christians of all denominations to see that one of their first duties is to be efficient in the activities of their particular trade union. I came across one such branch not long ago which had been dominated by three or four active Communists. Then three Christian men caught the vision of what their religion ought to mean, and began to go regularly to the meetings. At first it was boring; then as they began to speak out and take an active interest it became difficult—they were bullied; the Communists were rude to them; they were shouted down. They persevered, persuaded other men to come too and finally outvoted the Communists, and the branch became an efficient and truly representative branch. That was Christian action of a very Christlike kind.

I do not suggest that our society could be transformed by the multiplication of such actions, for the radical sin of human nature is deep and real, but it is indisputable that if Christians were really efficient in the business of daily life much of our present situation would be transformed. Instead of this far too many of us who call ourselves Christians believe we are better and more spiritual when we are praying than when we are working. The New Testament had no patience with such nonsense: 'Whatever you do, in word or deed, do everything in the name of the Lord Jesus. . . . Whatever your task, work heartily, as serving the Lord.'[9]

This challenge to Christlike efficiency will produce another very salutary effect. So often what prevents our efficiency are our sins. In business, for instance, there is prejudice against some new process or new idea. In international relationships we notice that an irrational antagonism toward or fear of rivalry from China or Russia prevents sound trade relationships. In personal life jealousy or a sense of shame hinders our actions.

[9] Colossians 3[17,23] (*RSV*).

55

When we really see that Christ means us to be efficient in all spheres of our living then we shall seek to be freed by the power of God from these hampering sins which prevent us giving ourselves, and being our best.

CHAPTER VI

Christlikeness

II—UNDERSTANDING

THE SECOND aspect of the development of Christlikeness is a growth in the *real understanding of human nature*. Jesus understood men in a remarkable way. He understood them because He knew what was in them, and He gave a true value to human personality. As we become understanding Christians we reveal something of the Spirit of Christ. We shall do this not by reading psychology, although I think many Christians, especially ministers, would do well to study more than they do the ways in which the human mind works. We shall develop this understanding, however, as we allow the Spirit of Christ to work within us and we find ourselves possessing a deepened sympathy with others. We shall learn to be good listeners, and to do what the prophet Ezekiel did—we shall sit where they sit, put ourselves in the place of other people, and get alongside them, trying to understand them.

This should be so obvious as to be a mere platitude, but there are far too few Christians who are really conscientiously and continually seeking to get alongside others in sympathy and in listening. Quite often a young Christian married couple will ask me how they can best witness for Christ in their new home. There are plenty of avenues, of course, but I often question them about the friends they invite in to their house. I ask them how many friends they have in at once. The answer is 'Three or four', or something like that. They look surprised when I point out that perhaps that is two or three too many.

I go on to say that one of the most helpful things a young couple can do is to invite just two others into their home, or even to have one friend in, and then one of the couple to slip into the kitchen so that two are left alone; or one to slip into the garden so that two can talk in the kitchen! Then there is a chance to listen, and to let the other talk.

Cardinal Newman understood this when he wrote: 'How many souls are there in distress whose one need is to find a being to whom they can pour out their feelings unheard by the world. They want to tell them, and not to tell them; they wish to tell them to one who is strong enough to hear them, and yet not too strong so as to despise them.' In this simple way of listening the young couple can make their home a place where their friends come to talk about themselves, to bring out their difficulties, and to open up their problems. In this sharing a Christian couple can have the opportunity of giving sympathy and understanding, offering their own experience, and in the end perhaps introducing their friends to Christ. This sounds so simple as I write it that I find myself wondering why thousands upon thousands more Christian people do not learn with God's help to give this very simple thing that anyone can give—a listening ear and a sympathetic mind.

We can examine this matter from another point of view. The New Testament makes it perfectly clear that part of a Christian's business is to help other Christians on in the Christian life. 'Admonish the idle, encourage the faint-hearted, help the weak, be patient with them all.'[1] The early Christian fellowship tried to do this when they confessed their faults one to another. The Methodist class-meetings were planned by Wesley for just this purpose. Today, however, in our modern Church life there is very little of this kind of activity. Certainly in the Anglican Church it is considered to be the business of the parson: the spiritual welfare of the congregation is his responsibility, and his alone. In the Church of Scotland the elders are charged with this very duty, to assist the minister in spiritual and pastoral work. I am sure, however, if the

[1] 1 Thessalonians 5[14] (RSV).

58

truth were known, it is sometimes a matter of theory than of practice. The fact is that by and large, in Britain as in America, lay Christians are nothing like concerned enough with helping each other forward in Christian living. This failure makes little sense of Christian fellowship. As I pointed out recently to the young people in my own church: 'You call yourselves Christians, but what have you done to help other Christians along? Your friends come to church; you worship together, you dance together, but do you ever help each other along in the Christian life? Perhaps you do by your influence and example, in fact I am sure you do, but do you go farther and try to help each other along by warning, by strengthening, by advising, by encouraging?'

This is a fair challenge by a minister to his own congregation. It is a still fairer challenge made by the people to the parson, for many of us who are parsons seem to be so busy that we forget that our first task is to look after the spiritual health of each member of our congregation.

If we are going to do this effectively, however, we must learn to understand human nature, and as I have already indicated, we shall learn to understand human nature by listening. We shall also learn the more faithfully we say our prayers, for the better we pray the more clearly we shall know God, and the more clearly we shall know ourselves, our real selves, and thus the more shall we know other people as they really are. I remember once a young seventeen-year-old public schoolboy saying to me: 'Why is it that when you talk I feel so bad? You seem to hit me all the time, as if you know what I am thinking.' 'Because I know what I think and what I am,' I replied, 'I know what you think and what you are.'

Another method that will help us to grow in a real understanding of human nature is if we try to see people as Christ saw people—realistically. He was never sentimental about people; he was always realistic. He saw people indeed as God's children, as God's sinful children. He saw much of the angel in man—the divine nature—but he also saw much of the devil—the self-centredness that spoils. A well-known politician once said: 'Human nature is essentially good.' That was sentimentality. Jesus saw people as sinners needing forgiveness. Nehru was nearer to the facts of life when he told an Indian friend of mine: 'Before I came to power I stood for nationalization, and as much as possible. Now I am doubtful, because as far as I can see nationalization doesn't work unless people are either coerced or conscientious.' That is most realistic. Man will work for the common good without incentive if he is coerced and forced to do so, or, on the other hand, if he is conscientious and really believes that co-operative living is the right way to live; but if he is neither conscientious nor coerced then he will not work co-operatively, for self-interest steps in. Self-centredness is the fly in the ointment. A growth in Christlikeness will give us increased understanding of men as they really are, and life as it truly is.

As our Christian understanding of human nature increases we begin to realize the possibilities of people. To use Paul's phrase, we shall see them as 'brothers for whom Christ died'. To put it another way, we shall begin to understand what is the Christian value of human personality. This is a real aspect of Christlikeness.

Some years ago, before the War, a play entitled 'The Mortal Storm' enjoyed a long run in London. Its theme centred on the Nazi régime, and its story concerned the break-up of a decent, happy, middle-class German family under the impact of the Nazi philosophy. The son, a young student, revealed the reason for the break-up when he said: 'There is nothing above the State, nor beside the State. The individual is of no importance save as a servant of the State.' There is plain atheistic philosophy. Man is no longer considered to be a child of God, with his own peculiar worth and value; he is just a unit to be used by the State—whatever that is—as it thinks fit. If a man is simply this and nothing more, if the State wishes to have some guinea pigs on which to try out some medical experiments and decides to light on the Jews, well, it doesn't matter—units have no rights, and have value only as they help the State. From this stemmed the vileness and beastliness of the treatment that individuals suffered. All powerful is the thing called the State (which on examination is a mere abstraction; it really stands for those who have power); in other words, some individuals treat the majority of individuals as mere things and units, giving to their personalities no real, intrinsic value at all. The majority are there to be used. In the same way in Communist philosophy the Party has the right to manipulate the masses for its own ends. This using of people for our own ends is the antithesis of the way that Jesus Christ saw individuals should be treated, for to Him each had a value of his own.

To be Christlike then we must seek to share the value that Jesus gave to human personality. What was it? In the first place, He believed that the human personality is meant to be a free personality—free to choose the ends of life, and to direct his action toward those ends. He was very particular to recognize this fact about men. He always treated people as having free will and the right to choose. This does not, of course, imply complete free will to do what I like. I live within society—a society of other free souls. You have no right to say to me: 'I choose to throw my rubbish over your back-garden wall.' My reply is clear: 'Thank you. I don't want it.' Your will may be free, but so is mine. There are, therefore, limits within a free society to an individual's free will. We have to live in community. There is a common good, as well as an individual good. But within these limits Christ placed a tremendous emphasis on the right, and indeed on the need, of a man to be free. In His eyes it was God's will that I should live and develop as a free-choosing personality. That is why He rejected the subtle temptation of the devil when he was standing on the platform of the Temple. He refused the suggestion to come floating down miraculously from the platform so that everybody would be overwhelmed by the wonder of it, and would be magnetized into believing in Him. He had no intention of dominating man's mind, of sweeping him off his feet by some emotion, of brain-washing him. Our

Lord's approach to the individual was to offer him truth, to offer him love. If truth was rejected, if love was refused, then He was content to be rejected and crucified. Christ lived and died to establish this understanding of the value of human personality.

If we seek to become Christlike we too have in practical daily life to stand for this value for the individual. What does this mean in practice? It means, for instance, that we must reject the possessiveness of power. We have no right to use undue and unfair influence over others for our own advantage and to further our plans. Parents must not be possessive of their children, but must be willing to allow their children to develop their own independence, to learn by their own experience, to make their own mistakes. We have no right to try to mould them to be like us, or to expect them to live the kind of life we would like them to live. We can offer them our best experience, give them our love, put before them the ways of goodness and truth—but then they must make their own choice.

It means, too, that generally speaking a Christian cannot be a revolutionary and support unconstitutional action backed by force. He must stand for the gradualism of persuasion.[2] Logically this will mean that Christians cannot contract out of political action, and that whether we like it or not we must play our part in the party politics of today even if it means only taking a thoughtful and responsible action when we vote. For some it may mean at a great deal of sacrifice 'going into politics'. One of the rather dismal features of today's life is to observe that both in national and local politics some of the best men of all parties refrain from standing for the local council or for Parliament. It may well be a Christlike action to do just this work and to do it because only in this way within the democratic structure can real freedom be maintained.

From another point of view this element of Christlikeness asserts the right of free speech, and the need to tell the truth

[2] This is generally true notwithstanding Bonhoeffer's agonized acceptance of a part in the Hitler plot, or the Presbyterian theology of tyrannicide, etc.

and to reveal the facts. We can never agree to liquidating opponents, to the suppression of facts by the Government, or by anyone else, to misrepresentation by the Press, and mass propaganda. People must be allowed to know the truth, and then to decide. It seems to me quite unchristian when Church people work up an agitation to keep agnostics off the television screen. I do not agree with their agnostic views, but as a Christian I believe they have a right to be heard and to be seen.

In business this idea means that as an employer I should try to explain as many facts as I can to the employees in my industry. They have a right to be told what is happening, and to be invited to contribute their thoughts to dealing with the situation. Christlikeness at this point is a very searching thing. It hits right against our love of power, and this love of power is one of the most menacing features of this age. We are moving into what has been called by Dr James Burnham an era of managerial revolution. In industry the managerial class is all powerful; in government it is the managerial bureaucrat; in social life the managerial technician or welfare officer. All these trends minister to man's love of power to dominate. Christlikeness would lead us, while accepting the need for change in this age of technology, to be on our guard against this temptation, and to fight it wherever it rears its ugly head. Today the battle is joined against economic and mental slavery as truly as it used to be against physical slavery.

All this may sound somewhat platitudinous, but if we search our own hearts and minds we cannot fail to see that the infection of the disease of love of power has in some way affected all of us, and that the remedy here is to allow the Spirit of Christ to heal and to strengthen us.

In the second place, Jesus saw the value of human personality not only in being a free-choosing being, but in the uniqueness of each individual. A man is of distinctive value and worth to God. We can remember how Jesus referred to the *one* lost son, the *one* lost sheep, the *one* lost coin, as mattering tremendously to the owner. Each was unique, and of its own particular worth. We may have our physical doubles in some part of the world, but there can never be a personality double. Each of us with all his own personal experience is himself, and God loves him as he is, for He has no favourites. I remember a small girl asking me once: 'How can God love everybody at once?' Any good mother with a large family could answer that. In an amazing way she can love her family as a whole, each individual specially, and everyone equally. The more she loves, the more she can love. God's infinite love can embrace all of us, and yet love me individually and in a special way.

It follows that if I am loved by God in this way, and have unique worth, then so has every other individual. Growth in Christlikeness will enable me to recognize the infinite worth of each person as a person. There can never be any 'herrenfolk' with a right to dominate others because they are of more worth. We cannot accept the idea held by some who call themselves Christians in South Africa that God predestined some people to hew wood and draw water, and so to serve the white man. The hymn is unchristian that says 'The rich man in his castle, the poor man at his gate', suggesting as it does that both are meant to stay where they are.

It is interesting to notice that when Jesus linked two commandments of the Old Testament together—'Thou shalt love the Lord thy God with all thy heart' and 'Thou shalt love thy neighbour as thyself'—he made clear two facts. First, that because God loves me in a true and personal way I should love Him back in return; and secondly, that I must love my neighbour whom God also loves, but I need not love him better than myself, but *as* myself. It is true that if I really respect myself, and believe that I am loved by God as an individual, it should follow that I should recognize that other individuals are my equals and I should treat them so.

This idea of equal worth and value does not lead us into the ridiculous idea that everyone has equal aptitudes, and that, therefore, all of us, for instance, ought to have equal pay, or equal this and that. The facts of life show this to be nonsense.

It does mean, however, that we cannot exploit individuals, for they are God's loved persons. We must not exploit them for fun, for expediency, for business, for politics. It means, too, that we must work to obtain for each of God's children equality of opportunity, and that as rising standards of human living are possible they are made available for all to enjoy.

We must recognize, however, that at any given point of history there will be certain differences, many inequalities, and some social separateness. There will be the under-privileged groups and the more privileged groups. Christlikeness in outlook will prompt us to work to remove this wrongness from human society, and to allow individuals to move freely from one group to another as they seize the opportunities they are offered. Repression and refusal to give equality of opportunity are sins.

Put like this in face of the world situation today the task looks gigantic and impossible. So it must have looked to the first Christians, a tiny minority in a pagan world. They sought first in the community of the Church to mirror what the Christlike life should be. As Paul grandly put it: 'There is neither Greek nor Jew, circumcision nor uncircumcision, Barbarian, Scythian, bond nor free: but Christ is all, and in all.'[3] I think it may well have been this real family spirit, this genuine fellowship, this deep and living sense that within the Christian community each was loved for himself and regarded as of equal worth, that attracted the outsiders toward Christianity. Women and children, rich and poor, clever and ignorant, good and bad, all were alike welcome.

Today, unfortunately, it still happens that the Christian Church can be a place of snobbery and class distinction. Money and reputation can still pull strings, and count for more than they ought within the life of the organized Church. The truth of this charge does not need to be proved. It is, unfortunately, open and apparent to all who know the life within all denominations. Here is a sin which Christians could deal with if they would; and if they did, they would enable the

[3] Colossians 3[11].

Church to bear a most attractive witness to the world outside, for power, position, money still count and mitigate against the true equality of man.

I well remember when I was Vicar in a West End parish in London one of the wealthiest ladies in my congregation coming to see me. She found fault with me—perhaps quite fairly—for all that I was trying to do for the young people who were starting to come to church. She complained that I was altering the services, and not using the Prayer Book fully. She preferred her Prayer Book services exactly as written, and demanded that I should have them so. I apologized and explained that some variation and adaptation was necessary if the young people were to be drawn into the Church and helped forward in their Christian lives. Her reply was unrelenting: 'I don't mind about the young people, whether they are helped or not. I like my own church as it always has been.' 'But, Madam,' I answered, 'you will soon be dead; and when you are there will be no Church if the young people are not built up in the Body of Christ.' 'Very well, then,' she retorted, 'I shall leave your church and withdraw my subscriptions.' This she did; but the story has a happy ending. Six months later she came back, and because at heart she was a grand old lady, she sought me out and told me: 'That other church was too dull, so I have come back to you.' She was a faithful member for another two or three years, and gave me a measure of her friendship until she passed on, a good Christian soul, into the fuller life.

She had got the wrong idea. She thought her money made a difference—it gave her position and influence, and therefore she had the right to call the tune within the Church of God. These distinctions must disappear from our thinking and our acting if we are to show any likeness to our Master.

In the third place Jesus recognized that if the true value of human personality is to be seen the individual must be treated as, and be able to live as, a responsible being. He showed this clearly in His story about the talents. What mattered was not how many talents a man had, but did he use the talents he possessed? In other words, a man cannot live as a true child of God unless he is working creatively with his talents upon the stuff of life. The socialist phrase, 'To each according to his need, and from each according to his ability', is basically true in its Christian idealism. We are suffering today from the selfish demand from individuals that each of them should receive not only according to need, but according to desire, and at the same time a refusal to give to the community according to ability. This decay of a sense of responsibility for being creative is sapping at the very foundations of modern life. Everywhere it is apparent; and what ought not to be surprising is that it is also becoming apparent that the world will not work this way, that life cannot be lived with a refusal of responsibility. Wealth—true wealth, which is the working upon natural resources for the welfare of mankind—cannot be produced without creativeness and the acceptance of individual responsibility for taking a share in the work. Yet blindly we stagger along, selfishly seeking to get rather than to give. It is no wonder that this modern civilization in such conditions creates strain and tension, stomach ulcers and neuroses. We are just not being our true selves.

Admittedly this is not altogether the fault of individual men and women. We have moved into the machine age, and machines tend to destroy creativeness and craftsmanship. They take away from the meaningfulness of daily work. Many people in a large industrial city like Birmingham 'Go to work to earn the cash to buy the bread to get the strength to go to work to earn the cash to buy the bread . . . etc.'—a kind of treadmill existence. There is no interest in their work, and it is largely repetitive.

I know, of course, that many operatives like this kind of labour. They find that as they do it automatically their mind can think of other things; they can dream dreams; they can talk to each other; but—and there is no escaping from this—they find no creative outlet in what they are doing as their daily work. For eight hours every day they are not acting as creative, responsible people. Automation will produce even more of this kind of work as it invades larger areas of industry. What can be done? We cannot get rid of machines, as I think Eric Gill suggested; yet something must be done.

In this connexion I remember some twenty-seven years ago that visionary and prophet, Canon C. E. Raven, saying in a sermon that leisure and the right use of leisure would be the problem for the latter half of this century. That he is right is beyond argument, but I wish I could feel that we were showing any success in helping the mass of the people to be creative in their leisure hours, and to live as responsible people. We seem to be floundering in a mass of inertia, realizing that we are sinking, but not knowing how to get out.

There would be some hope on the horizon if there were signs that we were acting responsibly in the one sphere where machines can never prevent us from being creative, that is in the sphere of personal relationships; but is there any sign of this responsible action—within the personal relationship of family life, between the different groups in society, between management and labour, between ourselves, and between the nations? In all these there seems little that is creative, and much that is irresponsible.

In these three aspects in which Christ underlined the value of human personality there is plenty of scope for action for Christians who seek in any measure to show within themselves the Spirit of Christ. If Christians are seeking for action, then action is surely open to them along countless avenues in everyday life.

CHAPTER VII

Christlikeness

III—WILLINGNESS TO SUFFER

A THIRD aspect of Christlikeness is *the willingness to suffer*. The New Testament is full of references to the suffering and sacrifice a Christian must be willing to face if he is to follow his Master. Paul writes that he is glad to share in the fellowship of His sufferings,[1] and goes on to point out that only if we are willing to suffer with Him shall we share in His triumph.[2] Part of the Christian experience is not only to receive the gift of faith, but to be called to accept sacrifice[3]—in fact, Paul could describe his experience in these words: 'I am crucified with Christ: nevertheless I live.'[4]

In the gospel story there is that delightful incident when the wise men came bringing their gifts to the infant Christ. Kneeling before Him, they opened their treasures and presented unto Him gifts—'gold, and frankincense, and myrrh'.[5] We are not being over-fanciful if we take these gifts as symbols of our offering to Christ, our King. He wants the truly valuable gold of our personalities yielded to Him; the daily frankincense of our prayer and worship must ascend to His throne; and then there is the myrrh. Myrrh typifies suffering and death, and part of the dedication of the Christian is the offering to God of our dying to self, and our willingness to suffer.

Christ specifically called us to this idea of sacrifice. 'If

[1] Philippians 3[10], 2 Corinthians 1[7].
[2] Romans 8[17], 2 Timothy 1[7,12].
[3] Philippians 1[29]. [4] Galatians 2[20].
[5] Matthew 2[11].

any man will come after me, let him deny himself, and take up his cross daily, and follow me. For whosoever will save his life shall lose it: but whosoever will lose his life for my sake, the same shall save it.'[6] Canon Streeter paraphrases this saying of our Lord thus: 'If you think to be one of my disciples you must say "no" to self, and remember that you are living with a halter round your neck.' A mark of Christ-likeness then is to live with a halter round one's neck. What does this mean, to live always wearing a symbol of death?

It is important first of all to clear out of the way any ideas of a false asceticism. There is no suggestion in the teaching of the New Testament that we are to seek suffering for suffering's sake, or to practise self-denial simply for the sake of saying no. The conception that God values the mutilation of the body, or the crushing of ordinary human desires, is pagan, and not Christian. Christ's religion is not a negation of life; it is the discovery of positive, real, eternal living.

Christian self-denial then is not practised by creating a list of taboos, fastings and abstentions. We shall not achieve it by refusing to eat meat on Fridays, or by abstaining from dancing or the theatre. Shutting ourselves off from the world in a monastery or convent, or leaving all the friends we love and rushing to darkest Africa are not in themselves necessarily the carrying out of our Lord's command to say 'no' to self and bear His Cross. The essence of Christian self-denial is when I seek to substitute His will for my will; to say 'no' to myself in order to say 'yes' to Him. There is something of active response and of glad acceptance in the spirit of the Christian who denies himself. Perhaps it is clearer if we think of the 'saying "no" to self' as being a preliminary to taking up the Cross, much as repentance is the gateway to faith. Dropping that which may hinder, I can grasp at that which is good.

There is a misunderstanding, too, in many people's minds about the Cross we have to carry in Christ's name. So often in pastoral work I come across, for instance, an old woman who tells me that with patience she is trying to bear her

[6] Luke 9[23].

cross; this turns out to be some illness, or the loss of some dear relative. But our Lord is not referring, in His challenge, to this kind of cross, for the pains and sorrows of life are not a cross we can take up or refuse to take up; they come upon us and hit us whether we choose them or not. They are part of the stuff of life in which we Christians have to live; we can neither accept them nor reject them. They have to be met when they come.[7] Our Lord was inviting us in His name and for His sake to take up a cross, and by implication infers that we can either take it up or refuse it. To what is He referring?

He means, I am sure, a deliberate saying 'no' to self, and the deliberate acceptance of the willingness to suffer in some particular way for a particular purpose so that we may carry out His will and further His kingdom.

Before we examine the implication of this more fully it is worth while noting in passing that this element of self-denial and suffering introduces into the Christian experience what I should like to call an element of iron or steel. So much Christian living is flabby, soft and comfortable. There is no real sacrifice involved, no real hardness to be endured. Many who read these words will, like myself, be neither Roman Catholics nor puritan Evangelicals. We specially need to heed this challenge of our Lord. In their own way Roman Catholics have an element of iron in their religion. Their rules of fasting, the need for regularity at Mass, the obligation of regular confession, the fear of hell, and the absolute authority of the Church over body and soul—here indeed are disciplines enough, and much sacrifice is demanded to respond as one ought in sincerity and truth. Alas, many Roman Catholics are never able so to respond.

The Puritan Evangelical feels that many things are wrong for him which others can enjoy. The list varies, but often includes dancing, cards, the theatre, films, and so on. We should never ridicule a young Christian who for His Lord's

[7] But perhaps facing an illness courageously and serenely for Christ's sake may deserve the title 'bearing the cross'.

71

sake turns his back upon the natural and good things of life. In so doing he expresses the depth of his love for his Lord, and there is a real element of iron in his religious faith. The danger for him lies in a later reaction when he may find that he has been renouncing things that need not be renounced, and clinging to things which he should have yielded.

Those of us, however, who pride ourselves that we are free from these narrow restrictions, and from what we regard as man-made restraints, must face with the utmost sincerity this demand of our Lord, otherwise there will not be the steel in our living which is part of being a Christian.

Examining the matter more closely we first have to face the suffering involved in a definite allegiance to Christ. Secret discipleship is not really possible. If I am to witness for Christ I must do it in the open, and that is where the suffering begins. In its stark nakedness we can see it more easily in other lands than our own. It is still true in a Muslim country that to be a Christian, and a baptized Christian, may cost a man his life. It will certainly involve social ostracism and utter loneliness. For an orthodox Jew to become a Christian will mean the rending of what to a Jew are the closest of all ties, the ties that bind him and his family together.

Some years ago there came to Birmingham Parish Church a young Hindu. His father was a lay Hindu high priest in Assam, wealthy and aristocratic. The young fellow came to our church, because an older brother had told him: 'When you go to England go along to a Christian Church. You will find the people there sociable and friendly, but they will not try to make you a Christian, so you need not worry.' He found with us, so he told me after a time, friendship and kindness; he was accepted by our young people, and made to feel at home. Two or three years passed. He prayed with us, and he worshipped with us. Some of our young people discussed religion with him, but nobody tried to convert him. Then the Gospel of Christ began to work in his heart and mind. At length he made his decision and accepted Christ as his Saviour and Lord. He came and asked me for baptism. 'I can never

72

return to my father's home, I know; it might even mean death if I did. As well as this exile I am willing to suffer anything in gratitude for the love of Christ.' One Whit Sunday morning I baptized him. As I did so, more vividly than before I understood something of the meaning of the suffering of allegiance.

This suffering may be seen more vividly in other lands, but exists most really in Britain today. Many a man working in a factory has to face ridicule when after a weekend he admits that he has been to church, and gets the reputation of being a practising Christian. The suffering is very real. It has nothing to do with being ashamed of naming the name of Christ. Most Christians are not ashamed of Him in the least—far from it. The hurt lies in being different, a sense of loneliness and estrangement from one's fellows. We hate the thought that they may believe that we think we are better than they are—if our friends are good, decent living people, we hate this. Yet we are different; we are living with a different purpose, we hope to live in a different spirit. We are with them, yet not of them. This is a very real mental and spiritual suffering.

This is particularly true and painful when it occurs within one's own family. In most Christian congregations today there are people of all ages who are the only members of their family to attend church, the only ones who profess to be Christian. Here is intense loneliness, for of all places where we hope to be understood, and want to be our natural selves without strain and stress, it is in our homes, but if one is the only Christian there that is not possible. We have to be on our guard; we do not want to let Christ down; we do not want to be misunderstood.

Jesus knew something of this from His own experience. His mother and His brethren did not understand Him, and that hurt. He shared with us His experience when He said: 'Think not that I am come to send peace on earth: I came not to send peace, but a sword. For I am come to set a man at variance against his father, and the daughter against her mother, and the daughter in law against her mother in law. And a man's foes shall be they of his own household.'[8]

Willingness to suffer must also show itself in the active acceptance of self-discipline. In a later chapter I shall try to show that the Christian life is a life of freedom, and that it is not bound by rules and regulations. This is true; but there is still a call to self-discipline. There may be no rules imposed from outside, but we must impose them on ourselves. Paul makes this point when he tells us: 'I keep under my body, and bring it into subjection.'[9]

It is a wise habit for a Christian to frame for himself some simple rule of life. For instance, the length of time that we spend on saying our daily prayers does not matter, but the rule to say them does. The frequency of attendance at the Holy Communion is not the main point; but the regularity is. The way of reading the Bible in private devotion can be varied; but the habit should be fixed. It is here that young Christians often need help, and in many Church guilds there is the practice of suggesting that each member should draw up his own rule of life after thought and prayer, and also, if necessary, after a quiet discussion with the minister, or some older Christian friend. However it is done, a simple rule is a good safeguard against becoming casual in spiritual exercises.

This idea of self-discipline, however, has wider implications. It embraces the control of my thoughts. Let me say at once I am not referring to training myself to abstain from thinking unkind, impure and other wrong thoughts; what I am suggesting is the need to find the discipline of concentration whereby I can keep my mind from wandering or from day-dreaming, and can fix it upon matters that need my attention. Frequently I am asked by some earnest Christian for help in concentrating during prayer time. I commonly begin by asking: 'Can you concentrate at other times?' This learning of thought-control is important not only to our devotions, but to our daily living.

We need self-discipline, too, over our feelings. Some of us are too prodigal with them, and let them run away with us.

[8] Matthew 10[34].   [9] 1 Corinthians 9[27].

74

We are moody, or we are passionate, but we are certainly not controlled.

Then there is our will. Hasty and impulsive action has ruined many a Christian's witness; retracing our steps is a hard and difficult business when we have acted wrongly. That is why it often helps to obtain discipline of will if we will practise doing something or not doing something which in itself is of no importance. The exercise of will in such a matter can help us to find the discipline we seek. It is said that John Wesley's mother made a practice of training her children's wills, so that they learnt this discipline. It is a valuable training.

There is, too, the willingness to suffer in the active acceptance of limitation. One of the amazing things about the Incarnation is the phrase of Paul's: 'He emptied Himself.'[10] What exactly this emptying or *kenosis* means has been the subject of endless debate among Christian scholars, but whatever it means, it shows the amazing self-limitation of God, His willingness to limit Himself that He might become one with us. The Christian in his turn has to be willing for this, and to accept it gladly.

I remember once reading the story of a wonderful priest who had given the best years of his life working amid terrible conditions in the east end of London. One day he returned to his Oxford college for a reunion with friends of his student days. He sat drinking coffee with two of his particular friends. They talked of their travels, of the countries they had seen, the picture galleries they had visited, and the music they had heard. The priest sat silent. He, too, was a cultured man, and he loved all these things of beauty; he, too, would have liked to have travelled, but he had had no time. He had been busy amongst his poor and suffering people; besides, he had no money. As he listened a shadow of wistfulness passed across his face. He felt limited; his capabilities could have reached so much farther; but even as the shadow fell across his face there were scores of people in his East

[10] Philippians 2⁷.

75

End parish who thanked God for him, and that he had been willing to suffer that limitation.

In some measure this challenge comes to every Christian. We have only so much energy, time, ability, and so on. If we are going to serve Christ, and for His sake to serve our fellow men, then some other things must go, and be laid on one side. It is doubtful if a true Christian can ever be a millionaire; not that for one moment am I suggesting that it is wrong to have money, if we use it wisely as a trust of which we are stewards. It is rather that money-making, if that is to be the great purpose of our lives, will hardly be possible if we are to find time and energy to serve Christ, and others for His sake. There may well be a call here to limit some activities for the sake of other and more worth-while activities.

This same thought of limitation may guide a young science student who could almost certainly earn a large salary in industry, but who because the need is greater, deliberately takes up the vocation of teaching. It might come to a scholar who could be a Fellow of his college, and enjoy the facilities of research and teaching in his own country, but who for the service of Christ goes out to Africa to teach in a theological college future African priests.

When I was in Ghana it was sad to meet a number of lecturers in the University there who seemed to me to be missing the point of vocation. Some of them would, no doubt, call themselves professing Christians, but it appeared that they were there largely for self-interest. The conditions of work and the salaries in the University were good; there was ample opportunity for them to complete their London University doctorates. They did their teaching no doubt adequately, but they showed little interest in their students. In the judgement of myself and others they were there for their own purposes, and not to serve the students in Ghana.

There were, of course, exceptions. Amongst these were a young married couple, both lecturing in different faculties. As Christians they had chosen to go to Ghana. Their home was open to the students, and they tried to identify themselves with their interests. This involved, to some extent, a limitation of their own interests, and certainly took up a good deal of their leisure time from their own work and social pleasure, but in accepting this limitation they were giving to those African students something utterly and completely worth while.

This acceptance of limitation often means that in love for God and our fellow men we are willing to accept that which is to us, from a natural and temperamental point of view, unpleasant and undesirable. I remember in Rhodesia meeting a young and cultured woman, vivacious and full of fun, who deliberately chose to visit lonely old ladies that she might talk with them and read to them. As she put it: 'I know it cheers them up, but I must admit I often find it boring.' Of course she found it boring, that was natural, but she deliberately decided to accept this that she might serve.

On that same visit a Government official was converted to Christ. He consulted me about his future. Opening his heart, he told me of the grave restrictions put upon him by the Government policy toward the Africans. He felt that now in the light of his Christian experience many things he would have to do according to the law would be repugnant to him. 'Shall I quit', he asked me, 'and find another job, or shall I stay where I am? Probably next year I shall become head of my department of native affairs, then, though obviously I cannot alter the law, I can administer it in as humane and Christian a way as possible.' I did not advise him; we merely talked and prayed together, but I must confess I was glad when he told me later that he was going to stay where he was, accepting the limitation of a difficult position for Christ's sake.

Another form of self-limitation is linked with Church membership. This may sound surprising, but it is true. In England, unlike America, it is not the conventional or done thing to be a regular church attender. A man who genuinely links himself with some branch of the Christian Church and regularly attends its local meeting-place is to some extent a marked man. His Church membership makes demands upon him which to some extent will limit his leisure time, and his energy for other pursuits. To be a real member of the Christian Church calls for the acceptance of the responsibility of belonging. This involves not merely regular Church worship, but a willingness, for instance, to offer one's expert professional services to look after the business of the local church, to become a sidesman or a deacon, to take up visiting; it may perhaps call upon a man to volunteer to help in a youth club, or to take a Sunday-school class—this latter is a wonderful privilege that calls for time for preparation as well as for teaching. In the Parish Church at Gerrards Cross there is a most flourishing Children's Church, and there a good number of fathers who were but loosely attached at the beginning now gladly share the duties of leading that Children's Church, or helping in some other way. This may limit their time in the garden or for playing golf, but it is quite certainly an acceptance of Christian responsibility. A responsibility such as this we are all tempted to evade especially if we are successful business men, yet it must not be evaded, just as the responsibility of parenthood must not be evaded.

A headmistress of my acquaintance told me recently about a difficult adolescent girl in her school. She was insubordinate, disobedient, lazy and thoroughly wild. After many attempts the headmistress finally talked the matter over with the parents. Her father said: 'I agree, something must be done. Will you please thrash her for me?' Quite apart from the advisability of corporal punishment, here was a plain evasion of fatherhood! Many Christians are quite willing to let other people run the Church family while they sit back and avoid the limitation of their time and energy which such a responsibility involves.

In the modern complex world of industry and business a Christian has to face the possibility of limiting his acquiring of money. The Bible nowhere suggests that to have money is wrong. What is sinful is when money 'has' us, or, as the Bible describes it, the 'love of money'. This implies that the Christian has to turn his back resolutely upon doubtful ways of gaining easy money. This is obvious, but what is not so obvious and is infinitely more difficult is to see when it is necessary to decide to make a stand and to refuse to compromise, though it may involve a financial loss. No one can tell any other to do this, but we need to ask for a sensitive conscience to discern it for ourselves.

One of the finest men in my congregation was faced with this situation. A newly elected director and secretary of a company, he found that under Government restrictions his firm was engaging in both illegal and non-moral practices. He protested, but any protest he made was of no avail. Finally he said he would resign and leave, if a change was not made. He had to leave. As a married man with two children this was a real sacrifice, for after much searching the only post he could get for which his qualifications fitted him was one with about half the salary.

This principle applies not only to a fairly clear case such as this, but also to matters concerning the choice of a house, the possession of television, the purchase of an expensive car. Clearly these things are legitimate for a Christian to acquire, but there is need to face the expenditure of our money on what is not absolutely essential. How far has the Christian the right to spend freely on himself and his family, when the cause of God needs financing, and the world is full of those living just on starvation line? There is no easy answer here, but there does seem to be room for us to face, for the sake of Christ, limitation that we may better serve the cause of our Master.

In all these examples the emphasis is not on limitation for limitation's sake, but on the willingness to be limited that we may be free fully to follow the way of Christ's service.

There is also the willingness to suffer the experience of alteration. In the same way as the Christian life is not static, but progressive, so Christian thought must never be static, but must always progress. When Jesus told us to love God He said that we had to love Him with all our mind, as well as with all our heart, and it is far too easy to get too fixed in our habits of thinking and acting. Jesus must have startled his contemporaries with His vivid ways of communication, and by His unorthodox methods of approach. New wine must be put into new wine skins, He told His disciples.

The Christian message is the age-old Gospel, but it needs to be expressed in new thought-forms, and in new methods, with each generation. We have only to study the New Testament to see how the writers of the different books struggled to use the word-pictures and thought-forms of their age, that through them they might be able adequately and clearly to bring the Gospel home to their hearers. The same demand is made upon the Christian Church in this generation, whether it be in Africa and Asia, or here in Europe.

It has been interesting to notice recently some of the television programmes in which scientific humanists such as Julian Huxley and Margaret Knight have been suggesting that humanism is sufficient to enrich the human experience and to save mankind, without any belief in God being necessary; morals are possible without religion. Paradise can be regained without faith. In these discussions I have observed that often the Christian protagonists do not seem able to reach the heart of the humanist argument. They make assertions and philosophical statements which had point and validity some decades ago, but do not seem logical nor relevant to the modern humanist. I cannot help wondering whether the Christian apologist of middle age has failed to move with the times in his thinking, so that his arguments are geared to another and earlier age.

I sometimes think that this is partly true in the theological colleges of all the Churches. I wonder whether the way in which Christian doctrine is expounded and taught is not really relevant to the climate of opposition and argument the minister of religion meets in the real world outside. I know that we cannot argue people into belief in God, but none the less it does become necessary that the Christian religion should make sense to thoughtful people. The mass of knowledge that they have acquired in other fields should not seem to have to be put in one water-tight compartment while their Christian faith and experience is put into another; rather it should be that within the whole range of their culture and knowledge the Christian faith in God should seem to make sense of the whole. To achieve this outlook we need to be willing to suffer the alteration of our ideas; and to some extent this is always painful. We like to cling to what we have always believed; we are afraid to face the struggle of doubt or the disturbance of questioning, so we refuse to alter our ideas or to broaden our thinking.

The same dislike of alteration applies to the changing of habits whether of worship or of practice. Examples leap to one's mind—where middle-aged church-goers have resisted suggestions of new methods, or where parents have insisted that their children should follow the habits of conduct and conventions of their own childhood. Fixity of habit can certainly have a stabilizing effect, and it is a good thing that after adolescence most of us settle down to regular lives based on accepted habits and ways of thought; but even in this stability there can be danger; we can refuse to face the need for alteration, to see a better and newer way, and to pursue it. One of the most heartening experiences is to meet some old person, a woman of deep saintliness and of active mind; as one talks with her one discovers that in spite of her age her mind is alert and eager; she welcomes and rejoices in new ways and new ideas; she doesn't accept them easily, for she has a long and solid experience of the past to guide her, but she is willing to see and to embrace that which is new, if it is really good and valuable. Here is a picture of what the Christian Church should ever be—drawing on the wisdom of the past, but willing to suffer the need of continual alteration.

The Christian must also be willing gladly to accept the suffering of pain and ultimate death. In themselves pain and disease are evil. The full range of the healing power of God extends not only to the healing of the soul from sin, but to the healing of the body from disease; but as long as we live in the body, so long we are liable not only to temptation and sin, but also to pain and physical illness. When this meets us the Christian attitude is not one of fatalism and resignation; it should be one of glad resolve that in and through the pain there shall be glory to God, and the learning of some lesson otherwise impossible to be learnt. Someone has said that here is the garden where God's best flowers can grow.

I remember talking some years ago to a very brilliant surgeon. For two years, through a finger cut and poisoned during an operation, she had suffered intense agony and pain. On several occasions her life had been despaired of, but now at last she had recovered. Simply and without melodrama she remarked: 'I would not have missed this experience of pain for anything. In it the presence of Christ has been more real than ever before.'

In his striking book, *Determined to Live*, my friend, Brian Hession, reveals the same kind of acceptance. Given three days to live because of cancer of the rectum he tape-recorded his thoughts about his approaching death. After a surprisingly successful operation his life was saved, and he picked up his work again. For three years now he has moved about the world lecturing and speaking about the power of faith to help people to conquer the fear of pain and disease. Thousands must be grateful to him for his ministry—a ministry only possible because he himself was willing to accept pain and death.

The same characteristic is to be seen in that remarkable book, *Margaret*, where a young girl of 16 was told she was dying of cancer. As she slowly became worse, she accepted it with faith and courage and a complete trust in the love of God; and thus her last months were a witness to all who came to her bedside. They found in her the God whom they were seeking for themselves, and quite a number were brought into a living experience of Christ. After all, Easter Day was only possible because Christ moved through Gethsemane to Golgotha.

Lastly, there is the willingness to care for people; and such real caring must always cause suffering. We cannot care without being hurt ourselves. Jesus, when He saw the city, wept over it.

The Bible calls Christians by different names, but one rather beautiful description is that we are 'a royal priesthood'. What then is a priest? The writer of the Epistle to the Hebrews describes him as one who 'stands on the godward side' of the world, showing that a true priest must firstly be God-appointed, and secondly one of ourselves. Thus only can he stand between us and God. The Christian, as it were, is placed in the middle as a mediator, even as Christ in a quite unique sense was the 'one mediator between God and man'. As His master did, so the individual Christian must make it his business—the Father's business—to lift up the world to God in prayer on the one hand, and then on the other to take the Word of God as he knows it for himself, and to offer it to the world that needs to know it. He stands on the godward side.

This is a position, however, of suffering, because we cannot really pray for people unless we are close enough to them to know their real needs, and these real needs, if we are sensitive, must hurt us. We cannot offer the Gospel of Christ unless we identify ourselves with those to whom we offer it, and live amongst them, sharing their lives. This is never easy nor free from pain.

If then we really care for people we shall suffer with them in their sufferings, even as Christ Himself suffered for and with us during His life on earth. All this is but another way of saying that it costs to love people. It is something like this that Jesus meant when He said: 'For their sakes I sanctify myself.'

Love is always difficult to define, but perhaps it can best be described as the giving of oneself, the outgoing of oneself to another, so that in a sense one belongs to the person whom one loves. This oneness which true love makes possible is seen not only in physical love between man and wife and in their deep and intimate belonging to each other, but in a lesser degree it can be seen in all true love. We cannot love anybody without making contact with them; such contact means to some extent a bodily proximity through exchange of looks, of activity, of conversation; but it means, too, so loving that we seek to give ourselves to their minds, to their emotions, and to their inner selves.

This kind of love and self-giving, which is real caring, would be at the very least the kind of love that costs the little extra, or, to use the words of Jesus, goes the 'second mile'.[1] The first mile, to help the postman to carry the mail bag, according to Roman law was obligatory on any person who was asked; but, says Jesus, do not simply do your legal duty, go all the way, do the extra mile. This is a real mark of Christian living, the willingness to care enough to do more than we need, than we are obliged to, for other people.

The story of the Good Samaritan illustrates this admirably. The robbers were essentially selfish, that is why they robbed the man and left him, not caring whether he lived or died. The Good Samaritan was essentially unselfish. He went beyond any obligation of race or relationship and got off his ass to help the man in need. The priest and the Levite were not bad men at all; they faithfully fulfilled their legal obligations, but could not be bothered to care enough to do the little bit extra, and go out of their way to help.

This caring love also shares what it possesses. I am not thinking now particularly of the sharing of the Gospel, though this is implied. As Mildred Cable said: 'I went out to Tibet because the people there had a right to know that Christ died for them.' I am referring rather to the need of every Christian to be a giving Christian, and every church to be a giving church. The Dead Sea is dead, because it takes in but never goes out. For myself I am sure that the principle of tithing as taught in the Old Testament, and in basic principle reaffirmed in the New, had this purpose in mind. If we learn to give to God a proportion of our possessions this symbolic act will help us to see firstly His claim upon all our

[1] Matthew 5⁴¹.

possessions, and also to become a giving person who will discover it is 'more blessed to give than to receive'.

It is strange, perhaps, that the giving of money should release springs of giving within us. It may well be that this is so because to most of us modern people money is a symbol to us of the work we have done to make it our own; it is part of us which we can use to build up our own lives, and all that belongs to us and surrounds us. Thus when our money is given in a genuine, thought-out proportion to God's work we are in the concrete, and not merely in the abstract, giving ourselves to God, or to express it in another way, putting ourselves through our money into circulation in God's service.

This caring love will also lead us to seek to understand. Elsewhere in this book I have referred at greater length to this need to understand our fellow men, but here I want to point out that it is costly really to sympathize and to seek to understand another human being, yet to understand all is to forgive all.

This spiritual discernment is one of the gifts of the Spirit for which Paul prays for himself and for his friends. Such understanding love will make a Christian a reconciling person, one who is able to help others to be right not only with God, but with their neighbours. It is here too that the Christian Church reveals its true self; it is the community of the forgiven, and therefore must show itself as a forgiving community. It is perhaps with this thought in mind that Jesus said a special blessing would rest upon those who are not simply peace-seekers, and looking only for their own convenience and ease, but upon those who at the cost of suffering and caring will become peace-makers. They shall inherit the Kingdom of God, which after all is the kingdom of love.

In this willingness to suffer we shall discover that it is a much deeper experience than mere unselfishness. It is a gradual dying to self that we may live for Christ, and for the 'brothers for whom Christ died'. It will lead us, not to self-glorification, or to self-gratification that we have been used to help others; we shall find instead a very deep sense of our own inadequacy, a wonder that God uses us at all, and the experience of pain, a travail of soul, that there is so much in God's world which is wrong, that our share in trying to redeem is but a drop in the ocean of need. Yet it will bring us assuredly again and again to that point where, as Peter said (though in different words) by the Sea of Galilee, we in our turn shall sincerely say:

> *Take my love; O Lord I pour*
> *At thy feet its treasure store;*
> *Take myself, and I will be*
> *Ever, only, all for thee.*

CHAPTER VIII

Christlikeness

GENTLENESS AND CREATIVE POWER

THE FOURTH aspect of development in Christlikeness is *the quality of gentleness*. We cannot read the Gospels without noticing how gentle Jesus was, tremendously gentle; not that for a moment I am suggesting the sentimentality so often thought to be expressed by the hymn, 'Gentle Jesus, meek and mild'—a picture of a kind, amiable person who is never disturbed, angry or passionate. That is no New Testament picture of Jesus, as all serious readers of the Gospel know; but gentleness was certainly one of His supreme characteristics. He was never pharisaical or censorious. He had time for the weak and the poor. It was said of Him: 'A bruised reed shall He not break; a smoking flax shall He not quench.' He displayed great tenderness to people nobody else wanted, the unloved and the unlovely. He went out of His way to give His friendship and He gave it with gentleness.

The early Church caught the spirit of its Master, and in the first century this made the Christian community very different from the world around them. Professor Butterfield, as a historian, treats this as very significant: 'Christianity must have an influence in every age. Christian teaching contains certain elements which will produce a softening of manners; in the ancient Roman empire it stressed the sanctity of human life, the importance of the family, the evils of sexual licence and divorce, the wickedness of suicide or the gladiatorial contests or the murder of infants. Christianity was standing

87

for a higher estimation of personality, based on the view of man as a spiritual creature. Furthermore the organization of charity was carried by the Christian Church to the point at which we can regard it as an original contribution to the life of the time. In the fundamental place which it gave to love, in its emphasis on gentleness, humility, joy and peace, the Christian was parting from the ethical ideas of the pagan world, and promoting a different kind of personality, a different posture for human beings under the sun.'[1]

This gentleness of manners springs from a deep sense of the wonder of God's forgiveness. What should matter most to the real Christian is the fact that Christ received him just as he was; with all his sins and weaknesses he was loved and forgiven. If this is so then how can he be ungenerous to other sinners? In face of God's forgiveness to me I must ask myself: 'Who am I not to forgive others?' The Lord's Prayer points out: 'Forgive us our trespasses as we forgive them that trespass against us.' We who have been really forgiven by God, accepted by Him as we are, must also accept other people and forgive them. I think it is true to say that a man cannot genuinely experience God's forgiveness for himself, and not be himself in his turn a forgiving person. There is something radically wrong with him if he is not. Jesus made this point in His parable about the man pardoned a hundred thousand pound debt who demands from his neighbour a £5 note. The hard, ungenerous, mean attitude was utterly condemned. The hall-mark of Christlikeness is to be a forgiving person. This generosity of spirit, this gentleness of attitude is the supremely important Christian characteristic.

Sometimes I am worried about the world-wide Church; what worries me is that sometimes it does not appear to be the place where above all else true forgiveness abounds. I can understand, and in a way—though do not misunderstand me—I am not unduly perturbed if the Christian Church contains amongst its members adulterers and jealous people and selfish people, and all other kinds of sinners, but it does

[1] *Christianity and European Civilization.*

matter terribly if the Christian Church has unforgiving people in its midst, people who call themselves Christians, but who are not gentle and generous toward others, for such people deny the very experience that has made them Christian.

I remember one Sunday night an unmarried lady, a regular member of my congregation, brought to the service with her a married man. His marriage was rather moving toward the rocks, and perhaps his friendship with this other lady was not altogether wise, though there was nothing fundamentally wrong. Before the service began another lady, also a regular member, leant across and said to the first: 'You know, you ought not to bring that man in here. He has no right to come to church.' How utterly opposed to the spirit of Jesus, who was described as the man who was always receiving sinners!

On the other hand, I remember with happiness a Christian lady who gave a warm welcome and her friendship to a man and a woman who began to worship in my church. This couple had lived together unmarried for seventeen years. They had two children, and were trying to make a real home for them. For many years they had stayed away from the Christian Church, but by chance we made contact with them, and they began to come back again. They could not get married, for his wife was still alive, and there was no divorce. I am not justifying that wrong relationship; it was, from a Christian standpoint, sinful; but what was a real happiness to me was the way in which the member of my congregation welcomed them, made them feel at home in church, and gave them the gentleness of her friendship.

Closely linked with the unforgiving spirit is the censorious attitude which negatives Christian gentleness. Smugness, self-righteousness, complacency, a better-than-thou attitude —these prevent us from showing the generosity toward others which we ought to show. This is a danger which besets many Christian enthusiasts. They are often found in the more evangelical congregations: they are full of evangelistic zeal, and serve the Lord most fervently; they are very keen, and they are very consecrated to Christ, but so often they tend to pass judgement on all their other fellow Christians. They refer to them as the 'weaker brethren' who must not be scandalized. They are quite sure in their own minds that *they* themselves could never be a cause of stumbling to anyone. They question the sincerity of the conversion of others, and speak doubtfully of the genuineness of their Christianity. There is a real spiritual danger lurking here. The enthusiasts may sometimes be quite right, and those whom they think are not converted may really not be converted. Often, however, they are showing a censorious spirit, and are lacking in gentleness as well as in spiritual discernment. Sometimes such an attitude casts a doubt on the reality of the conversion of the person who holds it, so that the weaker brethren are actually nearer the kingdom. Is not self-conscious righteousness the one really damning sin?

Many disciples of our Lord who are indeed the salt of the earth are the quite unassuming saints who have a deep love for their Lord, and constantly give themselves in simple, unpublicized selfless service. Many of the best Christians I know would not fit happily in with these fervent evangelists, and yet possess an attractive gentleness which quietly draws many of their friends toward God.

The fifth aspect of development in Christlikeness is the *desire to share the good news*. It cannot escape notice as we read the Gospels that Jesus, wherever He went, talked about God; He was always on His Father's business, telling people about the Father, and trying to bring people to the Father. To put it simply, He sought to share His Father with everyone else.

When a Christian starts growing in Christlikeness he will *desire* to share Christ with others. The word 'desire' is important. It is not the case that we must try to screw ourselves up until in an agony of feeling we think we really can say a word for God. This very sentence, and the phrase 'word for God' suggests something rather gruesome and unnatural, and quite beside my point. It is much rather along the lines of the Quaker saying: 'Never speak unless thou dar'st not keep silence.' We ought to be Christians of such a quality that we dare not keep silent. We should be so constrained by the love of Christ that we should be impelled to share Christ as opportunity offers. After all, the knowledge of Christ should be the best experience I have, the best secret I have; if I am friends with anyone I ought to want to share with him my best. This is quite natural and unembarrassing. There should be neither strain here, nor nervous stress. People I know only casually are not people with whom, as a rule, I share my intimate secrets. To such people, while taking every opportunity that naturally offers to bear witness for my faith, I shall not perhaps introduce the subject of personal religion. When, however, I know someone well enough to talk about any subject that crops up then I am beginning to be on a basis of friendship where I can share Christ with him.

Before the second World War when I was a Vicar in North London I chaired an interesting monthly open-air meeting. The three speakers were a Roman Catholic controversialist, a Congregational minister, and myself. We tried to answer any questions that were thrown at us. I remember on one occasion some Communist hecklers became very angry with us, and accused us of having a specious unity. They shouted: 'This unity of you Christians is phoney. Isn't it true that the Roman Catholic speaker wants to make you a Roman Catholic too, so where's the unity?' My answer came straight from the shoulder: 'Of course he wants me to be a Roman Catholic, because we happen to be very good friends, and therefore naturally as a friend he wants me to share the best he has got.' The Roman Catholic himself added: 'That's right. Of course I do; but I also want to add that we have a real unity in that I recognize that he, no less than I, belongs to the mystical spiritual Body of Christ.' The point is clear. Real friendship is sharing, and into this sharing comes the sharing of the best I know—the knowledge of Christ.

One of the most disastrous failures in this connexion, and one of the most common, is seen in the realm of marriage. I cannot understand how a real Christian can marry someone who is not. More amazing still is the infrequency with which ministers teach and warn against this mistake.[2] A Christian home is impossible unless both partners are Christians; the sharing of the body can be fully satisfying; the sharing of the mind real companionship; but unless there is also a sharing of the spirit there is something deep and real missing. On this the New Testament is quite clear; on this in theory all Christians would agree; but practice is something very different. The time to start is when a boy and girl, a man and a woman, have begun to become friends. As love begins to develop between them then is the time for the Christian to share his knowledge of God. It is no argument to say: 'I don't want to rush her; I don't want to disturb her; I don't want to push her into believing in Christ because I do.' Such an attitude is stupid and wrong. If the man loves the girl at all sincerely he should want to seek to give her the best he has to offer, and that is his faith.

Moreover, the argument that he does not want his girl friend to be influenced toward religion out of love for him is a poor argument. We are often in life influenced out of love for others toward something which is necessary and worth while. Human love can often be the gateway to the discovery of divine love.

My own daughter has a simple and genuine Christian faith, and one of the things I have always respected is her attitude to her boy friends who had little or no religion. She always tried to bring them to church and to win them for Christ. Many a time she has asked me for advice as to how best to answer the questions and difficulties of some agnostic friend. Such an attitude between friends is both sensible and dignified.

I must write plainly. I find it difficult to understand and to respect young people who say they love Christ, and yet never seem to do anything about trying to bring their friends to Him. I know we should not argue from our own experience,

[2] The Christian principle is clear, even though it does happen occasionally that a man or a woman finds faith in Christ through the love of the married partner.

yet sometimes we cannot help doing so. When, after a child-hood training in Christian things, I came gradually into a real conversion I remember that after I knew that I was Christ's, within a couple of months most of my real friends knew about it. Some did not like it, and a few friends I lost; but to me at that time it was tremendously important that my friends should share what I had experienced, and know what I knew. Looking back I am sure I was not always wise or tactful, but I was being very natural.

In some ways I would rather have a Christian at the age of nineteen a little too fanatical and over-enthusiastic; as he grows older he will cool down and mature, and in middle life will probably still be a definite and decided Christian. But if at nineteen he is luke-warm and unenthusiastic in his Christian faith, by the time he is middle-aged he will probably have lapsed into indifference and backsliding.

It is a real challenge which middle-aged Christians ought to face if they are seeking to be Christlike. Some of them have not spoken about Jesus Christ to anybody for years. Some have never even spoken to their children about the need to love and to serve Jesus. There will, of course, have been a few remarks about the value of religion, or suggestions that it is a good thing to go to church—but no plain, forthright talking about God and the need for faith in Him. This is a sin, a plain, downright sin, for it is a betrayal of Christ. Christians of all ages, if they really love their Lord and want to share Him, should be on the look-out for opportunities to do so.

I agree that we have got to be wise; we have no right to embarrass others foolishly; there must be a proper propriety; we have no right to intrude ruthlessly into the private life of others. All this is granted. It is also granted that about things that matter much to us we are shy and self-conscious. Perhaps the deeper our love and knowledge of Christ the more sacred and intimate it becomes, so that we find it difficult to share Him. We are afraid, to use the Bible phrase, to cast our pearls before swine lest they be trampled on and sullied. All this is understandable. But the way to deal with this is not by arguments with one's self, and forcing oneself to do one's duty. Self-consciousness disappears when we look away from ourselves, and centre our thinking upon the need of our friend, our love for him, our desire for his well-being; and then we can think of Christ and all that He can be to that friend. As we do this we shall find that we are forgetting ourselves, and in the richness of the consciousness of what Christ is and what He can be to others, we shall find ourselves sharing naturally and spontaneously in a way which wins and does not repel; which offers Christ, but does not thrust Him upon the soul of another.

The sixth and final aspect of Christlikeness that I want to notice is *a growth in creative power*. Jesus was never just dully good; He was always creative. I wonder why his friends asked Him to a wedding in Cana of Galilee, and why He accepted the invitation? I am sure He did not go just in order to do a miracle and to turn water into wine. I believe He was asked because His friends wanted Him there; He made a pleasant and happy guest. There are many hints in the Gospels that Jesus was often asked out to dinner, and this is noteworthy—he was often asked to have a meal with sinners and those on the fringe or quite outside the Church. Why did they ask Him? Because, to use our modern colloquialism, He helped to make the party go. When He was present people knew that He was; His personality was sparkling and attractive. It is this aspect of Jesus that I want to consider for a moment.

He had real creative power, and He took hold of situations and people and transformed them; and this is what His Spirit can do for us. We are not given in the teaching of Jesus a hard and fast blue-print for the Christian society, for the kingdom of God. The Koran, I believe, tends to lay down a plan, a code of morals, a fixed standard for living, and that is why its teaching so easily gets out of date; but Jesus gives us no pigeon-holed directions for living. There is no ethical code, all numbered, so that I can look up the appropriate number when I am at a loss to know how to act. There are no stereotyped answers. Christ gives us a spirit with which to face life, not a method with which to solve problems. That is what I mean by creative power.

The Living Christian possessed by the Spirit of Christ need not be pushed about nor broken by the stresses of life. He can react with Christlikeness to all that presses upon him. There is the difference. We may not have a blue-print, but we can have the Spirit of Christ within us to enable us to react Christianly and creatively to all that life brings.

This has always been true in Christian history. Initiative, as well as enthusiasm, have been marks of Christlikeness. New ideas have sprung into the minds of men led by the Spirit of God, and these ideas have been translated into action. That is what ought to have been happening continually. One of the great tragedies of organized religion, however, is that so often it takes men and women and canalizes their spiritual life, and conventionalizes their soul. This is perhaps the damning fact about institutional religion. We have turned out conventional Anglicans, or conventional Methodists, or conventional Evangelicals, or conventional High Churchmen. One of the most important tasks for Christian leadership today, as always, is to allow the disciples of Christ to develop their individuality under the creative guidance of the Holy Spirit.

Perhaps the most tragic illustration of this in my personal experience happened over twenty years ago. An Oxford woman graduate, after some years of agnosticism and very great intellectual struggle, had come into a real Christian experience. It was deeply mystical, and was changing her in a remarkable way. She joined other Oxford students on one of my missions. Once or twice she gave in public her witness to Christ. To hear her was to be greatly moved. There were no Bible words or clichés; she spoke simply and naturally out of her fresh mystical experience. Artistic by temperament, she painted a moving picture of what God had done and was doing for her. It fascinated the hearers by its originality and by its outreachingness.

After one such occasion a fine and most sincere Christian

leader came up to me, and pointed out that in her opinion the speaker needed Bible-teaching. 'Her theology's all wrong. Unless she gets her ideas straight she will cease to go forward, and will slip back in the Christian life. She ought to go to a Bible School.' I was inexperienced, and rather weakly agreed, though not very happily.

My friend went to a Bible College. It was good and it was sound; but in three months she had lost her hardly-won faith, and had gone back into an experience of doubt and difficulty. Eight years had to elapse before once more she had recovered her faith, but she never got back the freshness of the mystical experience she once enjoyed. The reason was the attempt, well-meaning, sincere and honest, but wholly misguided, to conventionalize, to standardize, to make sound, yes, even to make biblical, a rich, fresh, individual, inner experience of the Holy Spirit.

I know there is danger here in what I am trying to say, but the work of the Holy Spirit is never safe, in a very real sense it is dangerous. The first Christians were thought to be drunk, and they spoke with tongues and seemed to babble. It was mysterious, disconcerting, did not always seem to make sense; but it was a mighty and real experience of the creative power of the Spirit.

Today when Christians talk they often talk in a petty, trifling way. They do not challenge evil; they discuss and argue about secondary matters; they often seem to have no plan or purpose; they certainly do not thunder out in challenging, startling and dangerous tones the word of God over against the evil of the world. The organized Church is afraid to run risks, and if we prefer conformity and security to enthusiasm and the running of risks, then we can make our choice, but we shall certainly stifle the work of the Holy Spirit. Today visions can be awkward and misleading; but where there is no vision the people perish, and where there is no creative power of the Spirit the Church languishes and falls down on its objective.

Paul tries to give this vision to his friends at Corinth in his second letter. He starts by reminding them that the love of Christ should control them. No longer are they living for themselves; they must live for Him. Has He not done something remarkable for them? They are new people since God reconciled them with Himself through Christ, and through what Christ had done. Now they must live as ambassadors for Christ. God must speak His word to the world through them. By life and lip, everywhere and at all times, they must appeal to the world to turn to God, and to accept salvation in Christ. Then Paul ends: 'As workers together with God' they must seize the opportunity that is theirs.

What a phrase, pregnant with meaning! Christians must be activists. There is no room for drones in the hive of the Church. Here, too, is emphasis on the solidarity of all the redeemed—we are 'workers together'. Then come the last two words of Paul's phrase—'with God'. No doubt it can mean quite properly 'with God's help', with the working within us of God's Spirit. Certainly unless this is true we shall do no work of value for God; but I fancy that there is another meaning here. It is a truth which is plainly stated throughout the New Testament, and which is often implicit in much else. The strength of the Marxist philosophy lies partly in the vision it offers to the dedicated Communist. As Willie Gallacher says in his little book *The Case for Communism* there is an inevitability about the coming of the Socialist State. His book breathes the apocalyptic and messianic spirit of the New Testament, only with God left entirely out. The materialistic secular movement of history will bring in that promised kingdom of the Communist dream. Nothing can stop it. Come it will, and come it must. The true Communist lifts up his eyes to this vision, and then follows the Party line, for to him the Party line means something like this. Whether he lives, or whether he dies, whether he prospers or suffers, no matter; his task and privilege is to co-operate with the Party line, to work with this great movement of history, so that as he co-operates he will have a tiny share in helping to bring about this inevitable result of the movement at the heart of all things. Here is his confidence, and here is his hope.

Paul sees the same kind of vision, only he sees the kingdom of God—a purposeful movement within history, a movement guided by the hand of the living God which will inevitably bring, in God's own good time, the promised kingdom of God and of His Christ. He exhorts his fellow Christians to follow the Christian party line; whether they prosper or whether they suffer, whether they live or whether they die, their task and privilege is to co-operate with the will of God, to play their small part, each of them individually, and all of them together, in helping to bring in God's final purpose for the world.

Here is the Christian's confidence, and here is the Christian's hope. Seeing this vision and yielding himself to the Spirit of God, his life becomes creative with the power of God.

CHAPTER IX

A Life of Fellowship

THE FIFTH mark of the Christian life is that it is *a life of fellowship*, for in a very real sense there is no such person as a solitary believer. The old Roman Catholic doctrine 'There is no salvation outside the Church' is true, though not in the way that it is normally applied. To the Roman Catholic the 'Church' means his Church and none other, and therefore the doctrine is affirming that outside the Roman Catholic communion no one can be truly saved, in the sense of finding the fullness of Christian experience here on earth, while in the next life the non-Roman Catholic can find salvation only through the uncovenanted grace of God, and provided he has died in good faith.

If, on the other hand, we use the word 'Church' in what is to us the true biblical sense, the universal Body of Christ, then the dogma is a true statement of fact. Outside and apart from the Church man cannot find the Christian experience. If he turns to the Bible then he is using the Book of the Church; for apart from the Church writing, preserving and translating there would be no Scriptures. Does he look to the Sacraments? They are the Sacraments of the Church, originated within, and passed on through, its life. If he hears the preaching of the Gospel, that proclamation is made by a member of the Church. Only then through contact with, and through eventually coming within, the Body of Christ can an individual find the true salvation which Christ offers.

To put it rather differently. I cannot be a Christian by myself, for at the heart of the Christian faith and practice stands the Holy Communion, the fellowship meal—and I cannot have the Holy Communion by myself. It is a shared feast, with other believers.

It is clear, then, that the Christian Church is not simply an extra which I can enjoy if I care to; it is not an optional subject for the examination for Christian proficiency; it is not a club which I can join if I feel inclined to pay the membership subscription. It is, rather, a body to which I cannot help but belong if I am a Christian at all. The biblical phrase, 'a man in Christ', does not mean simply someone who personally believes in and shares in the divine life of Christ; it carries also the thought that I share in the life of Christ in and through Christ's Body, the Church.

At Pentecost when the Holy Spirit was given He was given indeed to individuals—'it sat upon each of them', but He came 'when they were all with one accord in one place'. Now the Church is the incarnate Body of Christ here on earth through which He still lives and works, through which worship is offered to God, and through which He shares His redeeming message to the world, and through which He reveals His divine life to those outside.

When I was born, whether I liked it or not, I was born into the Green family. I may now wish I had been born into the Smiths or Williamses, but it cannot be. I was born a Green and a Green I must remain. Moreover, my family was there before I was born, or else I never could have been born. So it is that the Christian Church, the family of God, gives me new birth into Christ. Without that previous family life I could never have been born into the Christian experience. Now that I am so born I am, whether I like it or not, a member of the family. In this way the individual Christian is inextricably bound up with the Church of God, and because we are members of that Body we are also members one of another, and must realize that fellowship.

If, therefore, it is true that outside the Church there is no salvation then the Christian Church is not simply a fellowship of sociability where we meet like-minded friends, nor is it a club of earnest-minded people who wish to serve the community for Christ's sake, though indeed the Church is both incidentally. It is first and foremost a fellowship or family of those who are saved by the precious blood of Christ, who meet as a community of the redeemed, as a society of the forgiven, with a deep gratitude to their Saviour, and a genuine love for each other. From this gratitude, and through this love, they are inspired and strengthened to serve their Lord in the world in which they live.

The expression of such a fellowship is a wide subject, and I can only draw attention to two or three salient points. If we keep this idea of fellowship in our minds then the habit of churchgoing is seen in an entirely different light. What is the motive? It is not that we go to church on Sunday because we think it will help us, or because we feel like it, or because it is good for the children, or because we have been asked to pass round the plate. These are all genuine motives, but the real reason for regular church attendance is plainly and simply because we are members of a family, and our place must not be empty at the family gathering.

The Roman Church often seems to members of the Reformed Churches to have many abuses and distortions of doctrine, but they have some great truths and practices from which we could most profitably learn a lesson. For instance, they plainly teach their people from childhood that to miss Mass on Sunday is a mortal sin, it is deadly to the soul to be away from your fellow Christians on the first day of the week when His Body is broken and His Blood shed in the Sacrament. I believe this is perfectly right and symbolic. It is a sin which imperils the soul wilfully to miss the family worship within the Christian Church on the first day of the week. It is our duty to be there, and we have no right to stay away; it is wrong to mutilate the family's worship by our absence.

Here is a conception of the solidarity of believers which would transform our Sunday worship. We should see the whole act as a family act; we should see the need to play our particular part within it; we should not test the value of this worship by whether we feel uplifted and inspired, or whether the sermon is helpful or not; we often should be inspired, and I hope the sermon often would be helpful; but the real joy and value to us would be that after worship we could look back and say: 'I was there, there in my place, part of the whole worshipping body of Christ's faithful people.'

This conception of fellowship would also save us from that parochialism which bedevils so miserably the Christian Church. So often one hears of little congregations of Christians refusing even to move their building from some down-town factory area into a developing suburb where thousands of people have no church building, and no openly worshipping Christian community. We see congregations raising thousands of pounds to beautify their own sanctuary, but ignoring completely the needs in Africa or Asia for the very essentials that are necessary for the building and developing of the Christian Church. I am sure the Roman Catholic Church too is bedevilled with parochialisms, with diocesan introversion, and other points of narrow-mindedness; but at least her people have a conception of Mother Church, the one same Church throughout the world.

The sinful divisions between the Reformed Churches make it more difficult for our members to grasp the idea of the one Church, yet if we could but grasp and put into practice the implications of this idea of the Christian life as a life of fellowship, then the world-wide Church of Christ would take on a new meaning, and we should see our part within it. Naturally, we should be concerned to heal the outward and visible divisions which keep us apart and make intercommunion difficult, but we should be able to see even now a unity which is greater than our separateness. In Slocum-on-the-Mud, a little village in Suffolk, as Christians we should begin to understand that our mission for Christ is to the whole world; we are His Church, and His Church is world-wide. The implications of this new sense of fellowship for Christian strategy and for Christian stewardship of money are obvious.

Another implication of fellowship is that it would re-emphasize the true meaning of the laity—the people of God.

In some branches of Christ's Church the division between clergy and people is too marked. In others, though theoretically the minister is only a person with a special function to lead worship, to preach the Word and to administer the Sacraments, in practice too much of the leadership and strategy of the Church is left in his hands. In part this is understandable, and springs not from any slackness or theory, but from the general pressure of life. The minister is the full-time professional; the lay people are, as it were, part-time volunteers, therefore on his shoulders must fall the larger burden of the Church's work.

This may be a part of the explanation, but the situation is none the less unhealthy. I doubt very much whether the Church in the twentieth century will ever regain her true vigour and drive until both ministers and lay people realize afresh that they are linked in an indissoluble fellowship, and are equally members of the family, for on each and all of them lies the responsibility for the life and witness of the Church; together they must shoulder this responsibility, otherwise there can be no advance.

This means a good deal more than merely suggesting that lay men and women take on further responsibility within the Church organization, the church building, and the church activities. It means that Christian lay men and women must see themselves as the Church active and witnessing in their neighbourhood, and in every part of their daily lives. They are the Church, and they are responsible for its witness.

There are signs in different parts of the world of an increasing acceptance of this responsibility, and a renewed understanding of fellowship. Nowhere is it more marked at present, perhaps, than in the new emphasis being laid upon the stewardship of money, and the practice of tithing. Certainly in America, the British Commonwealth, and now at last in Britain, this implication of belonging to the Church is being taken to heart.

It is clear that if we really belong to the family then each of us must be prepared to bear his share of the financial support necessary for the family's life. Right back in the Acts of the Apostles this element of fellowship is clearly seen. The first Christians brought their possessions and laid them at the Apostles' feet. Paul emphasizes the need to minister to the saints, and he urges Christians to lay aside for this purpose on the first day of the week money, as God had prospered them. Such giving of money, and the offering of our material resources is not to be thought of simply as a way of financing the Church. It is a deeply spiritual matter. Money is the symbol of work done. By the giving of ourselves and our labour, by working upon the stuff of life, we have made our money. In this sense it is part of us, the symbol of ourselves given in work, of our productivity. As we set apart a portion of our money for the work of the Church we are symbolically expressing the dedication of part of ourselves to the service of God. It is, of course, clearly true that all our money, just as all of ourselves, belongs to Christ; if we are His at all, then we are altogether His, but just as the man who says 'I can pray any time and all the time', but who never prays at a particular time generally ends up by praying at no time, so it is that the man who says 'All that I have is Christ's', but does not bother to dedicate a particular portion of what he possesses to God, ends up by giving very little, if anything.

It is for this reason that fellowship demands that each of us who is a Christian should give thought and care to discovering the proportion of our resources that should be dedicated in a special way to God and to His Church. For some the Old Testament principle of tithing may seem right; for others some other method may be preferable; but for all of us there should be some conscious and deliberate settlement of what we give week by week to the service of Christ and of His Church. Casual and impulsive giving may sometimes seem more generous and more spontaneous, but pledged, regular and thought-out giving is evidence of a truer sense of fellowship and shared responsibility.

These are some of the implications of the Christian life when it is seen to be a life of fellowship—a life in Christ, shared and lived within the unity and as a member of the family of those who belong to the same Lord and who own the same Saviour. The purpose of this unity in fellowship is not primarily for our own spiritual strengthening and happiness. It is outward-looking, and is meant to be a witness that the world may know through our oneness, our One Lord and Saviour and the One True God.

CHAPTER X

A Life of Discovery

THE SIXTH mark of the real Christian life is that it is *a life of discovery*. This note is very evident in the New Testament. In the opening words of his letter to the Christians at Ephesus Paul tells his friends that he is praying to God that they might receive 'the spirit of wisdom and revelation in the knowledge of him, that the eyes of your understanding being enlightened ye may know what is the hope of his calling, and what the riches of the glory of his inheritance in the saints, and what is the exceeding greatness of his power to us-ward who believe'.[1] He echoes the words of the Lord Jesus who promised that 'the Holy Spirit, when He is come, shall guide you into all truth'.[2]

As we grow in the Christian life we should come to discover something of what it really means to be a Christian, and what are the spiritual resources at our disposal. It will be given to us to know more about God, and more about man. Here is no standing still; here is the glorious adventure of possessing unsearchable spiritual riches, some of which we can always be discovering and appropriating. This is what gives to the Christian experience its freshness. There is nothing static; it is meant to be a moving forward into fresh insights, fresh knowledge, and fresh action.

There is no doubt that this is the climate of the New Testament, but I am not at all sure that it is the climate in which the modern Christian lives. In very many Christian communities the adventure of spiritual discovery seems to be absent.

[1] Ephesians 1[17].   [2] John 16[13].

There seems to be no life and movement. Spiritual fervour seems to be at a low ebb, and individual Christians stationary as regards any progress.

It is, therefore, important to emphasize this note of discovery very early on in the Christian life. In my evangelistic work I naturally meet many who have been privileged to have a dramatic conversion—a definite crisis in the process of their Christian experience. If I have the opportunity of seeing such people a little while after their conversion I have a question which I always try to ask. I do not say to them, 'Do you feel happy? Are you behaving better? Is it lasting?'—but I do ask, 'What have you discovered?' Far more important than any feeling of happiness or even than changed behaviour is the discovery of something new and fresh about God. If a man has become alive to God through Christ then he ought to expect to discover and find out more about the spiritual world as the days pass. The Christian life is meant to be a life of continuing discovery.

Some years ago I was asked to meet a brilliant young medical student, a girl of some eighteen years. Her parents never went near a church, and although in her very early teens she herself had gone for two or three years she had given it up from intellectual disbelief of what she heard taught there. She called herself an atheist.

During her early months at the university, being a strong personality, she had tackled some of her Christian friends, and badly confused them. They did not know how to handle her challenge. One day a fellow student, a Methodist, said to her: 'I can't argue with you, you are too clever for me, but I bet you would not argue with a parson.' Her retort was immediate: 'Of course I would, and I would love it.'

That was how I came on the scene. For three hours we argued. I certainly failed to convince her, though I was able, being older and more experienced, to expose some of the weaknesses of her position. The chief result was that we became friends. She had a good mind which I respected, and so we met and continued our discussion. In the end we got nowhere, and I concluded our final conversation with words something like these: 'Only when God and life break you will you really turn to Him'—and so we said good-bye.

I saw nothing more of her for some seven years, and then late one evening my telephone rang, and my caller asked if I remembered her name. I did not, and said so. Then she reminded me of our argument years before, and went on to ask whether she could come round and see me. The voice was urgent, and fortunately I was free, and so I invited her to come immediately.

When she arrived, and as she walked into the room, her first sentence was: 'Do you remember the last words you said to me?' At the time I did not. 'Well,' she continued, 'you told me that God would break me, and He has. Now I need help, and I don't know whether it is a psychiatrist or a parson that I need. I want one or the other, and I have decided to try you first.'

As we began to talk I found out that she was a qualified doctor, married, and that much had happened in her life in the intervening years. Now life had broken her. She felt lonely, frustrated, spiritually naked and defenceless, and she wanted God. That night God found her, very simply, very really.

During the next two or three months I saw her quite frequently, and each time I opened our talk with the words: 'What have you discovered now?' Every time there was something new she was longing to tell me. On the first occasion this is what she said: 'Do you remember what a tiny little bit of faith I had the other night? How very feeble my trust was when I genuinely turned to God? You told me that if I went on from that, to try to obey what God told me to do, my faith would grow. I have discovered that that is true. It is just what has happened.' She had never read her Bible before, but now she read it, and the whole picture came alive to her. A fortnight after her conversion she had read right through Luke's Gospel. She produced on a piece of paper a number of questions for me to answer. I found that they were the difficult questions and the difficult passages that were often set for scripture examinations! And so it went on. As she followed Christ in the simple obedience of faith so she discovered rapidly and amazingly some of the truths about the Christian life and faith.

This is God's intention for all of us who are Christians. We are meant increasingly to know more about God and His character, about Christ and His teaching, and about the Holy Spirit and the way He leads us.

I sometimes have it said to me rather sadly by a Christian man who has been arguing with a Communist that he has found that a genuine Communist knows more about his philosophy and dogma than the Christian knows about his. This is often distressingly true. *Why* is it? It is not necessarily because the Communist has read more books or listened to more lectures on Communism than the Christian has on Christianity. Part of the basic training of a Communist is that he must link learning about Communist theory with Communist action. As he does this he discovers the meaning and application of the theory in practice and in life. He discovers its relevance and meaning. The Christian so often when he reads the Bible fails to take its teaching and to obey it in action. It is when he does this that he will discover its meaning, and also will discover new truth.

This idea of discovery applies to other aspects of Christian practice. I remember a man of forty-five asking me about prayer, for, he said, he found his prayers difficult and unhelpful. I agreed with him that prayer would always be difficult, but as he pointed out, it was not just that his prayers were difficult, but they were utterly unreal and unhelpful. 'Excuse me asking,' I said, 'but what do you pray each night?' After a moment of hesitation he blurted out: 'Well, as a matter of fact, I only pray what I was taught to pray when I was a child —"Gentle Jesus, meek and mild, look upon a little child." ' 'How can that mean anything', I asked him, 'to a man of forty-five?' He had never discovered in all these years anything more in prayer. His prayer life had been standing still.

The Bible contains many promises that God will guide His people, and show them the way they should go. For many of us the discovery of God's guiding hand is one of the great joys of our Christian lives. Some lay a good deal of insistence upon the seeking of guidance from God, trying to find out before we make a decision what is the decision He wants us to make. That there is a real truth here I am sure, and certainly in my own experience there have been crises in my life when I needed God's guidance, genuinely sought for it, and, I believe, received it. Yet, on the other hand, there is something even finer and more real than this experience of the guiding hand of the heavenly Father. It was well expressed by a Warden of Keble College, Oxford, in a letter which I had the opportunity of reading. He was writing about guidance. He said that in all his years of Christian experience he had had very few, if any, occasions when he definitely knew of God's guidance before he made a decision. To him it was a case of trying to look at a situation with the mind of Christ, searching the Scriptures for any help that he could find, asking the advice of Christian friends, and in his prayers telling God that he was willing to do what He wanted. Then he had to make his decision and act. 'But', he added, 'for many years I have kept a diary, and never a year has ended when, reading back over the past twelve months, I have not been humbled and glad to see what I believe is the guiding hand of God upon my life.' Here was the discovery of guidance which brought with it confidence and trust concerning what lay ahead.

The Christian also learns to discover the breadth of God's love. As Dr Faber wrote:

> But we make His love too narrow
> By false limits of our own;
> And we magnify His strictness,
> With a zeal He will not own.
> For the love of God is broader
> Than the measures of man's mind,
> And the heart of the Eternal
> Is most wonderfully kind.

This is a discovery of great importance and practical value. In the early days of our Christian experience many of us tend to be somewhat narrow and dogmatic. Soundness in the faith means agreement with our own views. We find ourselves easily able to divide Christians up into the keen, the not so keen, and the dead. We put our fellow believers into categories of one kind and another. This perhaps does not do much harm in the early days, but unfortunately there are many who do not grow out of this narrowness through spiritual discovery. The advancing years do not mature and broaden their Christian understanding. Others discover the variety of God's ways with man. This may be a dangerous experience, but it is exciting and full of interest. Let me give one or two examples of what I mean.

Many Christians have looked at the people of other religions as if there is for them nothing real in the way of a knowledge of God, or of true spiritual experience. All that they believe is evil; their worship is false and idolatrous. Other Christians have discovered as they have come to understand God better that the God they know in Christ is a self-disclosing God; at the very heart of His being lies a forgiving love which for ever makes Him want to reveal Himself to all men everywhere. The discovery of this great fact about God's nature opens our eyes. We begin to realize that if God is like this, a self-disclosing God, then He is, and always has been, seeking to disclose Himself to men everywhere.[3] We should, therefore, expect to find amongst people of other religions here and there those who have caught a glimpse of God's self-disclosure, who have had some real spiritual insight, and who have had some genuine spiritual experience. True, it is not the full understanding and knowledge of God as revealed in Christ, but it is a real experience of God. This makes a very great difference to our attitude to the great religions of the world, and to our relationships with those who practise them.

The other example is somewhat similar. The fuller discovery of God's nature in Christ makes me question the

[3] Romans 2[14,15].

definitions of Christian dogma. Whereas before I was able to express my faith in simple black-and-white propositions, now I see this man-made formula to be only an approximation of what vaguely I know, and the Christian Church knows, by experience about God. It is not that I throw over the great affirmations of the Christian Creeds—I hold to them still, and genuinely believe them; but I see them as human expressions of great, ineffable truths, as feeble approximations which cannot really express or contain what they try to say. True, this can produce an attitude of doubt which inhibits a clear and firm proclamation of the Christian faith, but it need no do so. It should, rather, lead to maturity of Christian thinking and expression, and to a deep and genuine sympathy with the sincere agnostic, and for those on the fringe of the Christian Church who would like to believe, but cannot.

To sum up, let me underline my main point here. This maturity or mellowness of Christian experience is not the result primarily of intellectual broadmindedness, nor is it the product of conscious effort. It springs, as I have suggested, naturally and spontaneously from a continual and fresh discovery of the nature of God and His ways with men.

In the Psalms there is a lovely phrase which reads: 'All my fresh springs shall be in thee.'[4] The Holy Spirit will work in my life to give me fresh springs, fresh discoveries, fresh understandings and insights of God. Jesus meant much the same when He said: 'If any man thirst let him come unto me and drink. He that believeth on me, out of him shall flow rivers of living water.'[5]

[4] Psalm 87[7] (*PBV*).   [5] John 7 [37–8].

CHAPTER XI

A Life of Freedom

THE SEVENTH mark of the Christian life is that it is *a life of freedom*. Whatever else the Christian life is it is not primarily one to be lived under a series of rules and regulations. We are not under law, but we are under grace. Paul was always very clear about this, and the whole Epistle to the Galatians is largely a treatise upon this point. The Christians in Galatia had found the free forgiveness of God, and were rejoicing in their new experience of forgiveness and acceptance in the Beloved. Then the legalizers arrived, and tried to force them both to conform to certain ritual acts and ceremonies, and to accept the legal requirements of the Old Testament; all this above and beside the moral law which was fulfilled in Christ, and which the Galatian Christians gladly sought to obey. To them Paul gave his clarion call: 'Stand fast in the liberty wherewith Christ hath made you free.'[1] He goes on to say that in one sense there are no binding rules or commandments which are obligatory for Christians. We must resist the ever-present temptation that, having become Christians through simple faith in Christ and all He has done for us, we now seek to maintain our Christian life by the keeping of moral laws. 'Through the Spirit', he continues, 'we wait for the hope of righteousness . . . faith working through love.'[2] This is the great law, the one law, for the Christian, the law of love, for 'love is the fulfilling of the law'. In saying this, however, he is saying something tremendous, because there is

---

[1] Galatians 5[1].   [2] Galatians 5[5] (*RSV*).

H   113

no such thing, correctly speaking, as free love. Love is the most binding force on earth.

Here is a daughter going to Canada, let us say, for a year. She and her mother are devoted to each other. From one point of view it would be much easier for the girl, perhaps, if her mother gave her a list of twenty rules to keep if she was to be a dutiful daughter, pleasing her mother. That would leave the girl quite free to do anything she liked outside the ground covered by the twenty rules. But love is more binding than that. The mother gives her no rules, yet in the girl's mind and heart there is a consciousness of what would please her mother and what would not. This knowledge is inconvenient, for it covers the whole of life, both the known and the unknown situations, both the present and the future. Because she loves her mother she will always find the challenge and standard for her actions. She lives under love, and not under law.

So it is with the Christian life. Our main purpose, put quite simply, is to please God, or to put it in a more specifically Christian way, to please Christ. That is an enormously big task; there is no end to it, and there is no escape from it, if we really love Him.

From this point of view the Sermon on the Mount, for instance, becomes not a series of moral laws which must be kept exactly and explicitly, but an expression of the ideal life for man as Jesus sees it—the kind of human living that would please Him and make Him happy. If, therefore, we love him we shall seek to live that kind of life, not because it is an obligation commanded, but because it is a life that would please Him.

The Ten Commandments are binding upon the Christian in a similar fashion, not just as the law of God laid down which if we keep we have done our duty, but as a moral law which expresses the nature and character of God whom we seek to serve. Because these commandments help to make the world the kind of world that God wants, we must keep them out of love for Him, and because loving Him we seek to carry out His purpose in the world.

Is this just an academic argument, or does it really make a difference to think like this? I believe it does. In the first place our main question is: 'What will please God? How can I express my love for Christ?' Sometimes in life it may seem impossible exactly to keep one of the commandments or exactly and fully to live up to some ideal of the Sermon on the Mount. We may find ourselves in a situation in which we are so involved that any action we take falls short of the ideal. We still can test ourselves by our love for Christ. What in these circumstances, with these commandments and these ideals in our minds, will please Him best? We act then as an expression of our love for Him, though conscious of our failure to be perfect. He sees the offering of this love, and accepts it.

From another point of view this thought is a help. Seeking to please God is so great a task that if I am sensitive to what it means I shall know that I never can properly be well-pleasing in His sight. As Jesus pointed out to His disciples, when all is done we are still unprofitable servants. This means that part of the experience of Christian living is to have an ever-deepening sense of sin. We are always failing, and always will. Yet even as we know this we can rejoice in the fact that we are loved and forgiven by Him whom we fail perfectly to please. We know we love Him, though, with Peter, we hardly dare to say so.

This freedom from law and regulations is not licence, for most certainly it is not a freedom to do just what I like. Paul realized the danger of this misunderstanding when he wrote: 'You were called to freedom, brethren; only do not use your freedom as an opportunity for the flesh, but through love be servants of one another.'[3] Our freedom from rules needs certain checks if we are to live within the law of love. It is, as I have already written earlier in this book, freedom within a fellowship.

What, for instance, do we mean as Protestant Christians when we claim the right of private judgement? We certainly do not mean that every individual Christian can think just

[3] Galatians 5^{13} (*RSV*).

what he likes, and that his view is as true as that of anyone else. This is the false charge that the Roman Catholic often brings against us. 'Look', he argues, 'at your Protestant Churches. Everyone can think what he likes. Look at the mess you are in about doctrine, all your differences of views and differences of practice. What you need is to return to a Church which with authority will tell you what to think and how to act. You claim that you go to the Bible for your views. Well, it seems to me as if there are as many views as there are words in the Bible, judging by the results. You need an authoritative Church which will tell you the true interpretation of the Bible. Then, and then only, will you get uniformity, and have a faith which everyone will accept, and a Christian life which everyone can practise.'

This is the charge, and to it we must make a reply. First, we must admit that there is some truth in what is said. Some Protestants think and teach just as they individually choose to think and teach; but that is not what we mean by the right of private judgement. As a member of a human family each of us possesses within the family circle the right of private judgement. As an adult member we are ultimately free to think as we like, but not just casually or egotistically. If we are a real member of the family it is natural to pay careful regard to what the family thinks, to the atmosphere of the family life, to the practices and habits which make the family what it is. Then, and not until all this has been considered, is it our inalienable right to exercise our private judgement, to form our views, and to make our decisions.

This is no academic illustration. Some of us know to our joy the experience of seeing a child grow up in the family circle to adult life, and using private judgement in just this kind of way. She will be different a little from her parents both in views and practice, but there is a genuine similarity in her outlook and behaviour to that of the family in which she grew up. So it is in the Christian family. My private judgement can and must be exercised, but not without a real sharing of the life of the Christian family. This sharing will mean that I am forced to pay careful regard to what the Church thinks, not merely to the present thinking of the Church and to the Christian public opinion of the moment, but to the heritage of the past, to what the Church has been thinking for two thousand years. For example, in reading the Bible I must not say of a passage: 'I think it means this or that.' Before I come to a conclusion I must ask: 'What has the Church thought about this passage since it was first written? What do the scholars think it means?' Then, and not till then, I exercise my private judgement. Sometimes I may be right in repudiating the whole experience of the tradition of two thousand years of Christianity; sometimes I may be right, and the whole Church wrong; but this is most unlikely. Yet it does seem to be part and parcel of the genuine Christian experience that this inalienable right of private judgement should be asserted as part of the freedom of the Christian.

It is not only about what we think, but about how we act, that we have this right of private judgement. The privilege of conscientious objection is a Christian privilege, and we must be prepared to take our stand even to the point of martyrdom. But once again, we must recognize the public opinion of the Christian Church, and the accumulated wisdom of the past. It can only be in rare cases that the individual Christian is right and the whole Church wrong. For instance, there is no law that forces each Christian each day to say his prayers, but Jesus prayed regularly, and for two thousand years Christians have done the same. My private judgement leaves me free either to pray daily or not to pray, but it is not likely that I am behaving properly if I repudiate this accumulated experience and decide that I can manage without private prayer.

History is full of examples of the way in which this matter of private judgement has worked. There have been many cases where the single prophet has had a clearer insight into God's will than the Church of his day, and has stood out alone, and suffered for it. There will always be such occasions, and the freedom to be Christian as we see we ought to be Christian is a possession we should never give up.

One last example from within the Anglican Church. From time to time the Convocations—the Assemblies of clergy within the Church of England—pass what are called 'Acts of Convocation'. They concern matters of doctrine, of worship, and of morals. They rightly carry great weight, because they are the considered judgement of learned men, and are passed after careful consideration and sincere prayer. They are not, however, hard and fast binding rules upon any member of the Church of England, whether clergyman or layman. We can judge them to be wrong without spiritual peril, but we cannot ignore them easily or lightly. Humility would suggest that the individual clergyman or layman is more likely to be wrong in his judgement than Convocation, he will therefore give great weight and careful thought to these Acts; but in the last analysis he must exercise his own freedom of judgement, and if he disagrees then he must refuse to conform—and then he must be willing to suffer the usual penalty of being a non-conformist.

To sum up: Christian freedom gives me the position where I stand before God Himself answerable to Him alone, yet in humility I must give due consideration and weight both in my thinking and behaviour to what is the general public opinion of Christendom. In estimating this I must bear in mind not only the teaching of the Bible, but the tradition of the past, of Christian history. I must open my mind to be influenced not only by academic argument and thought, but by the spirit of Christian worship, and the accumulated experience of Christian living. Then I am free, free to obey my conscience, to exercise my private judgement, and to stand fast in the liberty wherewith Christ hath made me free.

Christian freedom is both dynamic and purposive. It is not only 'freedom from' or 'freedom in'. It is primarily 'freedom for' God's service. We are to be released from all bondage that all our powers and the deeps of our personality may be set free to be given gladly and used fully by Him who has made us free.

CHAPTER XII

A Life of Moral Struggle

THE EIGHTH mark of the Christian life is that it is *a life of moral struggle*. Scholars have argued a good deal about the seventh chapter of the Epistle to the Romans. Is Paul here describing his experience before or after he became a Christian? It is the story of a man conscious of a continual conflict going on within his soul. Deeply, at the centre of him, he accepts the law of God and longs to do it, yet he knows there is another principle at work within him, a sinful and evil principle which again and again seems to overcome his deepest desires and longing for holiness. In the agony of the conflict he cries out: 'The good that I would I do not; but the evil which I would not, that I do. . . . O wretched man that I am! who shall deliver me from the body of this death?'[1]

I think the body of opinion is in favour of this experience of Paul's being a post-Christian one. It is the moral struggle which, as every Christian knows, continues throughout the Christian life. This view is somewhat confirmed by what Paul writes in Galatians, Chapter 5, where having compared the works of the flesh with the harvest of the Spirit he makes the statement: 'The flesh lusteth against the spirit, and the spirit against the flesh; and these are contrary the one to the other, so that ye cannot do the things that ye would.'[2] Though this moral struggle is a fact that Christians must face, the experience of the eighth chapter of the Epistle to the Romans is the characteristic Christian note.

What is this spiritual struggle of which Paul writes, and for

[1] Romans 7[19, 24].　　　　　　　[2] Galatians 5[17].

that matter, all the other writers in the New Testament? The flesh and the spirit are opposite the one to the other. We must understand clearly that he does not mean by the 'flesh' our bodies. There have been those within the Christian Church, and there are still some, who seem to think that the body with all its appetites and instincts is evil in itself, that there is something inherently bad about the body. This is a form of an ancient heresy, and is not Christian truth. We are God's creation, and we are both body and spirit. Whatever we think of God's creation, whether by a special act or by evolutionary process, we must conclude that our body is in itself good, God has created it. My instincts and appetites can be distorted and warped, but in themselves they are good. This point can be supported also by the fact of the Incarnation. When the Word was made flesh, He became *our* flesh, He took *our* human body, He manifested Himself to the world through *our* human appetites, instincts and characteristics.

This fact that the human body, and our human mental faculties, are in themselves good is important, and if not clearly grasped can lead to unfortunate consequences. In the struggle for holiness, for instance, there have been those who have thought of fasting and mortification of the body as the drastic dealing with something that is evil in itself, whereas the true idea should be to regard the discipline of the body as a control of the physical part of us so that it shall be a better vehicle for the true expression of our thought and spiritual insight. We discipline a horse that we may ride him the better, not because the horse is bad in itself. There are still some Christians who seem to think that they ought not to enjoy bodily pleasures, that there is something wrong in the love of rhythm, in pleasure in eating, and in other joys which give bodily satisfaction. An extreme case is that of a young Christian man who thought it was wrong to play games, but added that he played tennis because it was good for his health; or another who believed dancing was sinful, and yet danced from time to time so that he might try to win the girl he danced with to a faith in God. Frankly, I should not like to be the girl, nor should I like to play tennis with that man! Somewhere in the mind in both these instances is an inner feeling, a hang-over of some misguided idea that the body and bodily pleasure are evil in themselves.

To take a more important instance, Roman Catholic theologians and some others hold that sexual intercourse between husband and wife is only legitimate when practised for the express purpose of the procreation of children. It is wrong to have the bodily pleasure and sexual feelings of intercourse just for themselves alone. The beauty and meaning-fulness of the act itself as a sacrament of the real belonging of love is therefore wrong as an end in itself, but right only if it is the means to something else. I believe that this moral dictum is based on a faulty theology of the body. It seems to me that all bodily desires and activities are good in themselves, and thus sexual intercourse is a beautiful, meaningful act if expressing true love and a deep personal relationship. Such instincts can, of course, be used selfishly or without meaning and purpose, and thus become wrong, but it is in their abuse and not in their natural use that the sin lies.

Having cleared away the necessary identification of the New Testament word 'flesh' with the body we can ask what does it mean? The best definition is probably 'the self', the old self-centred life in which everything is looked at from the egoistic viewpoint. When a man puts himself in the centre of his own life, when everything is looked at from the point of view of our own advantage, when life is based on self-interest, when in fact I am the centre of my being, then we are describ-ing basic self-centredness, or the old self-life, the flesh. In this connexion it is instructive to notice that what we would call 'spiritual' sins, such as envy, pride, and so on, Paul labels as 'of the flesh' so that the most carnal thing is conscious spirituality. No wonder Paul was hated!

So deep-rooted is our self-centredness that we even think and believe we can run our life without God. That is the true Bible definition of the root of sin. It is clear that flesh in this sense is absolutely opposed to the new life in Christ. The self-centred and the God-centred life are opposites. When a man finds a new relationship with God through Christ he begins a new life, a spiritual life centred round Christ, but the old life, self-centred and egoistic, is still in the experience of his personality.

It does not matter whether we describe these opposites within the Christian personality in psychological terms or in biblical phrases. There is this dichotomy in the Christian soul, and the two principles of life are contrary the one to the other. The result is a continual moral and spiritual struggle. That is why it is never easy or comfortable to live the Christian life. There is no room for spiritual or moral laziness. The negro spiritual sings truly: 'You can't get to heaven in a rocking-chair; My Lord won't have any lazybones there.' The struggle is costly and continuous.

This moral struggle is made all the more difficult and intense by the fact that though the Christian is not of the world he must needs live in the world amid the conditioning processes of modern life. Press, radio, television, business, shops and things to buy, standards of life, society and friends, all these tend to focus upon our desire to get and to have; they tip the scales of living in the direction of self-centredness and self-interest. God and the spiritual dimension are almost entirely absent.

We cannot help being affected by these conditioning processes. We are caught in the stream of them. It is this that makes the struggle of the spirit so hard. The way to fight in the struggle is not so much to oppose the evil in order to try to crucify the flesh, but rather to open our lives to spiritual influences, and to discover the expulsive power of a new affection. Instead of trying to destroy our self-centredness it is better through union with God to allow Christ to become the new and real centre of our living.

The secret here may seem obvious, but many Christians miss it. Learning to open one's heart and to submit one's will to the work of the Holy Spirit is infinitely more successful as a way of victory in the struggle than nerving oneself up to fight against what one knows to be wrong. It is possible to see the truth of this line of argument in a very human instance. It always amazes me when I see it, and fills me with joy and thankfulness.

Here is a young girl, modern in outlook, well educated, earning good money. She has a satisfying job, and many friends. She is a girl of high standards, full of *joie de vivre*. She exercises her opportunities to the full, travels abroad for her holidays, sees things and meets people. Then she meets the man she loves. She gives up her job, goes travelling no more, but settles down to married life. She adapts herself to housework, and does all the chores without grumbling. Quite magnificently she achieves the change, and fits in with serenity and happiness to the life of a married woman. How does she do it? It certainly is not because every morning she makes up her mind to renounce travel, to fight the longings for the old life, to push down selfish and indolent desires. It is rather that there has come into her life a new love—a love for him, and then a little later on a love for them—and it is this love which enables her to win the struggle over the old life, and to enter gladly into the new. It is, we must notice, a struggle, perhaps for some easier than for others; there are the old longings and there are the selfish desires, there is a wish for pleasure and travel, but the new love makes her more than conqueror.

So it is that the love of Christ constrains us, and the Holy Spirit leads us, and as this happens the old things will begin to fall away, and the moral struggle will begin to show signs of victory, until in the end all things become new.

CHAPTER XIII

A Life of Humility

THE NINTH and final mark of the Christian life is that it is *a life of humility*. By humility I do not mean absence of conceit; conceit in itself can be a minor sin, though it is unpleasant to others and disturbing to oneself; it is a stupid habit of mind and outlook rather than a major sin. I am reminded of the amusing story, probably apocryphal, of the Roman Catholic girl making her confession. She went regularly once a week. 'Father,' she confessed, 'I am sorry to say I have to confess the same sin again this week. It is my worst sin, and I can't get over it. It is a terrible sin, and I am very ashamed of myself. I must tell you, Father, it is the sin of conceit. I am always thinking of myself as so very good looking.' 'My child,' replied her confessor, 'that is not a sin, it's a mistake.' The girl left the confessional furiously angry, we are told.

No, humility is not an absence of conceit. Bishop Gore defined it like this: Humility is seeing myself at my true value, others at their true value, and God at His true value. It is when I see myself as I am, and God as He is, that I become really humble. It is not connected, you will observe, with conceit at all. It is connected with pride, the deadliest of the seven deadly sins. Humility is beautifully expressed by Paul when he wrote: 'By the grace of God I am what I am.' He put no value upon the accident of his birth, his strict religious upbringing, his fervent enthusiasm, all his other natural and cultural advantages. From one point of view they were valuable, but not to Paul as he thought of his Christian experience. What mattered there was that Christ loved him and gave Himself for him, and that forgiveness, free and gracious, was offered to him.

I am humble when in the depths of my consciousness I know that if I am a Christian at all it is because of God's love to me in Christ; it is His free and undeserved favour that has made me what I am; then I can say with the utmost truth: 'It is not I, but Christ that liveth in me.' Humility is the natural product of justification by faith. When a man realizes that he is utterly unworthy of God's acceptance, God's forgiveness, God's friendship, and then comes to know that all this can be his, utterly and only because Christ died for him, that everything that he knows of the experience of God is a free gift, that this free gift in no way depends upon his own efforts or his own merits, when he realizes that the Christian life can never be self-made, but that it has to be God-given, then within such a man is born the humble spirit and the contrite heart. With true meaning he can express the experience of his soul in the words: 'Nothing in my hand I bring, simply to thy cross I cling.'

This note of humility is the undertone of the real Christian's thinking and living. It is usually possible to detect it by the way a Christian talks and worships. As a rule in talking of his religion he does not emphasize his 'continued loyalty to Christ to whom he gave himself at Confirmation'; he does not speak much about his 'commitment' or 'personal dedication' to God's service. He talks rather, if he is sharing intimately his religious thinking, about his continuing acceptance of God's forgiveness—'I always need that'; he stresses his constant need to receive the help of God's Spirit. Notice the difference —not 'my dedication', 'my loyalty', 'my commitment', but 'receiving what He gives', 'accepting the forgiveness He offers'.

I remember once, many years ago, at a Keswick Convention listening to an interesting demonstration of the point that I am making. There must have been well over a thousand young people at this particular meeting, and a young man and a young woman gave their testimonies. Both, I am sure, were real Christians, but only one had humility. The first, an Oxford graduate, spoke of his past life and his moral failures; then told how he confessed his sins, sharing them with a friend and then telling them to God; how he made an absolute surrender; then how his life was changed; how he put this right and put that right. It was all very true, genuine and convincing. I do not doubt for a moment the truth of his conversion.

Then a young woman, a brilliant surgeon, spoke. Her life, too, had been one of irreligion and of moral failure, but her emphasis was that when she knew her need for God and a different life she could do nothing about it. Then she heard the story of the Gospel, the wonder of Christ's love and His death for her sins, the offer of God's forgiveness; simply she told how she came to God and asked for His forgiveness, and received the gift of new life. Her story was utterly centred in Christ and what He had done, and what He was doing for her. Humility and gratitude were the keynotes.

Humility, then, springs from a conviction of my utter dependence upon God, and that I am nothing except as He makes me something. It is no longer *my* faith that is of importance, but the object of faith that counts. This is true of the way in which a man enters into the experience of justification; it is just as true of the way in which he continues to live the Christian life. 'As ye have therefore received Christ Jesus the Lord, so walk ye in Him.'[1] By faith I received Christ as my Saviour and Lord, my heart crying out to Him: 'Lord, forgive me; I don't deserve anything; take me as I am.' Thus I took the Saviour by faith; so I must walk and live the Christian life by the same faith. At its heart the Christian life is a life of simple trust in God day by day, receiving as a little child all that God wants to be to me. That is why Jesus constantly stressed the need for a simple, childlike faith. Each day He means us, as it were, to stand before Him saying: 'Lord here am I. Be to me today all that you want to be as a Saviour, as a Friend, as a Guide, as a Master.' When this is a spontaneous and continuous attitude

[1] Colossians 2⁶.

our lives will become Christ-centred, because we are looking utterly toward Him all the time in trustful humility.

There is a delightful fable about the ocean. The sea, it is imagined, was one day feeling discontented. Disillusioned, it hated living at its low sea level when above it were drifting some delightful little white clouds scudding along before the wind. The sea grumbled to itself: 'I don't see why I should be living down here at this low level. Why can't I live higher up, up there where the clouds are?' And so in its discontent and anger the sea began to lash itself into fierce high waves, flinging the foam of its spray high into the air, yet always it fell down again to the same low level of living. Then one day the sun smiled down on the sea and said kindly: 'You want to live on a higher level? Then don't fret yourself, strain and struggle. Lie still and look up.' So the sea lay still, very still, and looked up. A warm wind arose, and the sun came down and carried some of the water up nearer to heaven, and presently there were seen some fresh white clouds moving overhead.

If we genuinely desire to live on a higher level of Christian life it is useless to strain and strive to reach heaven. Our business is to lie still and to look up to Christ, and then His Spirit will lift us up, enabling us to live a fuller and better Christian life.

An old-fashioned chorus that I learnt as a child expresses the same idea:

> *Moment by moment I'm kept in thy love,*
> *Moment by moment I've life from above;*
> *Living for Jesus, thy promise divine,*
> *Makes me quite certain, dear Lord, I am thine.*

And this prayer asks God to live out His life in us:
'O Lord, take our minds and think through them; take our lips and speak through them; take our lives and live out thy life; take our hearts and set them on fire with a love for thee; and guide us ever by Thy Holy Spirit. Through Jesus Christ our Saviour.'

Books for Lent and Easter

STENING AT THE CROSS
By Leslie F. Church, B.A., Ph.D.   5s. net

THEY MET AT CALVARY: WERE YOU
THERE . . . ?
By W. E. Sangster, M.A., Ph.D., D.D.   6s. net

ALL HIS GRACE
By Donald O. Soper, M.A., Ph.D.
Paper covers, 4s. 6d.; Boards, 7s. 6d. net

THAT THEY MIGHT HAVE LIFE
By Edward Rogers.
Paper covers, 5s.; Boards, 7s. 6d. net

HOLY IS HIS NAME
By Norman Hook, Dean of Norwich.   3s. 6d. net

WHY DID CHRIST DIE?
By Herbert G. Wood, M.A., D.D.   4s. 6d. net

THE RESURRECTION AND THE LIFE
By Leslie D. Weatherhead, M.A., Ph.D., D.D.   4s. net

CHRIST AND HIS CROSS
By W. R. Maltby, D.D.   6s. net

THE ADORATION OF THE LAMB
By J. Ernest Rattenbury, D.D.   6s. net

THE SEVEN WINDOWS OF CALVARY
By J. Ernest Rattenbury, D.D.   3s. 6d. net

WITH PETER TO CALVARY
By S. Val Green.   3s. 6d. net

LONDON: THE EPWORTH PRESS

5s. net

jamais eu de partis durables au centre. Il y a eu souvent en revanche des gouvernements du centre.

Combien dénombre-t-on de droites ? Dans un essai désormais classique, M. René Rémond repère la formation de trois familles idéologiques au XIXe siècle : le légitimisme (ou droite traditionaliste), l'orléanisme (ou droite libérale) et le bonapartisme (ou droite autoritaire) (1). Avec la crise politique de la fin du siècle on voit apparaître à l'extrême droite deux autres courants : le nationalisme conservateur et ce que l'historien Zeev Sternhell a appelé « la droite révolutionnaire » (ou préfascisme) (2). Au total, on peut distinguer deux grandes tendances, l'extrême droite et la droite classique, la première composée de trois courants idéologiques — le traditionalisme, le nationalisme et le fascisme— la seconde, subdivisée en droite libérale et droite autoritaire.

L'apparition successive de ces différents courants, leurs querelles, leurs oppositions, leurs alliances, leurs regroupements constituent l'histoire de la droite en France de 1789 à nos jours.

(1) René RÉMOND, *Les droites en France*, Paris, Aubier, 1982.
(2) Zeev STERNHELL, *La droite révolutionnaire, 1885-1914, les origines françaises du fascisme*, Paris, Seuil, 1978. A noter que Z. Sternhell n'a pas toujours su faire la distinction entre ces deux courants. Ainsi, sa conception trop extensive du phénomène fasciste — critiquée par de multiples historiens — l'a amené à assimiler sans nuance à ce système de pensée la plupart des mouvements non conformistes des années 30, qui malgré leur phraséologie étaient loin d'être « révolutionnaires » (Zeev STERNHELL, *Ni droite, ni gauche. L'idéologie fasciste en France*, Paris, Seuil, 1983).

LA DROITE ET LA RÉVOLUTION

Le 11 septembre 1789, les députés de l'Assemblée nationale se séparent en deux groupes. Les partisans d'un pouvoir royal fort disposant d'un droit de veto absolu sur les lois se placent à la droite du président. Les tenants d'un régime constitutionnel dans lequel le roi n'aurait qu'un rôle amoindri se groupent à gauche. Cette division topographique fournit le cadre dans lequel va désormais évoluer toute la vie politique française.

I. — La Contre-Révolution

1. Origines de la droite. — La division des esprits ne date pas de cette époque. Il faut remonter à l'Ancien Régime pour en trouver sa source. La droite se rattache idéologiquement à deux grands courants de pensée qui se sont opposés tout au long du XVIIIe siècle : le libéralisme conservateur et l'absolutisme monarchique. Le premier, qui s'incarne dans la haute aristocratie et les parlements, vise à l'institution d'une monarchie limitée par des corps intermédiaires indépendants du pouvoir et dont Fénelon, Saint-Simon et même Montesquieu, avec bien des nuances, ont élaboré la théorie. Il s'agit, par-delà le « despotisme » des Bourbons, de

9

revenir à la vieille monarchie médiévale et patriarcale, respectueuse des « lois fondamentales du royaume » et des privilèges de la noblesse. La réaction nobiliaire et la résistance des parlements sous Louis XV s'inscrivent dans la droite ligne de ce courant « réactionnaire ». Le second courant, celui de l'absolutisme, est antiféodal. Il fait de l'alliance du roi et de la bourgeoisie contre la noblesse la source de l'équilibre social. Son meilleur défenseur au XVIIe siècle est l'évêque de Meaux, Bossuet. Au siècle suivant il a perdu une partie de son audience. Ce n'est qu'avec la Révolution que l'aristocratie, durcissant ses positions, se convertira à l'absolutisme. Mais, au départ, le recours aux Etats généraux apparaît comme une manœuvre des corps privilégiés afin d'empêcher la refonte du système fiscal, avec l'arrière-pensée de profiter de la faiblesse de Louis XVI pour réformer l'Etat dans un sens à la fois libéral et oligarchique.

En septembre 1789 donc, les députés « du côté droit », ceux qu'on appelle les aristocrates, réclament le retour à l'Ancien Régime. Ils n'ont fait aucune concession à la révolution. Ils ont été contre le vote par tête et contre les décrets des 4 et 11 août 1789 qui supprimaient les droits seigneuriaux et l'ordre social traditionnel. Tout au plus certains admettent-ils le programme exposé dans la déclaration royale du 23 juin 1789, programme qui prévoyait l'égalité fiscale, la liberté individuelle, la liberté de la justice et l'élection dans toute la France d'Etats provinciaux.

Leurs représentants les plus célèbres sont le vicomte de Mirabeau, surnommé Mirabeau-Tonneau, frère du célèbre orateur, et l'abbé Maury, fils d'un cordonnier de Valréas, membre de l'Académie française. Le groupe compte également des esprits plus modérés, tel Cazalès, qui se rattachent au courant du libéralisme aristocratique (1).

Les députés du centre-droit, Mounier, Malouet, Bergasse, Lally-Tollendal, le comte de Clermont-Tonnerre, etc., ont d'abord soutenu le mouvement révolutionnaire, admettant notamment l'abolition de tous les privilèges. Mais les émeutes de l'été 1789 et le débat sur le veto royal les ont rejetés dans l'opposition. Ils veulent une monarchie inspirée des principes de Montesquieu et préconisent la création d'une seconde chambre à caractère aristocratique afin de contenir l'assemblée élue par le peuple (2). On les appelle les monarchiens ou anglomanes en raison de leur admiration pour les institutions britanniques. Comme leurs adversaires, aristocrates et monarchiens se retrouvent dans des clubs politiques (le Salon français, le Club des Impartiaux) et expriment leurs opinions dans de nombreuses brochures ou feuilles périodiques *(Les Actes des Apôtres, L'Ami du Roi...)*.

La droite va trouver un appui capital dans l'Eglise catholique ralliée au camp de la Contre-Révolution. Initialement, la Révolution française n'était pas antireligieuse ni même anticléricale. Des évêques, des prêtres avaient accueilli avec enthousiasme la convocation des Etats généraux et les premières réformes. La rupture s'est produite en juillet 1790 avec l'adoption de la Constitution civile du clergé qui organise une Eglise d'Etat dans le sens de la tradition gallicane, une Eglise indépendante du Saint-Siège. Le clergé se divise alors en « jureurs » qui prêtent serment à la Constitution

(1) Jacques de SAINT-VICTOR, *La chute des aristocrates, 1787-1792. La naissance de la droite*, Paris, Perrin, 1992.
(2) Robert GRIFFITHS, *Le Centre perdu. Malouet et les « monarchiens » dans la Révolution française*, Grenoble, Presses Universitaires de Grenoble, 1988.

civile et « réfractaires » qui demeurent fidèles à l'Eglise catholique romaine. C'est une sorte de schisme que vient aggraver en 1791 la condamnation pontificale. Dès lors la Révolution se trouve contrainte de pratiquer l'intolérance, de pourchasser le clergé réfractaire qui se tourne vers la Contre-Révolution. C'est une des causes de la fuite de Varennes et, pour une part, de l'émigration.

2. **La lutte contre la Révolution.** — A) *L'émigration.* — On estime à environ 150 000 le nombre de personnes qui quittèrent la France pendant les événements révolutionnaires. Cette émigration s'échelonne sur plusieurs années, en vagues successives. Au début, ce sont surtout les grands seigneurs et les membres de la haute bourgeoisie qui partent. Dès la prise de la Bastille, le comte d'Artois et les princes de Condé s'exilent. Ils sont bientôt suivis par des gentilshommes de moindre renom. Ensuite viennent les députés de la droite, les monarchiens qui ont perdu tout espoir de faire triompher leurs vues, les prêtres réfractaires menacés de déportation. A partir de juin-juillet 1793, les royalistes ne sont plus seuls à quitter la France. Ils sont imités par les girondins. D'autres vagues suivent, le 9 thermidor an II, le 13 vendémiaire an IV. Les émigrés se dispersent dans toute l'Europe, notamment en Rhénanie. En majorité, ils appartiennent non à la noblesse, mais au tiers état, à la bourgeoisie, au bas clergé et à la paysannerie qui redoutent les excès révolutionnaires. Au sein de l'émigration, les clans, les coteries de la cour se reforment. Le comte d'Artois, le comte de Provence ont chacun leurs fidèles qui nouent des intrigues, échafaudent des plans afin de libérer la famille royale, fomentent des révoltes en province. Par ailleurs, plusieurs

corps d'armée se constituent sur le Rhin : l'armée de Condé, celle des princes, la Légion noire de Mirabeau-Tonneau. Ces troupes, composées principalement d'officiers, sont peu disciplinées. Les premiers émigrés sont persuadés que la Révolution ne durera guère et que la reconquête sera une simple promenade militaire. Mais quand la guerre éclate en avril 1792, ils ne jouent presque aucun rôle. Ils sont très mal accueillis dans les régions qu'ils prétendent libérer et où ils rétablissent les impôts de l'Ancien Régime. Leur maladresse jointe à celle du duc de Brunswick sera la cause première de la chute de la royauté, le 10 août 1792. Ces émigrés n'ont pas le sentiment de trahir leur pays en combattant les troupes françaises. La notion de patriotisme telle que nous l'entendons de nos jours leur est totalement étrangère. Pour eux, la patrie n'est rien d'autre que la fidélité au roi, à un ordre social considéré comme immuable, à une certaine éthique politique où trouvent place les notions de hiérarchie, d'honneur et de service royal.

Il n'y a rien d'étonnant à voir les plus intransigeants dominer le monde de l'émigration. Le comte d'Antraigues, ancien député du Vivarais, devenu chef d'un important réseau d'espionnage, défend avec passion et violence les thèses aristocratiques. Une de ses brochures a pour titre : *Point d'accommodement*. De son côté le comte de Provence, qui prend le nom de Louis XVIII à la mort de son neveu, se propose de rétablir l'Ancien Régime, « moins les abus », concède-t-il. Et il lance des proclamations vengeresses à l'adresse des révolutionnaires. Ce n'est qu'en 1814, par la déclaration de Saint-Ouen, qu'il adoptera des positions plus modérées.

B) *Les soulèvements provinciaux.* — Au printemps de 1790, à l'instigation des émigrés, des troubles éclatent dans plusieurs villes et régions de France : à Nîmes, Toulouse, Montauban, dans la vallée du Rhône, en Provence, Poitou, Alsace, Franche-Comté. En août 1790, les royalistes se regroupent au camp de Jalès, en Vivarais. Mais l'insurrection la plus sanglante se produit en Vendée, au printemps de 1793, faisant suite à diverses conspirations organisées dans l'Ouest. La décision prise par la Convention de lever 300 000 soldats en est la cause directe. Les paysans vendéens s'arment. Ils veulent le retour à la monarchie et surtout de « bons prêtres », mais pas de milice. Des nobles (La Rochejaquelein, Charette, Lescure, d'Elbée, Bonchamps), des prêtres (l'abbé Bernier) et des roturiers (Cathelineau, Stofflet) prennent la tête du mouvement. Commence alors la tragique guerre de Vendée où les deux camps rivalisent d'horreurs. Aux cruautés des « blancs » répondent les représailles sanglantes des « bleus ». Après les prises de Saumur et d'Angers par les insurgés, la Convention s'alarme et, le 1er août 1793, décide la guerre « totale », c'est-à-dire le pillage systématique de la région. L'armée catholique et royale groupe environ 40 000 hommes sous la bannière du Sacré-Cœur. Elle est battue à Cholet (17 octobre 1793), au Mans (12 décembre) et anéantie à Savenay (23 décembre). La répression est impitoyable. Les « colonnes infernales » du général Turreau ravagent le bocage vendéen. La première guerre de Vendée opposait de véritables armées combattant face à face et au grand jour. La chouannerie qui prend la relève dans tout l'Ouest est une guérilla livrée par de petites bandes d'insurgés composées de faux-saulniers, de déserteurs, de prêtres réfractaires, de jeunes gens fuyant la réquisition militaire, de rescapés des guerres de Vendée. Ces bandes commettent des attentats contre les diligences, les acquéreurs de biens nationaux, interceptent les convois militaires, harcèlent les arrière-gardes des « bleus ». Une fois leurs embuscades ou leurs coups de mains accomplis, elles s'évanouissent dans les champs, se dispersent dans les chemins creux. Leurs chefs les plus célèbres sont Jean Cottereau, dit Jean Chouan, Puisaye, Georges Cadoudal, Louis de Frotté.

Les contre-révolutionnaires profitent des dissensions entre républicains. Le coup d'Etat des 31 mai et 2 juin 1793 élimine les girondins du pouvoir. Aussitôt éclatent de violentes insurrections fédéralistes en Normandie, en Bretagne, dans le sud-est de la France. A Lyon, Marseille, Toulon, les royalistes se mêlent aux insurgés et parfois prennent la tête de ces rébellions matées non sans difficulté.

C) *Les royalistes après Thermidor*. — La chute de Robespierre, le 9 thermidor an II (27 juillet 1794), marque un arrêt de la Révolution. Le pouvoir revient aux républicains du centre hostiles aux excès du jacobinisme. Les prisons s'ouvrent devant les royalistes. Les prêtres réfractaires sortent de la clandestinité. Le climat politique change, mais la violence persiste. A la « terreur rouge » succède alors une vague de « terreur blanche ». Des bandes de muscadins (compagnons de Jésus ou du Soleil) se livrent à des représailles et à des vengeances privées. Le club des Jacobins est mis à sac. L'année suivante, les émigrés pensent que l'heure est venue de porter un coup décisif à la République. Leur débarquement près de Quiberon tourne au désastre (juillet 1795).

A Paris, les royalistes, qui, contrairement aux émigrés, sont en majorité partisans d'une monarchie constitutionnelle, espèrent renverser le régime par les voies légales. Mais les thermidoriens, notamment les régicides, s'inquiètent du progrès de ces opposants qui ont réussi à noyauter un grand nombre de sections de la capitale. Par les décrets des deux tiers (22 et 30 août 1795), ils empêchent le renouvellement complet des députés. Le 13 vendémiaire (5 octobre), Bonaparte réprime la rébellion royaliste sur le parvis de l'église Saint-Roch. Les élections de l'an IV leur sont néanmoins favorables. Avec les républicains modérés ils ont près de 300 députés sur 750 aux Conseils des Cinq-Cents et des Anciens. Ils se réunissent à l'hôtel de la rue de Clichy, d'où leur nom de clichyens. Dirigés par le magistrat Dandré, ancien membre de la Constituante, par Dupont de Nemours, Boissy d'Anglas et Defermon, ils préparent activement les élections pour le renouvellement du tiers des Conseils en 1797. A cet effet, grâce aux subsides anglais, ils mettent sur pied, dans une soixantaine de départements, des « instituts philanthropiques » destinés à regrouper les républicains modérés et les royalistes. Comme les loges maçonniques, ces organismes comportent plusieurs degrés : le premier cercle comprend les citoyens effrayés par le babouvisme et désireux d'en finir avec l'anarchie révolutionnaire. Ils sont coiffés par un second cercle, celui des « fils légitimes », purs monarchistes, qui sont eux-mêmes en relation avec l'agence royale de Paris. Les instituts font une campagne active pour la paix et la fin des conquêtes.

Dans les assemblées la majorité revient aux monarchistes qui portent Pichegru à la présidence des Cinq-Cents et Barbé-Marbois à celle des Anciens. La fin du régime républicain semble proche. Un des cinq directeurs, Barthélemy, leur est acquis, un autre, Carnot, est neutre. Des mesures à caractère contre-révolutionnaire sont adoptées : abrogation de la loi contre les prêtres réfractaires, décrets en faveur des émigrés, élimination de l'administration des jacobins, réorganisation de la garde nationale. Mais les trois directeurs restés républicains, Larevellière, Reubell et Barras, réagissent le 18 fructidor an V (4 septembre 1797) par un coup de force. Les chefs royalistes sont arrêtés et 53 députés condamnés à la déportation.

La conquête du pouvoir par les voies légales leur étant désormais interdite, les royalistes se réorganisent dans la clandestinité. Leur plan consiste à déclencher une insurrection généralisée en France tandis que les armées coalisées franchiront la frontière. Par manque de coordination, les soulèvements éclatent non pas simultanément mais successivement à Toulouse, à Bordeaux, en Vendée et en Bretagne. Les Républicains n'ont ainsi aucune peine à les réprimer.

3. **Théorie de la Contre-Révolution.** — Comment délimiter la droite sous la Révolution ? La poussée vers la gauche a été si brutale en l'espace de quelques années qu'elle a modifié radicalement la physionomie politique du pays esquissée sous la Constituante. Les amis de La Fayette, les partisans de la Constitution de 1791, les tenants de la Révolution bourgeoise, les girondins, les dantonistes ont été rejetés à droite par l'apparition à l'extrême gauche de nouvelles factions pratiquant la surenchère révolutionnaire. Les thuriféraires de Robespierre ont eux-mêmes trouvé plus « enragés » qu'eux. Les groupes, les tendances politiques se sont en quelque sorte télescopés à droite. Ce n'est que lorsque la Révolu-

tion se stabilise après Thermidor que les partis tendent à retrouver leur position d'équilibre, les forces politiques à se décompresser, la situation à se clarifier. On ne saurait tenir pour de droite tous les mouvements qui ont été à un moment ou à un autre hostiles à l'orientation de la Révolution, les feuillants ou les brissotins par exemple (1). Même parmi les clichyens résolus à restaurer la royauté ne figurent pas que des hommes de droite. Certains qu'on peut situer au centre ou au centre-gauche penchent pour une monarchie constitutionnelle qui reprendrait à son compte l'œuvre de 1879. Il n'y a à vrai dire sous la Révolution qu'une droite pure, celle qui s'est constituée autour des « aristocrates » dès 1789, au moment du débat sur le veto royal, droite que sont venus renforcer les monarchiens et le clergé réfractaire. Elle seule mérite l'appellation de contre-révolutionnaire. Elle trouve son unité profonde dans une philosophie politique, le traditionalisme, né en réaction directe contre la philosophie des Lumières.

Pour les traditionalistes, l'homme est un « animal social » qui ne peut exister hors de la société, cadre naturel qui l'éduque, le façonne, le protège. Cette société ne s'édifie pas selon la fantaisie, l'imagination ou les principes abstraits d'égalité ou de liberté : à l'idéalisme optimiste des Lumières qui insiste sur le volontarisme humain, la pensée traditionaliste oppose un réalisme pessimiste fondé sur la soumission de l'homme à la nature. La seule diffé-

(1) Pour caractériser les résistances populaires et leur aspect de « révolte primitive » sans contenu idéologique précis (ce qui n'est bien entendu le cas ni de la Vendée ni de la chouannerie), M. Colin Lucas a suggéré pour la première fois d'utiliser le terme d' « anti-Révolution » plutôt que celui de Contre-Révolution (C. LUCAS, Résistances populaires à la Révolution dans le Sud-Est, colloque *Mouvements populaires et conscience sociale (XVIe-XIXe siècle)*, Paris, Maloine, 1985.

rence avec le monde physique réside dans le fait que les lois sociales peuvent être transgressées par le libre arbitre humain. Mais le prix payé à cette vaine liberté est incalculable : il s'appelle désordre, anarchie, dérèglements moraux. La Révolution, en modifiant les conditions sociales et les hiérarchies naturelles, en voulant changer l'homme lui-même, a offensé la nature : péché sans rémission. Tôt ou tard elle reprendra ses droits. L'ordre naturel retrouvera sa place après les révoltes de l'orgueil humain. Cet ordre naturel, comment le connaître ? Par l'observation attentive des faits. L'Histoire devient la seule école de vérité, la « politique expérimentale » par excellence. Il s'agit de dégager de l'observation attentive des faits les vérités éternelles. Nourri de l'expérience des générations successives, le traditionalisme prétend se modeler plus aisément sur la vie que tout autre système. Il est réformiste, préférant aux brusques à-coups révolutionnaires les adaptations lentes, souples, presque instinctives.

Tel est le fond commun du traditionalisme auquel on peut rattacher une assez grande diversité de théoriciens. On distingue parmi eux au moins deux écoles, l'école théocratique et l'école historique.

La première, illustrée par Bonald et Joseph de Maistre, voit dans la Révolution française le châtiment par Dieu du péché des hommes, la sanction de la décadence morale et religieuse qui s'est produite au xviiie siècle. Comme pour Bossuet, l'Histoire n'est rien d'autre pour eux que la réalisation des desseins de la Providence sur la terre. La Contre-Révolution ne doit pas être la restauration de l'Ancien Régime mais l'édification d'un régime nouveau, basé sur l'Eglise, une théocratie. L'ultramontain Joseph de Maistre soumettrait volontiers les trônes de la Chrétienté à la magistrature spirituelle de la papauté. Bonald, au contraire, incline vers une forme atténuée de gallicanisme, consacrant l'indépendance des rois de France à l'égard du souverain pontife. Il préconise une « monarchie royale absolue et héréditaire » qui sauvegarderait toutefois les libertés locales et familiales, les privilèges municipaux et provinciaux.

La seconde école, agnostique, pragmatique, procède des théories politiques de l'Anglais Edmund Burke exposées dans ses *Réflexions sur la Révolution française*. Burke en Angleterre, Montlosier en France défendent l'image d'une monarchie un peu archaïsante, patriarcale, tempérée comme chez Montesquieu par une série de corps intermédiaires formant écran et protégeant les individus.

Le traditionalisme devait être la doctrine politique que les contre-révolutionnaires opposèrent au mouvement révolutionnaire né des idées du siècle. Mais il faut se garder d'imaginer que, dès 1789, les deux idéologies se soient affrontées. L'esprit du XVIIIe avait trop profondément marqué la société pour qu'il en fût ainsi. Les premiers contre-révolutionnaires — Rivarol, Mallet du Pan — étaient imprégnés de la même pensée politique que leurs adversaires. Ils firent d'abord le procès de la Révolution française au nom de la Raison et de la philosophie des Lumières. Ce n'est que progressivement que s'élabora la philosophie traditionaliste et par là même la première forme de droite en France.

II. — Un centrisme instable : le bonapartisme

Bonaparte allait-il être le Monk de la République française qui placerait Louis XVIII sur le trône ? D'aucuns le pensèrent. Dès l'établissement du Consulat, les émigrés rentrent à la suite d'amnisties successives. C'est le cas de Chateaubriand, de Fontanes. Les chefs chouans se soumettent les uns après les autres. Le Concordat rétablit la paix religieuse et permet une renaissance catholique dans les campagnes. La prospérité économique revient, le spectre de la terreur s'éloigne. Mais à Louis XVIII, qui dans plusieurs lettres lui rappelle ses droits, Bonaparte répond par une fin de non-recevoir. « Je suis la Révolution française », aime-t-il à répéter. Il ne souhaite pas rétablir l'Ancien Régime, mais veut faire l'unité nationale autour de sa personne et s'efforce de concilier le besoin d'ordre ressenti par le peuple et l'essentiel des conquêtes politiques et sociales de la Révolution. Le Consulat, peut-on dire, est, comme le Directoire, un régime centriste, mais dont les bases ont été sensiblement élargies par les victoires militaires, la paix d'Amiens et la réorganisation judiciaire et administrative du pays. Le Premier Consul va plus loin que le « centrisme parlementaire » des thermidoriens, en appuyant son régime sur le peuple. Les référendums-plébiscites donnent au nouveau césarisme une apparence démocratique. Ce gouvernement centriste n'en reste pas moins condamné à lutter contre les extrêmes. Bonaparte n'hésite pas à faire exécuter Cadoudal et les royalistes qui avaient conspiré contre lui, à faire enlever puis assassiner le duc d'Enghien, à exiler les plus fanatiques des jacobins.

La proclamation du Consulat à vie puis de l'Empire ôte aux partisans des Bourbons leurs dernières illusions.

Le régime accentue progressivement son caractère monarchique. En 1808, on remplace sur les monnaies « République française » par l'inscription

« Empire français ». Une noblesse impériale est créée. Une partie de l'aristocratie de l'Ancien Régime ne dédaigne pas les dignités impériales. Par son mariage avec Marie-Louise, Napoléon devient gendre de l'empereur d'Autriche et cousin de Louis XVI. Les préfets jacobins cèdent peu à peu la place à d'anciens royalistes. L'équilibre semble rompu entre la France ancienne et la France nouvelle. A vrai dire, Napoléon, entraîné dans les guerres européennes, ne parviendra jamais à consolider son régime à l'intérieur. L'opinion reste muselée. La conscription devient de plus en plus impopulaire. La bourgeoisie commerçante des grands ports qui souffre du Blocus continental se détache de l'Empire. Une opposition libérale naît au sein du Corps législatif tandis qu'une opposition catholique fait son apparition avec le conflit entre l'empereur et la papauté. A nouveau, les catholiques sont rejetés dans les bras des royalistes. Le régime ne se maintenant que par la gloire des armes, la défaite engendre inévitablement sa disparition. Lorsque, le 6 avril 1814, l'empereur est contraint d'abdiquer sous la pression de ses maréchaux, nul ne songe à élever sur le trône le roi de Rome. Le retour des Bourbons, la maladresse des émigrés, les violences de la réaction nobiliaire et cléricale, la démobilisation d'une partie de l'armée sont à la racine du profond mécontentement qui suit le départ de Napoléon pour l'île d'Elbe. En quelques mois les maux de l'Empire sont oubliés. Quand revient l'exilé, c'est le Bonaparte jacobin, le « général Vendémiaire » qui est acclamé par le petit peuple. L'expérience d'un bonapartisme populaire semble possible. Mais Napoléon refuse de donner trop de gages aux jacobins et cherche l'appui des classes moyennes et de la bourgeoisie. Benjamin Constant rédige l' « Acte

additionnel aux constitutions de l'Empire », sorte de
« charte améliorée » qui reconnaît la souveraineté
nationale, et confie le pouvoir législatif à une
Chambre des Pairs (l'ancien Sénat transformé en
Chambre héréditaire) et à une Chambre des Représentants élue au suffrage censitaire. Un très grand
nombre d'électeurs s'abstient de ratifier par plébiscite la nouvelle Constitution. Quant aux élections
législatives, elles donnent une écrasante majorité
aux libéraux qui sont loin d'être fidèles à la dynastie
impériale, comme ils le prouveront après Waterloo.
Cet échec n'était-il pas prévisible ? Le bonapartisme,
forme de césarisme démocratique, est par essence
antilibéral et anti-parlementaire. Il ne pouvait
renier ses principes sans se condamner lui-même.

Napoléon, à Sainte-Hélène, reconnaîtra l'erreur
qu'il a commise de ne pas s'être appuyé en 1815
sur le jacobinisme populaire. Son exil contribuera
à forger la légende qui fera de lui l'héritier et le
défenseur naturel de la Révolution démocratique.
Le bonapartisme, après avoir hésité sous l'Empire
à basculer à droite, représentera à partir de 1815
une force de gauche. Ceci explique sous la Restauration l'étroite association du bonapartisme et
du libéralisme contre l'ordre établi.

CHAPITRE II

LA DÉFENSE DE L'ORDRE

I. — La Restauration

Après quinze années de despotisme, l'opinion éclairée souhaite le retour à un régime libéral tout en refusant l'anarchie révolutionnaire. La Charte de 1814 traduit cette aspiration. Réaliste, Louis XVIII reconnaît désormais une partie du legs révolutionnaire. Il admet l'égalité des Français devant la loi et l'impôt, l'admissibilité de tous aux emplois civils et militaires, les libertés politiques, le droit de propriété. Enfin il garantit l'amnistie pour les faits passés. En même temps, il entend « renouer la chaîne des temps que de funestes écarts ont interrompue » et rattacher la monarchie restaurée à l'Ancien Régime. La Charte récuse le principe de la souveraineté nationale. Elle est une Constitution « octroyée » par le roi, qui tient toujours en théorie son sceptre de Dieu.

1. **Les ultras.** — Cette volonté de réconcilier la France ancienne et la France nouvelle se heurte aux partisans trop zélés de la monarchie qui n'ont, selon la formule du chevalier de Panat, « rien oublié ni rien appris ». Une vague de vengeance populaire contre le personnel de l'Empire se propage alors dans tout le pays. C'est une nouvelle « terreur

blanche », encouragée par les « ultra-royalistes ».

A ces derniers, les élections d'août 1815 donnent une écrasante majorité : 350 élus sur un peu plus de 390 députés. La plupart sont de petits gentils-hommes provinciaux ou d'anciens émigrés. Ils n'aiment pas par principe les constitutions écrites et trouvent la Charte beaucoup trop libérale, sans préconiser pour autant le retour à l'absolutisme. Prenant conscience de leur force parlementaire, ils sont même amenés à défendre le principe du gouvernement représentatif (Chateaubriand : *De la Monarchie selon la Charte*, 1816) à l'encontre du roi qui préfère choisir ses ministres en dehors de la majorité.

L'idéologie des ultras reprend fidèlement les thèmes de la Contre-Révolution. Pour eux, l'Histoire s'arrête en 1789. La Révolution française, produit d'un complot maçonnique contre la religion et l'ordre social, est radicalement mauvaise. La Restauration, ils se l'imaginent sous les traits d'une monarchie tempérée, limitée par les corps constitués, respectueuse des traditions et des antiques « lois fondamentales du royaume », bienveillante à l'égard de tous et principalement de la fidèle noblesse. La société ne sera plus égalitaire mais composée d'un tissu de corps intermédiaires hiérarchisés — familles, ordres professionnels, corporations, communes, provinces, clergé, noblesse héréditaire... —, jouissant tous d'une relative autonomie dans leur propre sphère. A leur manière, les ultras sont des libéraux, mais des libéraux d'Ancien Régime. Ils sont ennemis du jacobinisme, de l'organisation militaire issue de la Révolution, de l'Université impériale et généralement de toute forme de centralisation contraignante.

Enfin, ils ambitionnent de rétablir l'Eglise dans ses droits et privilèges, veulent arracher le pays à

l'influence pernicieuse des philosophes du XVIIIe siècle, reconstituer la société chrétienne d'autrefois et
rêvent d'unir le trône et l'autel.

Cette droite traditionaliste, nous l'avons vu, n'est
pas rigoureusement homogène. Elle est traversée
par des courants divers. Les rapports de l'Eglise et
de l'Etat, par exemple, ne sont pas envisagés par
tous de la même manière. Certains, comme le jeune
abbé de La Mennais (*Essai sur l'indifférence en
matière de religion*, 1817-1823), sont ultramontains,
d'autres, comme Louis de Bonald, gallicans. Sur le
plan littéraire, le jeune romantisme royaliste (Lamar-
tine, Hugo, Nodier, Vigny) coexiste difficilement
avec le classicisme hérité du siècle passé.

Le parti ultra, sans avoir la forte structure des
partis modernes, est relativement bien organisé.
Ses dirigeants (Bonald, Corbière, Villèle, Vitrolles,
La Bourdonnaye, Clausel de Coussergues, Haussez,
Maccarthy, Castelbajac, Chateaubriand...) se réunissent périodiquement chez l'un d'entre eux, le
député Piet, où ils délibèrent des grandes questions du parti et arrêtent les consignes de vote.
Les ultras prolongent leur action en province
grâce à des comités royalistes qui jouent un rôle
actif dans les départements lors des élections. Leur
organisation est doublée d'une association occulte,
Les Chevaliers de la Foi ou *de l'Anneau*, animée
par F. de Bertier. Leur presse est florissante : *La
Gazette de France*, *La Quotidienne*, *L'Etoile*, *Le
Drapeau blanc* (intransigeant), le *Journal des Débats*
(plus libéral). Au milieu de cette constellation, *Le
Conservateur* (1818-1820) brille d'un éclat tout particulier. Animé par Villèle, Martainville, La Mennais et surtout Chateaubriand, il critique avec
véhémence l'arbitraire du gouvernement et — paradoxalement — défend la Charte.

L'assise sociologique des ultras se trouve dans la grande et la petite aristocratie, le clergé, mais également dans une bonne partie des masses rurales. À cette époque subsiste encore un royalisme populaire qu'on aurait tort de négliger. En revanche, les classes moyennes semblent plutôt acquises aux idées modérées ou libérales. Ceci explique que les ultras réclament un suffrage à deux degrés avec un cens relativement bas (cinquante francs de contribution directe). Ils veulent diluer les voix de la bourgeoisie libérale.

Leurs bastions sont en province : le Midi (Provence, Languedoc, Aquitaine), l'Ouest (Bretagne, Vendée), le Lyonnais, la Franche-Comté.

2. Le gouvernement des ultras. — La « Chambre introuvable » de 1815 était ingouvernable, le roi se refusant à faire appel au parti majoritaire. En septembre 1816, Louis XVIII la fait dissoudre. De nouvelles élections permettent le gouvernement des modérés du centre (Richelieu, de Serre, Dessolle, Decazes). Les ultras, qui voient le pouvoir leur échapper aux élections partielles de 1817 et 1818, se jettent alors dans l'intrigue et le complot. Ils mettent leur espérance dans le comte d'Artois qui doit normalement succéder à son frère Louis XVIII et dont ils connaissent les opinions.

Mais l'assassinat du duc de Berry, le 14 février 1820, jette les modérés dans les bras des ultras. Louis XVIII, qui se rend compte qu'une trop forte libéralisation du régime risquerait de menacer son trône, renvoie Decazes et rappelle Richelieu qui s'appuie en partie sur les ultras. Le système électoral est modifié. Par la loi du double vote on assure la prédominance des grands propriétaires terriens (30 juin 1820). Les élections partielles de novembre 1820 et d'octobre 1821 redonnent la majorité aux ultras. Richelieu, jugé tiède, est remplacé par Villèle. Celui-ci n'est pas un fanatique, mais un homme réaliste, un politicien avisé et un remarquable technicien des finances publiques. Pour réaliser le programme de son parti, il va bientôt disposer d'une majorité écrasante que lui donneront les élections générales de mars 1824 : 410 ultras environ sur 430 députés. C'est la « Chambre retrouvée ». L'avènement, la même année, de Charles X permet d'escompter une rapide et profonde contre-révolution. Après des années d'opposition, voici les ultras parvenus au pouvoir. Le clergé et le roi les soutiennent ; ils disposent de l'administration et de l'armée. Nul obstacle ne peut leur barrer la route. Par la loi de septennalité, la Chambre a décidé de proroger sa durée. La vraie restauration peut commencer. Le sacre de Reims renouant avec les plus vieilles traditions, la loi du sacrilège, le vote d'une indemnité de près d'un milliard pour les émigrés, la mise au pas de l'Université libérale par Mgr Frayssinous en sont les premières étapes.

Mais la victoire des ultras est trop belle. Ils ne tardent pas à se quereller. Une extrême droite intransigeante derrière La Bourdonnaye trouve encore trop timorée la politique de Villèle. A cette opposition vient se joindre la « défection » de Chateaubriand et de ses amis. « Congédié comme un laquais », l'ambitieux écrivain forme une contre-opposition de droite qui reprend les thèmes déjà développés dans *Le Conservateur* : liberté de la presse, alliance de la monarchie et du peuple, lutte contre l'autoritarisme gouvernemental. La Bourdonnaye et Chateaubriand représentent les deux pôles entre lesquels le traditionalisme va évoluer dans les années suivantes : une forme contre-révolutionnaire, autoritaire et intransigeante, qu'illustreront, par exemple, un Blanc de Saint-Bonnet ou un Louis Veuillot, et une forme plus modérée alliant la monarchie traditionnelle et les principes parlementaires, qu'on retrouvera dans la pensée d'un Falloux ou d'un Albert de Mun.

Le gouvernement subit un troisième assaut de la part d'un indépendant, le comte de Montlosier. Ce vieux légiste gallican, à la fois « féodal » et libéral, s'inquiète du progrès des idées ultramontaines, de l'ardeur du clergé à étouffer les libertés et de la puissance occulte des Jésuites. Dans un *Mémoire à consulter* (1826), qui rencontre un succès considérable, il dénonce le « parti prêtre » et une mystérieuse franc-maçonnerie cléricale, la Congrégation (1). Ces attaques soulèvent une vague anticléricale d'une violence inouïe. Villèle escompte ramener le calme en dissolvant la Chambre, mais les élections de 1827 sont désastreuses pour lui. A contrecœur, Charles X le remplace par un modéré du centre, le comte de Martignac, mais en août 1829 constitue un nouveau ministère ultra avec Polignac, Bourmont, La Bourdonnaye et Capelle. Par 221 voix contre 181, la Chambre réplique par une « adresse » au souverain lui demandant de respecter la Charte. L'épreuve de force est engagée. Le roi renvoie la Chambre. Malgré les pressions électorales, l'opposition enlève à nouveau la majorité. Charles X estime que, la Charte étant octroyée, il lui est loisible de la modifier. Le dimanche 25 juillet il signe les célèbres ordonnances. A ce coup d'Etat le peuple de Paris répond par les barricades.

(1) Montlosier confondait en réalité un ensemble d'œuvres pieuses, n'ayant aucune activité politique, avec la société des Chevaliers de la Foi.

II. — La monarchie de Juillet

La révolution de 1830 aurait peu d'importance au regard de l'histoire des idées politiques si elle n'avait fait que remplacer au pouvoir une famille régnante par une autre, la dynastie des Bourbons par celle des Orléans. A la vérité, elle a fait bien davantage. La monarchie qui s'installe en juillet diffère sensiblement de la précédente, non pas tant par ses institutions que par l'esprit qui l'anime, par une assise sociale et une idéologie nouvelles.

1. Caractères de la monarchie de Juillet. — C'est une autre conception de la monarchie qui s'instaure. De la monarchie chrétienne de l'Ancien Régime on passe à une monarchie laïque, adaptée à une société elle-même sécularisée par la Révolution de 1789. La prestation de serment à la Charte remplace l'onction sainte des sacres de Reims. Le roi n'est plus un souverain de droit divin tenant son sceptre de Dieu, il est monarque en vertu d'un contrat passé entre les représentants du peuple et lui. Ce qui n'empêchera pas Louis-Philippe, issu de la lignée des Capétiens, de souffrir d'un « complexe de légitimité » vis-à-vis des autres souverains de l'Europe, refusant toujours de se considérer comme un simple mandataire du peuple.

Le régime inaugure également une nouvelle conception du parlementarisme. La Charte révisée de 1830 supprime l'article 14 qui donnait au roi le pouvoir de faire des ordonnances. Toutefois, elle ne reconnaît pas officiellement la responsabilité politique des ministres devant les chambres ni le principe de la solidarité ministérielle ; ce sont là des conséquences de la révolution de Juillet que la pratique parlementaire instaurera progressivement.

L'orléanisme parlementaire n'a cependant pas pour effet d'annihiler tout pouvoir royal. Le ministère doit avoir en principe la double confiance du roi et des chambres (orléanisme dualiste). Louis-Philippe lui-même ne veut pas que le trône reste « un fauteuil vide ». Il entend à la fois régner et gouverner. Ainsi se forment, derrière Molé puis Guizot, un « parti du château » et un « ministère de la cour », qui seront combattus par les groupes parlementaires. La faible importance du corps électoral permettra d'ailleurs l'emploi, sur une échelle assez large, de la corruption et des manœuvres administratives (décorations, nominations de fonctionnaires-députés, chemins de fer électoraux, etc.).

La loi du 19 avril 1831 a, en effet, supprimé le double collège électoral, mais n'a élargi que modestement le suffrage censitaire. Le corps électoral passe au début de la monarchie de Juillet de 94 600 à 167 000 électeurs. L'enrichissement de la moyenne bourgeoisie permettra en août 1846 d'en dénombrer 241 000.

2. **Le règne de la bourgeoisie.** — Cette étroite assise du pays légal incite à définir en première approximation le nouveau régime comme celui de la bourgeoisie. En effet, il profite particulièrement à la grande bourgeoisie d'affaires (Laffitte, « roi des banquiers et banquier des rois »). Mais il s'appuie aussi sur une aristocratie libérale : noblesse d'Empire (Soult, Mortier, Gérard...) ou noblesse de robe (Molé, Pasquier...). Il importe de souligner la place prépondérante qu'occupe la richesse foncière dans une société qui n'est que très partiellement industrialisée. La base de la richesse bourgeoise est encore la rente foncière. Dans sa thèse sur *Les grands notables en France (1840-1849)*, A.-J. Tudesq a

souligné le rôle dans les départements des grands propriétaires fonciers, issus généralement de l'aristocratie, qui ont su préserver leurs biens au cours de la Révolution. Au côté de la bourgeoisie et de la noblesse, il faut aussi réserver une place aux élites intellectuelles. La révolution de 1830 n'a pas seulement été faite par des banquiers, mais surtout par des universitaires, des étudiants, des journalistes. Considérant l'importance occupée par le corps enseignant sous la monarchie de Juillet, Thibaudet a qualifié celle-ci de « monarchie de professeurs » (Villemain, Guizot, Cousin, Sylvestre de Sacy...). Il aurait pu ajouter aussi « de journalistes ». Le *Journal des Débats* ne fut-il pas élevé à la hauteur d'une institution quasi officielle de l'orléanisme ? Par le biais du journalisme, il devient désormais possible d'accéder au gouvernement. Il suffit de songer aux équipes rédactionnelles du *Globe*, du *Courrier français* qui se retrouvent après 1830 associées au pouvoir à des titres divers.

Il serait donc injuste de ne voir dans la monarchie nouvelle que le règne méprisable des intérêts, le vil triomphe du dieu Argent. La célèbre phrase de Guizot : « Enrichissez-vous par le travail et par l'épargne », est beaucoup plus l'affirmation d'une morale d'austérité et d'acharnement que le conseil cynique d'un parvenu. A côté de la richesse, les orléanistes pensent que le mérite personnel doit trouver sa juste place. L'égalité des droits, l'égalité des chances sont ouvertement reconnues.

Et c'est sans doute cette reconnaissance théorique de l'égalité (en droit mais non en fait) qui donne au régime son audience dans une large fraction de la société française. Le garde national des faubourgs et le grand brasseur d'affaires se reconnaissent dans la paisible monarchie du roi-citoyen.

Balzac nous le fait découvrir, peu de classes sociales offrent une telle diversité de conditions : bourgeoisies parisienne et provinciale, bourgeoisies d'affaires, universitaire, parlementaire, sans compter la petite et moyenne bourgeoisie, celle des riches artisans, épiciers et autres boutiquiers. Et, cependant, l'idéologie bourgeoise présente une grande unité, une uniformité, une homogénéité que l'on trouve rarement ailleurs.

3. L'opposition des droites. — Désormais, le traditionalisme ne se confond plus avec la droite ; du moins n'est-il plus toute la droite. L'événement politique majeur des années 1830 est la formation d'une autre droite qui s'oppose à la précédente par sa doctrine, son programme et son personnel politique.

A) *L'orléanisme.* — C'est un ancien centre-gauche, celui des constitutionnels et des doctrinaires de la Restauration, qui a glissé à droite après son accession au pouvoir. M. René Rémond (1) situe très exactement ce glissement en mars 1831, date à laquelle l'orléanisme, après avoir essayé de faire une politique d'ouverture par son aile gauche, le parti du Mouvement (Laffitte, Odilon Barrot), revient à une politique plus conservatrice avec le parti de la Résistance (Casimir Périer, Broglie). L'orléanisme s'identifie alors pleinement à la Résistance. La division de celle-ci en plusieurs tendances assez floues (une aile gauche avec Thiers, une aile droite avec Guizot et un tiers parti avec Dupin) ne modifie en rien son unité. Ces nuances relèvent

(1) R. RÉMOND, *op. cit.*

plus de la divergence des tactiques et de la rivalité des hommes que des clivages politiques fondamentaux.

« L'orléanisme, a dit Thibaudet, ce n'est pas un parti, c'est un état d'esprit. » Aussi n'est-il pas surprenant qu'il ait survécu à tous les régimes qui se sont succédé depuis le XIXᵉ siècle. Tout compte fait, son nom est impropre. La fidélité à la famille d'Orléans n'est qu'un aspect secondaire de son idéologie. Les orléanistes ne l'ont été que par accident ou, si l'on préfère, ils ont constitué la forme première d'une droite destinée à se perpétuer au-delà de la monarchie de Juillet, la droite libérale ou droite conservatrice.

Libéraux, les orléanistes le sont pleinement, aussi bien au plan philosophique, religieux, politique qu'économique. Disciples de Voltaire, ils font confiance à la raison individuelle pour trouver la mesure de toute chose. Leur rationalisme se garde toutefois de verser dans le matérialisme. S'ils supportent difficilement la rigueur dogmatique du catholicisme, ils s'accommodent volontiers du protestantisme libéral d'un Guizot ou de l'éclectisme d'un Victor Cousin, qui est, peut-on dire, la philosophie spiritualiste du régime. Ils se veulent tolérants en matière religieuse, ce qui ne les empêche pas pourtant d'être anticléricaux et même, certains, anticatholiques. Guizot aura de sérieux démêlés avec l'Eglise à propos de l'enseignement et Thiers portera des jugements sévères contre les Jésuites. Mais, dans l'ensemble, après la forte poussée d'anticléricalisme consécutive à la révolution de Juillet, ils éviteront d'envenimer leurs rapports avec le clergé. A partir des années 1840-1845, on pressent même dans la haute bourgeoisie orléaniste le revirement qui la conduira dans la seconde moitié du siècle à retrouver la foi catholique et à répudier son scepticisme voltairien.

Politiquement, l'orléanisme affecte d'être un centrisme en lutte sur deux fronts, l'extrême droite légitimiste et l'extrême gauche républicaine. Même si depuis son identification au parti de la Résistance il n'occupe plus tout à fait « le juste milieu », il n'en défend pas moins des idées modérées. Il s'agit tout d'abord de réconcilier les Français autour d'une monarchie tricolore alliant l'héritage royal de l'ancienne France au legs révolutionnaire de la France nouvelle. La Charte révisée de 1830 réalise la fusion harmonieuse de ces deux forces ; elle est le « point fixe » qui achève l'ère révolutionnaire, apporte une solution définitive aux luttes séculaires entre Français. Ces libéraux qui sont souvent des historiens pensent avec Guizot que l'avènement de la bourgeoisie, consacré en 1789, est l'achèvement d'un long et inévitable processus de prise de conscience qui a commencé au Moyen Age avec le mouvement communal. A leurs yeux, vain était le caractère réactionnaire de la contre-révolution ultra. 1830 efface cette parenthèse chimérique pour rétablir et clore le mouvement de 1789. Il s'agit bien des principes de 1789 et non de 1793, car les orléanistes tiennent à faire une nette distinction entre la phase libérale et la phase égalitaire de la Révolution. La première est sage et utile, la seconde, criminelle et négative. A ceci les radicaux répliqueront plus tard avec Clemenceau : « Messieurs, que nous le voulions ou non, la Révolution est un bloc dont on ne peut rien distraire. »

Tout en sacrifiant au culte de Napoléon (le retour des cendres de l'empereur), ils ont en haine le centralisme bonapartiste. Ils sont décentralisateurs. C'est peut-être leur seul point commun avec

les ultras. Mais les réformes dans ce domaine resteront en deçà de leurs idées, essentiellement par
crainte d'un retour du fédéralisme. En politique
extérieure, ils sont hostiles à toute aventure et
pratiquent une politique de paix qui mécontente la
gauche révolutionnaire et romantique.

En matière économique, ils adoptent les grands
principes du libéralisme, le « laissez faire, laissez
passer » des « classiques » (J.-B. Say, Bastiat). Pour
eux, le rôle de l'Etat doit être réduit au minimum :
celui d'un « Etat gendarme » au budget rigoureusement équilibré, dont la mission est de faire respecter
l'ordre et la légalité en se gardant bien de fausser les
lois de la libre concurrence. Un abîme sépare la
théorie de la pratique. Les principes du libéralisme
économique sont vite oubliés lorsque de puissants
groupes de pression n'y trouvent pas profit. Beaucoup plus que le désir de maintenir l'Etat en dehors
du champ économique, les orléanistes ont cherché à
lui arracher le maximum d'avantages, quitte à faire
des entorses à la doctrine (le protectionnisme doua-
nier, la loi de 1842 sur les chemins de fer).

Les orléanistes, en effet, ne sont pas uniquement
libéraux. Ils sont aussi conservateurs. C'est un des
traits caractéristiques du libéralisme français au
XIXᵉ siècle que de devenir de plus en plus conservateur. Une formule célèbre résume leur credo
politique : l'ordre et la liberté. Réactionnaires, ils
ne le sont pas, en ce sens qu'ils ne veulent pas, à la
différence des ultras, d'un retour en arrière. Ils
souhaitent simplement maintenir l'ordre politique
et social dans lequel ils ont trouvé leur épanouissement moral et financier, limiter au strict nécessaire
les réformes afin d'empêcher toute nouvelle explosion populaire. Ils ont été effrayés par la force
libérée en 1830, qu'ils ont réussi à canaliser à leur

profit. Leur peur d'être débordés a fait avorter une politique appuyée sur le parti du Mouvement et avec elle la formule originale d'un orléanisme de centre-gauche, populaire et anticlérical. De la démocratie, ces grands bourgeois louis-philippards ne veulent pas, car, pensent-ils, le nivellement égalitaire qu'entraînerait l'établissement du suffrage universel mettrait fin au gouvernement des élites, des notables, auquel vont leurs préférences. C'est pourquoi le régime réprimera avec tant de sévérité les émeutes populaires des années 1831-1835, jugulera la liberté de la presse et rejettera même, en 1847, la proposition pourtant modérée de Duvergier de Hauranne d'abaisser le cens électoral.

Il semble difficile assurément, lorsque l'on fait le bilan de la monarchie de Juillet, de laver les orléanistes des reproches d'égoïsme social et d'immobilisme que leurs détracteurs n'ont pas manqué de faire. Cela paraît évident en matière sociale. Le sort misérable des ouvriers ne leur inspire aucun sentiment de pitié. C'est à la charité privée, répètent-ils, qu'il revient de s'occuper des plus défavorisés. Il faudra attendre 1841 pour qu'à la suite d'abus inimaginables une loi vienne interdire le travail des enfants de moins de huit ans.

B) *Le légitimisme*. — La révolution de Juillet a éliminé du pouvoir les traditionalistes. En prenant leur place, les orléanistes les ont rejetés à l'extrême droite. Ils n'en demeurent pas moins une force politique très vivante qui prend le nom de légitimisme. C'est avant tout le parti de la fidélité, fidélité dont Chateaubriand a exprimé avec une amère désillusion le noble désintéressement. Fidélité chevaleresque à la branche aînée des Bourbons, fidélité pieuse à l'Eglise catholique, fidélité nostalgique à une forme de société rurale et artisanale menacée de déclin. Refuser avec indignation les lois de « l'usurpation » est pour eux une question d'honneur. Aussi ne verra-t-on aucun ancien ultra arborer en 1830 la cocarde tricolore à son chapeau. Rares également seront ceux qui, à l'image de l'avocat royaliste Berryer, accepteront de poursuivre une carrière politique sous le régime abhorré. La noblesse légitimiste, dans son ensemble, se réfugie dans une boudeuse abstention, se retire sur ses terres. C'est le mouvement inverse qui, un siècle et demi plus tôt, l'avait amenée à la cour du Roi-Soleil. Cette « émigration de l'intérieur » facilite évidemment la tâche des orléanistes en précipitant le renouvellement des cadres politiques, administratifs et militaires du pays. Mais, ce que l'opposition perd dans le présent, elle le regagnera dans l'avenir. En s'enracinant à nouveau en province, la société aristocratique trouvera un regain d'influence au sein du monde rural et provincial, prélude à de nouvelles percées politiques.

Entichée de préjugés nobiliaires, retranchée dans ses demeures féodales ou ses hôtels du faubourg Saint-Germain, l'éternelle noblesse frondeuse peut à loisir ressasser ses griefs et donner libre cours à sa naturelle amertume. Elle peut se gausser des nouveaux riches, se moquer avec impertinence des travers du bourgeois, sourire avec mépris de sa méconnaissance des usages du monde, elle ne met pas sérieusement en danger le pouvoir. La satire mondaine n'a jamais réussi à ébranler un régime.

De graves dissentiments séparent le camp des légitimistes. Certains défendent les droits au trône du duc d'Angoulême (Louis XIX), d'autres, plus nombreux, ceux du duc de Bordeaux, futur comte de Chambord (Henri V). Des sociétés secrètes se constituent. Des complots chimériques se nouent dans l'enthousiasme et sombrent dans le ridicule, comme la romanesque équipée de la duchesse de Berry en Vendée (1832). Les régions de l'Ouest, du Sud-Ouest et du Midi où se trouvent les fidèles aux princes en exil ne bougent pas. L'Eglise elle-même qui a des sympathies avouées pour la cause légitimiste juge plus prudent de se tenir à l'écart des luttes dynastiques.

Mais, à côté de ce légitimisme déclinant, existe un néo-légitimisme populaire, animé par une équipe de jeunes gens enthousiastes et généreux qui réclament des réformes politiques et sociales audacieuses. Ce mouvement est résolu à utiliser pleinement les moyens légaux à sa disposition. C'est ainsi qu'il se dote d'une presse nouvelle, parfois brillante, toujours satirique : à Paris, *Le Populaire* et *La Mode* du vicomte Walsh, en province, de très nombreuses gazettes locales. Certains (Falloux, La Rochejaquelein) se font élire à la Chambre. Tous, avec Chateaubriand, rêvent d'unir légitimité et liberté. Ils réclament l'abaissement du cens, l'accession à l'électorat de tout citoyen acquittant une contribution foncière. Dans *La Gazette de France*, l'abbé de Genoude se fait le champion de ce traditionalisme libéral et populaire, essayant de gagner à cette cause les travailleurs en révolte contre l'ordre bourgeois. D'une façon générale, la critique sociale s'intensifie à l'extrême droite. Dans sa thèse sur *Les débuts du catholicisme social en France (1822-1870)*, J.-B. Duroselle a montré qu'au moins à l'origine celui-ci plonge ses racines dans la droite traditionaliste. Représentants d'une société précapitaliste, les légitimistes dénoncent avec force l'avènement du machinisme inhumain, soulignent les effets nocifs de la suppression des corporations par la Révolution. En 1834, Villeneuve-Bargemont, ancien préfet de Louis XVIII, rédige un traité d'*Economie politique chrétienne*, s'attaque aux méfaits du capitalisme sauvage et propose des remèdes. Six ans plus tard, c'est un autre légitimiste, le Dr Villermé, qui effectue la première grande enquête sur les conditions tragiques dans lesquelles vivent les ouvriers de la grande industrie. Ces précurseurs seront par la suite relayés par d'autres chrétiens sociaux qui se rattachent tous au même courant de pensée, Armand de Melun, Frédéric Le Play, Albert de Mun, La Tour du Pin, etc.

III. — Du parti de l'ordre
à l'ordre moral

1. **Le parti de l'ordre.** — La soudaine révolution de février 1848 semble ouvrir une ère de « bons sentiments ». La république nouvelle, humanitaire et pacifiste, réconcilie vaincus et vainqueurs, « républicains du lendemain » (légitimistes et orléanistes) et « républicains de la veille ». Elle instaure le suffrage universel, supprime l'esclavage, se préoccupe du sort misérable des ouvriers et des chômeurs. Mais l'illusion romantique d'unanimité nationale est de courte durée.

Les élections générales d'avril 1848 font passer brusquement le corps électoral de 250 000 à 9 millions d'électeurs. Politiquement, la majorité appartient aux 500 républicains nationaux, issus de la petite et moyenne bourgeoisie, qui représentent un centrisme modéré. Toutefois, les partis de droite sont loin d'être éliminés par le suffrage universel. Là réside la surprise. L'emprise des notables sur les masses paysannes souvent illettrées est restée très puissante. Les orléanistes sont environ 200, les légitimistes, qui ont refait leur unité, une centaine. Désunies hier, les deux droites se trouvent désormais associées dans l'opposition. La sanglante répression des émeutes ouvrières de juin consacre la rupture entre la gauche radicale et socialiste et les républicains du centre. Elle prépare de ce fait la victoire des droites coalisées dont les élections locales et les législatives partielles de l'été 1848 manifestent la remontée dans le pays.

Légitimistes et orléanistes forment alors le parti de l'ordre. Son comité, dirigé par Thiers, Molé, Berryer et Rémusat, siège rue de Poitiers. Ce sont les orléanistes qui dominent largement la coalition et imposent aux légitimistes minoritaires leur style et leurs opinions : défense de l'ordre et de la propriété. Ce premier effort d'unification des monarchistes est récompensé : aux élections présidentielles, leur candidat officieux, Louis-Napoléon Bonaparte, est élu avec 5,4 millions de voix contre 1,4 million au général Cavaignac, candidat des républicains du centre. Le premier ministère de la Seconde République est confié à l'un des leurs, Odilon Barrot, ancien chef de la gauche dynastique. Aux élections législatives de mai 1849, après une active campagne contre le péril « rouge » des « démoc. soc. », les députés du parti de l'ordre se retrouvent majoritaires (450 environ sur 713). Les légitimistes, qui ont près de 200 élus, renforcent leurs positions dans l'Ouest, une partie du Sud-Ouest, le Languedoc et le département du Vaucluse. D'une façon générale, la province se trouve placée au centre de la vie politique. Ceci explique pourquoi la forte poussée d'extrême gauche (200 élus de la « Montagne »), venue des milieux ruraux, inquiète particulièrement les vainqueurs : le socialisme agraire apparaît dans une France à prédominance paysanne comme un mouvement de révolte directe contre les notables.

Pour la majorité, il s'agit de mener une politique antirépublicaine. Impitoyable est la répression des émeutes fomentées en juin 1849 par les Montagnards. A Paris, la troupe disperse les manifestants ; à Lyon, il y a de véritables batailles de rue. La loi du 31 mai 1850 revient sur le suffrage universel en posant comme condition à l'exercice du droit de vote trois années de résidence au même lieu, ce qui élimine de l'électorat les couches sociales dangereuses sur lesquelles les notables ont le moins d'influence : artisans et journaliers contraints à de fréquentes migrations (1). La mort, le 26 août 1850, de Louis-Philippe fait naître chez certains l'espoir d'une fusion des deux branches dynastiques. Pure illusion ! Associées mais rivales, les deux traditions de droite subsistent avec leur doctrine, leurs passions et leur personnel politique. Tandis que les légitimistes rêvent toujours d'une Contre-Révolution catholique et royale qui ferait revenir la France à un état antérieur à 1789, les orléanistes acceptent pleinement la société moderne issue de la Révolution. Les uns sont profondément réactionnaires, les autres n'ont jamais été aussi conservateurs.

2. **Le bonapartisme.** — En soutenant discrètement la candidature de Louis-Napoléon qui leur semble un terne aventurier, un « crétin » dira Thiers, les apprentis sorciers du parti de l'ordre n'ont pas conscience de libérer une force politique imprévue, le bonapartisme.

A) *Les idées bonapartistes.* — Dès les élections de mai 1849, les partisans du neveu de l'empereur

(1) Un tiers des citoyens sont ainsi écartés de la vie politique.

ont fait une campagne indépendante du parti de l'ordre. Ils ont des élus sous leur propre drapeau, notamment en Champagne et dans les Charentes. Ce n'est que lorsque le péril radical est localement puissant que le mouvement bonapartiste s'allie aux défenseurs de l'ordre. Ailleurs, il représente autre chose que le simple conservatisme. La légende napoléonienne qui, nous l'avons vu, était restée associée à l'idéal de la gauche libérale a conservé un pouvoir magique sur l'électorat paysan. Dans les campagnes certains illettrés ont cru élire le grand empereur lui-même ! Voter l'année suivante pour les candidats bonapartistes signifie bien souvent voter contre l'emprise des notables et pour le maintien des conquêtes de la Révolution.

Les bonapartistes, en effet, n'ont pas le même programme que les partisans de l'ordre. Ils se présentent comme une force politique moderne, soucieuse de développer la civilisation industrielle, d'enrichir le pays grâce au progrès économique et social. Dans leur profession de foi ils parlent volontiers de réformes à accomplir, de routes à tracer, de chemins de fer à construire. Le 31 octobre 1849, le prince-président déclare : « Tout un système a triomphé le 10 décembre, car le nom de Napoléon est à lui seul un programme. »

Ce système n'est ni à droite, ni à gauche. Le bonapartisme est encore à cette époque un centrisme instable, pouvant aussi bien verser dans un bonapartisme de gauche, populaire, démocratique et anticlérical, que dans un bonapartisme de droite, conservateur, clérical, défenseur de la propriété contre la menace des « rouges ». Il ne se confond en tout cas avec aucune des deux traditions de la droite.

Autoritaire et par conséquent antiparlementaire,

le bonapartisme étale un profond mépris des notables et de la bourgeoisie censitaire. Il cherche à s'enraciner dans les milieux populaires en faisant éclater le carcan des cadres traditionnels, en éliminant les influences patriarcales, les liens de clientèle. Sur le plan social, Louis-Napoléon est resté proche de l'idéalisme humanitaire de 1848. Auteur d'une brochure sur *L'extinction du paupérisme*, il a le désir sincère d'améliorer la condition ouvrière.

Le césarisme plébiscitaire du prince-président apparaît donc incompatible avec le libéralisme parlementaire du parti de l'ordre. Le président ne pouvant plus légalement briguer un second mandat, il lui faut obtenir la révision de la Constitution ; une course de vitesse ne tarde pas à s'engager entre l'Assemblée et le président : tous deux rêvent d'une restauration, mais il ne s'agit pas de la même.

B) *Le bonapartisme autoritaire*. — Le coup d'Etat du 2 décembre 1851 prend l'aspect d'une opération de police destinée à éliminer l'opposition de droite plutôt que celle de gauche. A Paris, le peuple réagit peu. En province, après quelques soulèvements républicains rapidement étouffés, le calme revient, non sans avoir effrayé les électeurs du parti de l'ordre. Le rétablissement du suffrage universel semble ouvrir la voie à un bonapartisme démocratique. Il n'en sera rien. La dynamique interne du coup de force, la répression de l'agitation républicaine (hâtivement qualifiée de socialiste) qui a suivi, la nécessité de trouver des cadres que seuls les conservateurs peuvent lui fournir condamnent immanquablement le régime à pencher vers la droite.

A l'exubérance de 1848 succède la mise en sommeil de la vie politique. La presse est étroitement surveillée. Les ministres ne sont que de simples exécutants, responsables devant le prince-président qui deviendra bientôt empereur. Les préfets, rouages essentiels de tout système autoritaire, ont pour mission d'organiser les élections, de « bonnes » élections. En matière économique, les idées saint-simoniennes, débarrassées de leur caractère utopique, tiennent une grande place. Le Second Empire sera une époque de développement économique, mais également d'enrichissements scandaleux. Pour la première fois libéralisme politique et libéralisme économique seront dissociés.

Les ralliés à l'Empire sont nombreux : les militaires, cela va de soi, les milieux d'affaires, car le maintien de l'ordre est la condition essentielle de leur prospérité, les paysans qui apprécient les sollicitations du pouvoir à leur égard, et enfin les chefs du « parti catholique », Louis Veuillot en tête, qui espèrent profiter de la nouvelle dictature pour faire abolir les articles organiques et rétablir l'Eglise dans une partie de ses privilèges d'antan.

En revanche, les cadres des anciens partis restent réfractaires au régime. Les légitimistes qui n'ont que quatre élus aux législatives de mars 1852 se retirent sur l'Aventin. Ils prennent — comme ils en ont désormais l'habitude — le chemin de leurs manoirs provinciaux, s'occupant de leurs domaines, consacrant leurs loisirs à la chasse ou à la lecture de *La Gazette de France* et de *L'Union*. L'Eglise, qui seule aurait pu leur apporter un appui efficace, s'est ralliée à l'Empire, à l'exception de quelques prélats, dont Mgr Pie, évêque de Poitiers, et Mgr de Dreux-Brézé, évêque de Moulins.

Quant aux orléanistes, qui ont perdu le soutien de la bourgeoisie d'affaires, ils sont naturellement choqués par l'aspect policier du régime et le luxe un peu vulgaire de la cour. Ils se contentent d'une boudeuse opposition de salons. On les retrouve à l'Académie française où siègent Montalembert, Duvergier de Hauranne, le duc de Broglie, Sylvestre de Sacy, Lacordaire et Prévost-Paradol. L'Empire qui a confisqué les biens des Orléans ne parviendra jamais à se défaire totalement de cette fronde intellectuelle et mondaine qui a inscrit sur son drapeau la défense du libéralisme.

Un nouveau phénomène affecte à cette époque l'orléanisme. C'est son rapprochement avec le catholicisme libéral (1). La loi Falloux sur la liberté de l'enseignement (mars 1850) en a été la première manifestation. Après 1848, une fraction importante de la bourgeoisie, élevée dans le culte de Voltaire, a redécouvert la morale religieuse qu'elle utilisera consciemment ou inconsciemment comme un moyen de protection de l'ordre social. Le gallicanisme rejeté par la droite ultra après 1830 trouve refuge dans le camp du libéralisme. En retour, l'alliance du catholicisme ultramontain et du légitimisme se réalise aisément. Au *Syllabus* de Pie IX, catalogue des « erreurs modernes », répond l'anathème de Henri V contre la société révolutionnaire. Les zouaves pontificaux qui se battent pour défendre le pouvoir temporel du pape unissent dans une même foi la défense du catholicisme et du royalisme, du trône de Saint-Pierre et du trône du roi légitime.

C) *Vers l'Empire libéral.* — Dans les années 1859-1860, le régime connaît un important tournant politique. La question romaine détache de l'Empire les catholiques qui pardonnent mal à

(1) Une partie des orléanistes restera encore spiritualiste, comme Thiers et Rémusat.

Napoléon III d'avoir laissé amputer les Etats de l'Eglise. Mgr Pie qui ose parler de Ponce Pilate est déféré au Conseil d'Etat. *L'Univers* de Louis Veuillot est suspendu. Le comité central des Conférences de Saint-Vincent de Paul est dissous. La bourgeoisie capitaliste, protectionniste par principe et par intérêt, s'irrite de la signature en janvier 1860 du traité de libre-échange avec l'Angleterre. Cela suffit à aviver chez elle des nostalgies orléanistes.

Perdant ainsi l'appui des notables, le régime cherche à trouver un second souffle en multipliant les avances à la classe ouvrière et à la petite bourgeoisie. Cela se traduit par la politique scolaire anticléricale de Victor Duruy, la reconnaissance du droit de coalition (1863), la tolérance de candidatures ouvrières (Tolain). Le bonapartisme qui a su arracher des voix populaires aux partis de gauche ne parviendra pas néanmoins à provoquer de ralliements notables dans la classe ouvrière. Il semble irrémédiablement se fixer à droite.

L'opposition profite de ces contradictions pour relever la tête. Aux élections de 1863, les républicains modérés et les libéraux orléanistes créent une « union libérale » qui obtient une trentaine de sièges. Bientôt se forme au sein des élus bonapartistes un groupe d' « indépendants » réunissant des conservateurs catholiques et protectionnistes. C'est le *tiers parti*, décidé, non pas à renverser le régime, mais à l'infléchir dans un sens parlementaire. Il s'agit de prévenir toute politique d'aventure. On pense alors que l'expédition du Mexique n'aurait jamais eu lieu s'il avait existé un ministère responsable devant le Corps législatif. Thiers formule le programme de cette opposition libérale. En 1864, dans un discours resté célèbre, il réclame les « cinq libertés nécessaires » : liberté individuelle, liberté de la presse, liberté des élections, liberté d'interpellation et responsabilité parlementaire. Napoléon III ne peut donner entière satisfaction à ces revendications. Il assouplit cependant le régime de la presse et accorde le droit de réunion. Aux élections de 1869, après une campagne animée, le tiers parti a près de 120 élus, les orléanistes en comptent une quarantaine. Les grands perdants sont les bonapartistes autoritaires (les « mameluks ») qui n'ont pas 100 représentants. Ce succès des libéraux est un peu la revanche du parti de l'ordre sur le 2 décembre. L'empereur cède. Il se sépare de l'anticlérical Duruy, des autoritaires Haussmann et Rouher. C'est alors qu'on peut réellement parler d' « Empire libéral ». Le ministère Emile Ollivier rencontre partout bien des difficultés. Il est attaqué par les républicains et les bonapartistes autoritaires, menacé par la défection de certains orléanistes (Buffet, Daru) pour qui l'évolution libérale reste encore insuffisante.

Un bonapartisme orléaniste était-il possible ? Pouvait-on concilier les principes de la monarchie parlementaire et ceux du gouvernement plébiscitaire ? Les événements n'ont pas permis la poursuite de l'expérience. Le plébiscite du 8 mai 1870 par lequel le peuple approuve massivement les réformes libérales implique par sa nature même leur négation pure et simple.

La guerre ramène au pouvoir les autoritaires. On les surnomme désormais les « arcadiens », du nom de la rue où se trouve leur comité, ou encore les « ratapoils » (Jérôme David, Duvernoy). C'est à eux que l'impératrice fait appel en août 1870 pour constituer autour du général Cousin-Montauban le dernier ministère de l'Empire. Cette tendance d'extrême droite du bonapartisme sera pour ainsi dire la seule à subsister après la défaite.

Le Second Empire a fixé définitivement un système politique qui sous Napoléon Ier conservait encore son caractère hybride. Ainsi lui a-t-il permis de dégager sa nature profonde. Le bonapartisme est un césarisme à la fois conservateur et démocratique qui se propose de concilier sur le mode autoritaire, comme l'orléanisme sur le mode libéral, l'ordre et le progrès.

« L'empereur, disait Napoléon III de son oncle, fut le médiateur entre deux siècles ennemis. Il tua l'Ancien Régime en rétablissant tout ce que ce régime avait de bon. Il tua l'esprit révolutionnaire en faisant triompher les bienfaits de la Révolution. »

Le bonapartisme allie au souci de l'Etat fort le désir de s'appuyer sur le peuple sans le concours des notables. Ses velléités de réformes sociales, qui ne sont pas suffisamment audacieuses pour effaroucher les possédants, lui permettent de séduire et d'attirer dans son orbite une fraction de la clientèle de gauche. D'où, comme le note R. Rémond, l' « ambiguïté » fondamentale de ce courant de pensée qui prétend arbitrairement échapper à la division droite-gauche. André Siegfried parle même de « fausse droite ». Sous des formes et avec des dosages différents, on retrouvera l'ensemble de ces éléments dans les avatars ultérieurs de la droite autoritaire.

3. **La république des notables.** — Une fois de plus, Paris est en avance d'une révolution sur la province. Le dimanche 4 septembre 1870, une insurrection balaie le personnel de l'Empire et amène les députés républicains de la capitale à proclamer à l'Hôtel de Ville, selon un rite désormais traditionnel,

la formation d'un gouvernement de défense nationale. La nouvelle équipe prend le pouvoir dans une situation militaire désespérée qu'elle ne parviendra jamais à rétablir en dépit d'efforts héroïques. Le 28 janvier 1871, un armistice de trois semaines est signé pour consulter le pays.

A) *L'Assemblée de Bordeaux.* — Les élections du 8 février offrent au pays un choix clair entre monarchistes pacifistes et républicains patriotes, entre Thiers et Gambetta. Non moins évidente est sa réponse. Sur environ 650 sièges à pourvoir, les républicains n'ont pas 200 élus. La province a désapprouvé massivement Paris républicain. La rentrée en force des notables sur la scène politique, précédée il est vrai par leur progressive émergence à la fin de l'Empire, signifie le retour à une certaine sagesse terrienne après la folle politique d'aventure.

Les légitimistes, fidèles au comte de Chambord, sont près de 200. Réapparition étonnante après une éclipse d'une vingtaine d'années. Sur les bancs de l'Assemblée on découvre les grands noms de l'aristocratie et de la bourgeoisie parisiennes. Mais la plupart sont des hobereaux, sans passé ni expérience politique, élus par les campagnes catholiques. Ils incarnent la vieille France rurale de l'Ancien Régime que n'a pas encore entamée la civilisation industrielle et mercantile. Les méfaits du capitalisme accroissent leurs préoccupations sociales. A la stérile lutte des classes ils opposent la collaboration sociale et le corporatisme d'association. A cet effet Albert de Mun crée au lendemain de la Commune des Cercles catholiques d'ouvriers.

Les orléanistes qui sont près de 200 reflètent l'image d'une France plus moderne, celle des affaires, de la richesse mobilière. Entre les aristocrates libéraux et les nouveaux barons de l'industrie (« les dynasties bourgeoises » dont parle l'historien Beau de Loménie) des liens étroits se sont tissés. Au vrai, peu de choses séparent encore ces orléanistes des grands bourgeois républicains. Sur le plan doctrinal, l'orléanisme n'offre guère de nouveauté par rapport à la période précédente. « Les réformes sociales de 1789 et le gouvernement parlementaire, répète Augustin Cochin, bon gré mal gré, c'est là ce qu'on appelle la civilisation. »

Mais ces libéraux ont perdu leur bel optimisme. Ils s'enquièrent de trouver des contrepoids au suffrage universel, réclament le renforcement des libertés locales et surtout la constitution d'un Grand Conseil ou Sénat, composé de notables, qui viendrait tempérer les emballements populaires.

Quant aux bonapartistes, hier encore prépondérants, la défaite les a totalement discrédités. On a peine à en dénombrer une vingtaine à l'Assemblée, qui se dissimulent sous des étiquettes diverses. La mort en janvier 1873 de Napoléon III, le vaincu de Sedan, leur redonnera quelque espoir d'un rétablissement de l'Empire au profit du jeune prince impérial.

Si l'accord se fait pour signer la paix et confier le pouvoir exécutif de la République à Thiers, les divisions réapparaissent sur la forme définitive à donner au nouveau régime. Aussi l'Assemblée convient-elle par le pacte de Bordeaux de repousser ce débat à plus tard. Mais, en même temps, le provisoire accrédite en France l'idée républicaine qui, après la répression sanglante de la Commune, se trouve pour la première fois dissociée de la révolution sociale. La république a rétabli la liberté des cultes, signé la paix. Elle a pour elle le fait d'exister, de rassurer. La monarchie en revanche commence à représenter l'aventure. Le pays ne s'y trompe pas et, aux élections partielles, accorde ses voix aux républicains. Tirant la conséquence des événements, Thiers se rallie à la république. Il se verrait volontiers chef d'une république consulaire et conservatrice. « La République existe, dit-il le 13 novembre 1872 devant l'Assemblée, elle est le gouvernement légal du pays ; vouloir autre chose serait une nouvelle révolution et la plus redoutable. » Les monarchistes n'ont pas la sérénité du « libérateur du territoire » ; ils s'inquiètent de la montée du radicalisme. Le 28 avril 1873, à Paris, le radical et franc-maçon Baraudet l'emporte sur M. de Rémusat, républicain modéré et ami de Thiers. On y voit la preuve de l'impossibilité d'une république conservatrice. Une coalition des trois droites monarchistes se forme autour d'un orléaniste, le duc de Broglie, qui, le 19 mai 1873, demande à interpeller le gouvernement sur la nécessité de faire une politique « résolument conservatrice ». Le duc présente Thiers comme un otage des radicaux. Celui-ci réplique par un plaidoyer en faveur de la république, « régime, dit-il, qui nous divise le moins ». Le 24 mai, l'Assemblée rejette l'ordre du jour de confiance au gouvernement par 368 voix contre 344. Le soir même, elle porte à la Présidence de la République le maréchal de Mac-Mahon, duc de Magenta. Ce soldat loyal et courageux, sans grande compétence politique, confie aussitôt au duc de Broglie le soin de diriger un nouveau cabinet composé de représentants des trois droites.

B) *L'Ordre moral.* — Commence alors le régime dit d'*Ordre moral* dont le maréchal définit l'esprit dans son premier message à l'Assemblée : « Avec l'aide de Dieu, le dévouement de notre armée qui sera toujours l'esclave de la loi, l'appui de tous les honnêtes gens, nous continuerons l'œuvre de libération du territoire (1) et le rétablissement de l'ordre moral dans le pays. »

L'armée, l'Eglise, la magistrature, les notables sont invités à se mobiliser pour la défense de la moralité publique. Les enterrements civils doivent désormais avoir lieu avant le lever du jour, les débits de boisson sont réglementés, les instituteurs radicaux surveillés par les préfets et les journaux républicains poursuivis. Des fonctionnaires sont révoqués. Une loi de janvier 1874 confie au gouvernement la nomination des maires.

L'atmosphère est à un cléricalisme tapageur qui reçoit la bénédiction du clergé légitimiste et ultramontain. Processions, manifestations et missions religieuses sont encouragées dans les campagnes. La Congrégation des Augustins de l'Assomption œuvre dans le sens d'un catholicisme de combat, à la fois mystique et ligueur, unissant les préceptes de la Contre-Réforme aux thèmes de la Contre-Révolution. Les pères assomptionnistes organisent d'immenses pèlerinages populaires (Lourdes, La Salette, Paray-le-Monial) et disposent d'une presse moderne et bien organisée (*La Croix* et *Le Pèlerin* notamment). Leurs prédicateurs insistent sur la pénitence que la France doit faire pour obtenir le pardon des fautes commises. A cette préoccupation répond la dévotion nouvelle au Sacré-Cœur. La basilique de Montmartre qui se dresse dans le ciel de Paris est consacrée à « l'expiation des crimes de la Commune ».

---

(1) La convention d'évacuation des troupes allemandes a été signée le 15 mars 1873.

La renaissance d'un catholicisme populaire satisfait les légitimistes, mais heurte la sensibilité discrète des orléanistes qui conçoivent une forme de piété plus personnelle, plus intime. Aussi refusent-ils de s'associer à la campagne lancée par certains pour la restauration du pouvoir temporel des papes. Gallicans, ils pensent que les deux pouvoirs ne doivent pas se confondre et redoutent l'effet de retour de l'anticléricalisme.

L'Ordre moral ayant fait disparaître les insignes républicains des mairies et proscrit le mot même de république, tout semble prêt pour la restauration du trône. En août 1873, le comte de Paris, petit-fils de Louis-Philippe, reconnaît pour roi Henri V, comte de Chambord, qui à son tour le prend pour héritier. Mais la fusion bute sur la question du drapeau tricolore, symbole de la souveraineté nationale, que le prétendant légitimiste refuse maladroitement d'admettre. « Je ne puis consentir, dit-il, à inaugurer un règne réparateur et fort par un acte de faiblesse. »

Une fois encore, l'Assemblée se résigne à organiser le provisoire en attendant la mort du comte de Chambord. Par la loi du Septennat (20 novembre 1873) Mac-Mahon est nommé président pour sept ans. Mais la coalition des droites royalistes ne survit pas à l'échec de la restauration. Les légitimistes, qu'on appelle les chevau-légers, pratiquent selon leur habitude la politique du pire. Le 16 mai 1874, ils mêlent leurs voix à celles des radicaux, contribuant ainsi au renversement du ministère de Broglie. L'événement qui précipite la conjonction des orléanistes et des républicains modérés est la remontée spectaculaire du bonapartisme aux élections partielles. Réorganisé par Rouher sous le nom d'Appel au peuple, disposant de puissants journaux *(Le Pays, Le Gaulois, L'Ordre)*, le parti bonapartiste possède en outre de sérieux appuis dans l'armée et l'administration. Quatre ans après Sedan, le rétablissement de l'Empire entre à nouveau dans l'ordre des possibilités. Les orléanistes peuvent accepter par tactique le concours des bonapartistes pour s'opposer à Thiers ; ils ne sauraient admettre la démagogie du césarisme plébiscitaire. Mieux vaut se résigner à la république parlementaire et conservatrice. L'amendement Wallon, voté le 31 janvier 1875 à une voix de majorité, fonde de façon définitive la république. Les lois constitutionnelles adoptées ensuite établissent un régime parlementaire, équilibré par une Chambre haute — le Sénat — et un exécutif influent, réalisant une sorte de monarchie orléaniste sans monarque.

C) *La crise du 16 mai 1877*. — Le renversement de tendance en faveur de la république s'effectue à la même époque dans le pays. Les élections législatives de mars 1876 donnent aux républicains 360 élus. Les monarchistes ne sont plus que 150, dont moitié de bonapartistes. A mesure que la gauche investit l'Etat, la droite incline à l'antiparlementarisme. La division des républicains rend cependant possible le gouvernement des centres (Dufaure, puis Jules Simon). A la suite d'un désaccord avec J. Simon, Mac-Mahon lui retire sa confiance et rappelle le duc de Broglie. C'est la crise du 16 mai 1877. Trois jours plus tard, l'Assemblée refuse la confiance au nouveau ministère « d'ordre moral ». Le président maintient le cabinet et, s'appuyant sur le Sénat, renvoie les députés devant les électeurs. Le débat se situe sur deux plans. A l'opposition droite-gauche se superpose un problème d'interprétation constitutionnelle : le président peut-il avoir une politique personnelle contraire à celle de l'Assemblée ?

Une campagne très animée s'engage, à laquelle le président prend une part active. « La lutte, dit-il, est entre l'ordre et le désordre. » Le duc de Broglie ne répugne pas à employer les méthodes autoritaires : 40 préfets, 1 743 maires, des centaines de fonctionnaires suspects sont révoqués, plusieurs journaux poursuivis. On ressuscite même les candidatures officielles : « Vous voterez pour les candidats que je recommande à vos libres suffrages », déclare le président.

Le 14 octobre 1877, les républicains ont 323 élus et les droites 208 (dont moitié de bonapartistes). 54 % des électeurs français ont choisi la république : c'est le tournant décisif. De Broglie démissionne et Mac-Mahon, après une tentative de résistance, reconnaît que le droit de dissolution ne saurait être érigé en « système de gouvernement ». Ainsi s'achève la Constitution orléaniste.

En 1879, le Sénat passe aux républicains. C'est la conséquence des mutations qui se sont lentement opérées dans le pays. Les notables s'effacent devant ces « couches sociales nouvelles » dont parlait Gambetta. La France est mûre pour la démocratie. Le 30 janvier 1879, Mac-Mahon démissionne. Il est aussitôt remplacé par le républicain Jules Grévy. A la république des ducs succède celle « des Jules » (H. Guillemin).

Ainsi, quelques années ont suffi pour effacer le triomphe du 8 février 1871 et chasser les droites des marches du pouvoir. La disparition tragique du prince impérial, le 1er juin 1879, porte un coup mortel au parti bonapartiste qui se divise en partisans du prince Jérôme (anticlérical) et tenants du prince Victor (conservateur clérical). Le 24 août 1883, Henri V meurt à son tour. Avec lui s'éteint quelque chose de la France de l'Ancien Régime. Aucun obstacle ne s'oppose plus au ralliement des légitimistes qui n'ont jamais eu confiance dans le prétendant orléaniste. Le rameau contre-révolutionnaire subsistera mais étiolé. La désagrégation des droites est cependant loin d'être complète. Elles conservent des positions enviables dans l'Eglise, l'armée, la marine, le corps diplomatique, l'administration, le monde des affaires, les professions libérales et n'attendent que la revanche.

Chapitre III

LA DROITE ET LA RÉPUBLIQUE

I. — Les grandes crises

Maîtres du pouvoir, les républicains se consacrent en premier lieu à consolider leur conquête et à rendre impossible toute restauration monarchique. C'est l'époque des grandes lois républicaines, de la création de l'enseignement gratuit, obligatoire et laïque. La droite assiste impuissante à la laïcisation en profondeur de la société. Aux élections de 1881, elle ne totalise que 88 sièges sur 545. Mais elle ne perd aucune occasion de relever la tête. Profitant de la division des républicains, de la lassitude de l'opinion devant l'instabilité ministérielle et de la dépression économique qui affecte le pays à partir de 1881, royalistes et bonapartistes s'unissent derrière le baron Mackau, bonapartiste rallié à l'orléanisme. « L'Union des droites » ne présente qu'une liste aux élections d'octobre 1885. Elle se garde habilement de poser la question du régime (1) et organise sa campagne autour de la défense de la religion et de l'ordre social. Elle recueille 3,5 millions de voix et a 201 députés contre 4,3 millions aux républicains et 383 élus ; il en résulte qu'il n'y a plus de majorité possible. Les ministères se succèdent ; leur fragilité alimente directement une vague d'anti-

(1) Les royalistes préfèrent se dissimuler derrière l'étiquette discrète de conservateurs.

parlementarisme qui sera portée à son comble en octobre 1887 avec le scandale des décorations (affaire Wilson).

1. **Le boulangisme.** — A) *Le général « Revanche ».* — C'est alors qu'un officier sans grand talent militaire mais doué d'un prodigieux sens de la mise en scène, excitant la fibre patriotique des Français, exploitant leur antiparlementarisme, devient en quelques mois un personnage aussi prestigieux peut-être que le furent en leur temps les deux empereurs. Le mythe du général Boulanger, du « brav' général », héros empanaché, à la belle prestance et à la barbe blonde légendaire, contraste étrangement avec la médiocrité, la naïveté et la sotte vanité du personnage. Boulanger est vite dépassé par le boulangisme.

Officier de gauche, soutenu par le jacobin Clemenceau, le général a réalisé en tant que ministre de la Guerre dans les cabinets Freycinet et Goblet des réformes populaires (amélioration de la condition des soldats, radiation des cadres de l'armée des princes de la maison de France, incorporation du clergé : « les curés sac au dos ! »). Lors de l'incident Schnaebelé (avril 1887), Boulanger passe pour avoir fait reculer Bismarck et devient aussitôt une sorte de héros national — le « général Revanche » — que vont renier les républicains opportunistes et une partie des radicaux. Muté, puis rayé de l'armée, il entame alors une campagne contre le régime parlementaire corrompu et se fait plébisciter triomphalement à l'occasion de plusieurs élections partielles. Autour de lui se groupent les mécontents : des radicaux (Naquet, Rochefort), des blanquistes, des bonapartistes (Thibaud), des antiparlementaires ou « solutionnistes » (Paul de Cassagnac) et surtout les militants de la Ligue des Patriotes de Paul Déroulède. Les monarchistes sont d'abord hésitants : pacifistes, ils ne veulent pas de la revanche. Mais ils se sentent débordés par leurs électeurs qui votent massivement pour cet inquiétant général de gauche. Le baron Mackau, prêt à toutes les combinaisons possibles pour renverser la république, prend contact avec l'apprenti dictateur en qui il espère trouver un nouveau Monk.

Un vent d'autoritarisme gagne la droite fiévreuse. Le comte de Paris, répudiant la tradition orléaniste, se met à prôner des théories pour le moins surprenantes, alliant le principe plébiscitaire, la monarchie autoritaire et la démocratie parlementaire. Albert de Mun, dans un discours enflammé, s'exclame : « L'ennemi, c'est le parlementarisme ! » Le boulangisme devient le lieu géométrique des oppositions au régime. Seules demeurent réfractaires à cet engouement passager une partie des anciens légitimistes, catholiques et contre-révolutionnaires, ainsi qu'une frange des orléanistes pour qui le respect du gouvernement parlementaire importe plus que la restauration du trône.

Le programme du Parti républicain national — tel est le nom du nouveau mouvement — tient en trois maîtres mots « Dissolution, Révision, Constituante ». Les idées politiques du général, pour autant qu'il en ait, sont des plus vagues : il réclame l'élargissement du collège électoral du chef de l'Etat, l'incompatibilité des fonctions ministérielles et parlementaires, le recours à la procédure du référendum. Il ne faut pas lui en demander davantage. A un député qui se soucie de savoir quelle serait la responsabilité du Président de la République, il répond évasivement : « Nous nous perdons dans les détails ! » Sur le plan social, Boulanger se prononce pour l'amélioration du sort des ouvriers et en matière religieuse pour une politique libérale.

L'appui que leur apporte généreusement la duchesse d'Uzès permet aux « révisionnistes » de monter de vastes campagnes à l'américaine. Le 27 janvier 1889, élu triomphalement à Paris contre un candidat radical, Boulanger est pressé par la foule qui l'acclame de marcher sur l'Elysée. L'agitation est à son comble. « C'est Boulange qu'il nous faut ! » scandent les manifestants. La république n'a jamais été aussi menacée. Mais le général, sûr de son succès aux prochaines élections, refuse de s'engager dans la voie de l'illégalité. Un instant décontenancés, les républicains se ressaisissent vite. Ils entament des poursuites contre la Ligue des Patriotes, modifient le mode de scrutin et laissent croire à l'arrestation imminente du général. Celui-ci prend peur et s'exile volontairement. Les élections d'octobre 1889 opposent à nouveau deux blocs : les républicains (opportunistes et radicaux) et la coalition des conservateurs et des boulangistes. Ceux-ci ont 40 élus, ceux-là 170. C'est une fois de plus l'échec des droites coalisées et surtout l'effondrement du mouvement boulangiste. Par crainte des invalidations l'habile Mackau abandonne ses alliés de la veille et se rapproche des opportunistes.

B) *Conséquences du boulangisme.* — Tout éphémère qu'elle ait été, l'épopée boulangiste n'en a pas moins marqué profondément la vie politique française. Quelle est sa véritable signification ? Assurément, le boulangisme du début n'a pas la même nature ni le même aspect que le boulangisme des dernières heures ; celui de l'état-major du parti ne correspond pas au boulangisme populaire mis en vers par le chansonnier Paulus, et ce dernier courant est loin d'avoir la même signification selon qu'il apparaît en milieu urbain ou en milieu rural. Ces contradictions internes n'empêchent pas le mouvement révisionniste d'avoir une unité profonde et de représenter une force politique originale.

Le général Boulanger a regroupé sous sa bannière les autoritaires de tous les partis : jacobins, blanquistes, bonapartistes, conservateurs, catholiques, à l'exception des guesdistes (marxistes) et de quelques contre-révolutionnaires que leur rigidité doctrinale a maintenus à l'écart de ce phénomène passionnel. Idéologiquement, le révisionnisme boulangiste réunit toutes les composantes de la droite autoritaire, dont le bonapartisme fut, comme nous l'avons dit, la première manifestation en France : l'appel au soldat, l'antiparlementarisme, le patriotisme jacobin, les idées de réformes sociales, la tentative de fédérer les droites et la tendance à attirer une partie de l'électorat populaire. Analysant les scrutins boulangistes, Adrien Dansette remarque d'ailleurs des similitudes frappantes entre les résultats obtenus dans certaines circonscriptions par le général Boulanger et le candidat Louis-Napoléon Bonaparte. A quarante ans de distance, on assiste à la résurgence d'un même courant idéologique.

Les conséquences politiques du boulangisme seront durables. Issu de l'extrême gauche, il a entraîné dans son sillage fulgurant une partie de son électorat radical : le petit peuple de la capitale qui votait « rouge » par tradition et qui désormais va glisser progressivement à droite. A ce moment, le radicalisme évolue vers le centre-gauche et se rapproche de l'opportunisme, abandonnant son nationalisme pointilleux et son programme de révision constitutionnelle. Faiblissant sur ses positions urbaines, il gagne du terrain en province et dans les campagnes. Plus à gauche, on assiste à la naissance d'un antimilitarisme virulent sous l'influence de la propagande marxiste. Le culte de la revanche qui était resté jusqu'alors l'apanage des héritiers de la grande Révolution se déplace vers la droite. Les chassés-croisés de ce genre sont fréquents dans l'histoire de la France. Cette fois l'évolution sera particulièrement importante pour l'avenir. Le nationalisme français s'était, en effet, toujours confondu avec la tradition révolutionnaire dont il semblait former un élément inséparable. Tout au long du siècle il se trouve greffé sur le libéralisme. A la fois humanitaire et belliciste, mystique et centralisateur, il était une vivante protestation contre les traités de 1815 et les régimes « obscurantistes » qui persistaient en Europe. Ce premier nationalisme qu'illustrent Béranger, Michelet et plus tard Victor Hugo est à l'origine de la légende napoléonienne. « Pensez-y, disait Godefroy Cavaignac à Louis-Philippe, le 31 juillet 1830, c'est une révolution nationale. » Pourtant le nationalisme semble fuir le pouvoir. Lorsque les libéraux triomphent, il devient une force d'opposition avec les républicains puis les socialistes. A certains égards, la Commune fait figure d'une vibrante insurrection nationaliste contre les « traîtres » pacifistes qui s'apprêtent à livrer à l'ennemi l'Alsace-Lorraine.

Après 1871, le nationalisme ne change pas de nature. Il conserve son aspect jacobin ; le désastre militaire lui a seulement fait perdre toute résonance humanitaire. Il devient plus nettement xénophobe et militariste en même temps qu'il se divise sur la manière de préparer la revanche. Au nationalisme ouvert sur la conquête coloniale de Jules Ferry s'oppose le nationalisme « continental » de Clemenceau. Pour le premier, la politique coloniale semble le plus sûr moyen après la défaite de retrouver une gloire nouvelle. Pour le second, rien ne doit détourner la France de la « ligne bleue des Vosges ».

En mai 1882, se crée la Ligue des Patriotes dont le président est l'historien Henri Martin et le vice-président Félix Faure. Son but ? « L'organisation de l'éducation militaire et patriotique par le livre, la gymnastique et le tir » (article 2 des statuts). Bien qu'elle se veuille totalement apolitique, la Ligue se réclame de l'idéal démocratique de défense des droits de l'Homme. A l'époque du boulangisme, elle compte environ 200 000 membres. C'est à ce moment que, profondément déçue par le régime républicain, elle verse dans l'antiparlementarisme, sous l'impulsion de son animateur Paul Déroulède, le poète de la revanche. L'idée se fait jour que, pour récupérer les provinces perdues, il convient d'instaurer un pouvoir fort à l'intérieur. Se plaçant sur le terrain de la lutte contre la république, il était naturel que la Ligue évoluât vers la droite.

Parallèlement, le nationalisme trouve écho dans des milieux qui lui étaient restés réfractaires. Légitimistes et orléanistes s'étaient toujours montrés attachés à la paix européenne et hostiles à toute entreprise belliqueuse (1), fût-ce au prix d'une humiliation. En 1885, un seul député de droite, Mgr Freppel, prend la défense de la politique coloniale de Jules Ferry et vote contre l'évacuation du Tonkin. A partir du boulangisme, la situation va se renverser. La droite se teinte de nationalisme et d'antiparlementarisme. Le scandale de Panama en 1892 suffit à déclencher une nouvelle éruption.

2. **Le ralliement.** — L'aventure boulangiste dans laquelle les royalistes se sont fourvoyés a large-

(1) Exception faite lorsqu'il s'agissait de défendre le pouvoir temporel du pape.

ment discrédité le principe monarchique. Une restauration du trône apparaît à beaucoup comme utopique. Une partie de la droite est prête à se rallier à la forme républicaine du régime.

En 1885, l'orateur légitimiste, Albert de Mun, avait esquissé une première tentative en créant un parti purement catholique à l'image du *Zentrum* allemand. Le Vatican, jugeant cette initiative peu souhaitable dans le contexte religieux de l'époque, avait fait tourner court l'opération. Cinq ans plus tard, le 12 novembre 1890, le cardinal Lavigerie, en accord avec le pape, invitait les catholiques à admettre la république au cours d'un toast porté à la flotte française en visite à Alger. Léon XIII reprend le même appel dans son encyclique *Au milieu des sollicitudes* (16 février 1892) : les catholiques doivent « accepter la Constitution pour changer la législation », faire évoluer le régime de l'intérieur. La reconnaissance du fait républicain n'entraînait aucunement l'acceptation des principes de 1789. « Sur ce terrain nous ne nous entendrons jamais », disait Mgr d'Hulst. C'est dans cet esprit que se constitue autour d'Albert de Mun, de Jacques Piou et d'Etienne Lamy un parti catholique et républicain, l'Action libérale. Il s'agit, en se plaçant sur le terrain électoral, d'associer les masses catholiques à l'édification d'un ordre social chrétien dont l'encyclique sociale *Rerum Novarum* trace les grandes lignes.

L'initiative pontificale a pour effet de provoquer un trouble profond parmi les catholiques habitués à unir dans une même ferveur le trône et l'autel. Si les troupes orléanistes se rallient à la république par réalisme — des liens de famille et d'intérêts ne les rapprochent-ils pas des opportunistes ? —, les légitimistes, dont la fidélité est chez eux comme

65

une seconde nature, boudent les conseils pontificaux, à l'exception d'une petite phalange derrière Albert de Mun. Ils vont jusqu'à faire courir le bruit que le souverain pontife est franc-maçon, et, en tout cas, lui dénient le droit de dicter leur conduite politique. Un vent de gallicanisme souffle à nouveau sur la droite ultra. Entre le ralliement et la fidélité aux princes, la position hésitante de certains journaux catholiques comme *La Croix* traduit l'embarras des milieux traditionalistes.

Apparemment les élections de 1893 sont un échec pour les ralliés qui n'ont que 35 élus contre 60 aux monarchistes. A. de Mun et J. Piou sont battus. Le ralliement a cassé la droite. Mais, hormis dans le Nord et l'Ouest, les voix catholiques, qui habituellement se portaient sur les candidats royalistes, vont en force au second tour aux « républicains de gouvernement », opportunistes ou progressistes. Ceux-ci, effrayés par le triple danger radical, socialiste et anarchiste, commencent à évoluer vers le centre-droit et, pour gagner l'appui des électeurs modérés, mettent un frein aux mesures de laïcisation. C'est la naissance de « l'esprit nouveau » qu'illustre une génération nouvelle de républicains plus conciliants à l'égard de l'Eglise : Poincaré, Barthou, Georges Leygues, Deschanel (1).

Les catholiques semblent sortir du ghetto politique dans lequel ils ont été maintenus depuis le départ de Mac-Mahon. L'affaire Dreyfus va retarder cette évolution décisive.

3. L'affaire Dreyfus. — A) *Les caractères de la crise.* — La déportation à l'île du Diable, au début

(1) Le rapprochement des progressistes de la droite entraîne une petite dissidence, l'Union progressiste, qui refuse de se couper de la gauche.

de 1895, du capitaine Dreyfus, condamné pour crime de haute trahison, n'avait soulevé aucune émotion dans l'opinion publique, pas plus que la campagne en faveur de sa réhabilitation, menée quelques mois plus tard par des parents et amis du prisonnier. Ce n'est qu'à la fin de 1897, après les révélations du colonel Picquart, puis la mise en cause d'un officier hongrois, Esterhazy, que le doute commence à naître dans les esprits sur sa culpabilité. C'est alors que se déchaîne un torrent de passions sans commune mesure avec le fond du débat. Malgré la volonté d'apaisement du gouvernement, le pays se trouve bientôt déchiré en deux camps, les dreyfusards et les antidreyfusards.

Pour la première fois depuis le boulangisme, la politique descend dans la rue. Elle n'est plus ce champ clos où s'affronte en des joutes chevaleresques la caste des politiciens professionnels. L'affaire Dreyfus marque la fin de « l'aristocratie républicaine » (G. Sorel). Elle révèle la toute-puissance de la presse, qui devient un quatrième pouvoir. Elle conduit à l'engagement des écrivains et des « intellectuels » (à gauche : Zola, Péguy, Lucien Herr, Proust, Anatole France, Seignobos ; à droite : Barrès, Coppée, Lemaître). D'un côté l'Université, de l'autre l'Académie.

Enfin, elle modifie les formes du combat politique : des organisations de masse (les ligues) supplantent et débordent les vieilles formations représentées au Parlement : la Ligue des Droits de l'Homme chez les dreyfusards, la Ligue des Patriotes, la Ligue antisémitique française et surtout la Ligue de la Patrie française chez les antidreyfusards.

B) *Les conséquences politiques*. — Les partis de droite soutiennent l'autorité de la chose jugée. Ils sont hostiles à la révision du procès qui porterait atteinte à l'honneur militaire et préfèrent l'éventualité d'une injustice au désordre, à la ruine du sentiment patriotique, à la démoralisation de l'armée (1). Retrouvant l'éclat tapageur du boulangisme, ils se laissent gagner par un nationalisme pointilleux et — fait nouveau — par un antisémitisme virulent. Déroulède essaie d'entraîner le général Roget à l'Elysée. Aux courses d'Auteuil, le président Loubet est frappé à coups de canne par le baron Christiani. Pendant trente-huit jours, Jules Guérin tient tête aux forces de l'ordre dans le « fort Chabrol ».

L'engagement de la majorité des catholiques aux côtés des antidreyfusards, les campagnes antisémites de *La Croix* et de la presse assomptionniste raniment l'anticléricalisme qui va servir, fort opportunément, de ciment à une gauche divisée sur la question sociale.

L'affaire Dreyfus a rendu impossible la réconciliation des droites avec le régime et la poursuite de « l'esprit nouveau ».

En juin 1899 se constitue une majorité de « défense républicaine » (le « bloc des gauches ») qui, derrière Waldeck-Rousseau et Emile Combes, va reprendre le flambeau de la politique anticléricale. Les républicains de gouvernement, qu'on appelle encore progressistes, se trouvent séparés en deux. La minorité (Barthou, Leygues, Poincaré), qui redoute maintenant davantage le péril clérical que la menace « collectiviste », se tourne vers la gauche et forme l'Alliance démocratique. La majorité est

(1) A partir des années 1870, comme le remarque le Pr GIRARDET *(La société militaire dans la France contemporaine)*, le recrutement des officiers se modifie et devient plus aristocratique. L'armée cesse d'être à gauche à la fin du siècle.

rejetée dans l'opposition (Méline, Dupuy) et s'organise dans la Fédération républicaine. Une partie des fondateurs de la République est donc passée à droite. Ils occupent la place des orléanistes dont ils ont repris la tradition affairiste et l'idéologie libérale du « juste milieu » : l'ordre et la liberté, le protectionnisme, la tolérance en matière religieuse.

C) *Les conséquences idéologiques.* — L'affaire Dreyfus provoque à l'extrême droite l'apparition d'une nouvelle famille politique : le nationalisme. Le terme est en lui-même équivoque, car il recouvre des réalités sensiblement différentes. Il importe de distinguer au moins deux types de nationalisme : un nationalisme de sentiment et un nationalisme de doctrine.

Le premier ne constitue pas en soi une idéologie autonome. C'est une attitude politique qui peut entrer comme un corps simple en chimie dans la composition d'éléments plus complexes ; c'est une pièce d'un ensemble plus élaboré. Il apporte sa coloration, son style aux idéologies les plus diverses. Ainsi a-t-on pu voir le patriotisme exacerbé, le chauvinisme cocardier faire bon ménage avec le libéralisme pendant la première partie du XIXe siècle. En 1887, on décèle sa trace aussi bien chez les révisionnistes du général Boulanger que chez les jacobins amis de Clemenceau. Il imprégnera plus tard le parti socialiste et même le parti communiste.

Le nationalisme de doctrine, en revanche, forme à lui seul une véritable idéologie. C'est ce nationalisme d'extrême droite qui s'élabore à l'occasion de l'affaire Dreyfus (1). Sa bruyante apparition sur la scène politique modifie la géographie électorale. A

(1) En 1898, les nationalistes ont 15 élus, auxquels il faut ajouter 4 députés « antijuifs ». En 1902, ils sont 59 à siéger à la Chambre des Députés.

partir de cette époque, la Lorraine, républicaine, vote à droite. A Paris, les radicaux perdent la majorité au Conseil municipal. Tandis que la bourgeoisie et les classes moyennes se rallient à la droite, les paysans s'émancipent des notables et adhèrent au régime républicain.

Ce nationalisme est une réaction instinctive, passionnelle, brutale, qui fait de la grandeur nationale sa préoccupation essentielle. Antiparlementaire par principe, il n'a qu'un respect limité de l'ordre établi. Le mouvement le plus représentatif de cette tendance est la Ligue des Patriotes, dissoute en 1889 mais reconstituée en 1898 par Paul Déroulède, député d'Angoulême. Cette formation, hostile à la république opportuniste, se montre beaucoup plus virulente que son alliée, la Ligue de la Patrie française de Jules Lemaître, qu'on peut rattacher au courant de la droite nationale (d'essence bonapartiste) et qui, avec ses 500 000 membres, aura quinze à vingt fois plus d'adhérents qu'elle.

A côté de ce nationalisme de doctrine, activiste au plan politique mais très conservateur dans le domaine économique et social, on voit s'élaborer progressivement un courant plus radical encore, celui du nationalisme révolutionnaire et antisémite, qui préfigure déjà par bien des aspects le fascisme. Par haine des puissances d'argent et des féodalités financières, cette « droite révolutionnaire », pour reprendre l'expression de Zeev Sternhell, se déclare volontiers anticapitaliste. Elle prend la défense des pauvres, des ouvriers, des petits épargnants français trompés par le capitalisme apatride. Elle est xénophobe et violemment antisémite, puisant aux deux sources de l'antisémitisme français dont Edouard Drumont a fait la synthèse (*La France juive*, 1886) : celle de gauche liée à l'anticapitalisme

(Fourier, Proudhon), celle de droite liée au catholicisme. Au péril juif est associée la dénonciation de la franc-maçonnerie.

Cherchant à dépasser les réactions confuses et passionnelles, Maurice Barrès tente de donner à ce mouvement une assise intellectuelle plus solide. Pour lui, le nationalisme est « l'acceptation d'un déterminisme », la prise de conscience du poids que représente le passé — la terre et les morts — sur le présent. L'homme n'est pas libre, il est solidaire de l'œuvre sacrée de ses ancêtres, qu'il a reçue en héritage et qui lui commande d'agir en conformité avec elle. En admettant cette réalité, il trouve son plein épanouissement : « C'est tout un vertige où l'individu s'abîme pour se retrouver dans la famille, dans la race, dans la nation. » Le nationalisme ne doit donc arracher aucune page de l'histoire, pas même celle de la Révolution. Mais, à la différence du jacobinisme niveleur, il doit défendre les libertés locales, préserver les particularismes régionaux.

Ces idées se trouvent favorisées par l'apparition dans le dernier quart du XIXe siècle d'un nouveau climat intellectuel qui affirme le primat du sentiment et de l'instinct sur la raison (Gustave Le Bon notamment). Certains appliquent au domaine social les principes de Darwin. Chez l'anthropologue Vacher de Lapouge et chez le Pr Jules Soury, le darwinisme social devient même l'élément central d'une théorie raciste opposant la race supérieure des Indo-Européens à celle inférieure des Sémites.

Amalgamé par ailleurs au traditionalisme contre-révolutionnaire, le nationalisme devait produire un nouveau mélange explosif.

4. L'Action française. — Au printemps 1898, un petit groupe d'intellectuels antidreyfusards, venus d'horizons très divers, se réunit autour d'un professeur de philosophie, Henri Vaugeois, et d'un critique littéraire, Maurice Pujo, pour chercher les bases politiques d'une rénovation française à partir du « postulat nationaliste ». L'année suivante est créée une modeste revue à couverture grise, *Bulletin* puis *Revue d'Action française*, destinée à répandre les idées du nouveau groupe qui ne se convertira à la monarchie qu'après l'arrivée de Maurras.

Charles Maurras est un jeune poète méditerranéen, né à Martigues en 1868, disciple de Mistral, admirateur des lettres classiques, de la clarté latine, passionné d'ordre et n'ayant que mépris pour les rêveries romantiques et les « nuées germaniques ». Venu à la politique par l'esthétique, il découvre pleinement les méfaits du régime républicain et la splendeur de la monarchie d'Ancien Régime au cours d'un voyage en Grèce effectué en 1896 à l'occasion des premiers jeux olympiques. De retour en France, la tempête de l'affaire Dreyfus ne fait que fortifier ses convictions. La France, pays de tradition catholique et royale, se trouve au bord du précipice par la faute de gouvernants méprisables. Il entreprend alors une enquête sur la monarchie pour le compte de *La Gazette de France*, organe de la fine fleur de la réaction.

Quelques mois suffisent à ce théoricien passionné pour convertir à ses vues les rédacteurs de *L'Action française* et se poser en chef incontesté de cette école qui allait régénérer (mais sans doute aussi altérer) la pensée traditionaliste en France.

L'originalité du néo-royalisme tient dans la puissance de sa construction dogmatique, synthèse de courants de pensée jusque-là différents et souvent contradictoires.

Premier courant : le nationalisme « intégral », qui répudie toute référence démocratique. Nationalisme décentralisateur, comme celui de Barrès, nationalisme de défense, de repli, xénophobe et violemment antisémite, qui peut se résumer par la formule maurrassienne de « la France seule ».

Second courant : le traditionalisme, dont Bonald, de Maistre et Le Play sont les principaux théoriciens. Les idées-forces de ce courant anti-individualiste et organiciste sont reprises par l'Action française qui proclame fièrement : « Réaction d'abord ! »

Troisième courant : le positivisme. Maurras qui est agnostique (il ne se convertira au catholicisme qu'à sa mort) ne fonde pas ses convictions monarchistes sur le droit divin auquel il ne croit pas. Son monarchisme a perdu le sens de la mystique royale. Il veut être « scientifique », comme le socialisme marxiste prétend l'être.

« La volonté de conserver notre patrie française une fois posée comme postulat, tout s'enchaîne, tout se déduit d'un mouvement inéluctable... Si vous avez résolu d'être patriote, vous serez obligatoirement royaliste... la raison le veut. »

L'Eglise n'est pour lui qu'un temple de définition des devoirs, un magnifique modèle d'ordre et de hiérarchie, un tuteur de la société civile. Si cela avait été possible, Maurras eût volontiers conservé un catholicisme expurgé de toute référence judaïque et biblique, un catholicisme sans christianisme. L'Action française ralliera néanmoins un très grand nombre de croyants. Disciple d'Auguste Comte, Maurras s'appuie sur une méthode scientifique d'observation des faits, « l'empirisme organisateur », qui consiste à déduire de l'expérience historique les lois de la société politique. Il invoque la raison, non pas la raison destructrice du XVIIIe siècle, mais la clarté logique et majestueuse du XVIIe.

Dernier courant : le socialisme anti-étatique. Anticapitaliste, anticonformiste, l'Action française se rapprochera à ses débuts des syndicalistes révolutionnaires, des anarcho-syndicalistes et des socialistes nationaux en soutenant les grévistes et le mouvement ouvrier. Georges Sorel disait lui-même que les vrais ennemis de l'Action française étaient à droite, au sein de « la bourgeoisie falote et réactionnaire ». Et Maurras d'ajouter : « Un socialisme libéré de ses éléments démocratiques et cosmopolites peut aller au nationalisme comme un gant bien fait à une belle main. »

L'incontestable génie doctrinaire du maître de Martigues est d'avoir su fondre ces éléments disparates en un système intellectuel apparemment logique et cohérent, et, en tout cas, profondément corrosif : un « bloc » contre-révolutionnaire en littérature, en politique et en philosophie s'opposant aux trois formes de la subversion, la Réforme, le Romantisme et la Révolution. La république étant le règne des quatre « états confédérés » (juifs, protestants, francs-maçons et métèques), seule une monarchie traditionnelle, héréditaire, antiparlementaire et décentralisée pourra redonner à la France sa gloire et sa grandeur passées. Dans ses profondeurs le pays n'est pas corrompu : le « pays légal » est artificiellement plaqué sur le « pays réel ». Pour accomplir la restauration, tous les moyens sont bons, « même légaux », ajoute Léon Daudet. « Politique d'abord » sera la devise de ces jeunes royalistes machiavéliens.

L'originalité de la Ligue d'Action française, créée en 1905, tient à son double caractère d' « école » de formation (l'Institut d'Action française dispense comme une Faculté un véritable enseignement) et de groupe d'agitation permanente (les « camelots du roi »). En 1908, la revue se transforme en un quotidien, autour duquel gravitent des périodiques, des organes de presse, professionnels ou régionaux.

Dans le camp royaliste, les « bonzes » orléanistes sont scandalisés par ces « trublions » qui prétendent servir la même cause qu'eux. Ils sont vite débordés. L'Action française intervient alors bruyamment sur la scène politique (affaires Thalamas, Bernstein...) et fait de nombreux adeptes dans les milieux intellectuels et universitaires, beaucoup plus d'ailleurs en raison de son nationalisme que de son monarchisme. Ce succès a de multiples causes : l'effondrement des autres ligues nationalistes après 1902, les persécutions dont sont l'objet les catholiques sous le gouvernement Combes, la montée du péril allemand, l'attrait d'un système cohérent, le goût renaissant d'un certain esthétisme, les qualités intellectuelles de l'équipe dirigeante (Maurras, Jacques Bainville, Real del Sarte, Lucien Moreau, Funck-Brentano, Léon de Montesquiou, Jules Lemaître, etc.).

Le mouvement connaît son apogée vers 1925-1926. Il abandonne alors ses idées avancées pour se replier vers des théories sociales nettement plus conservatrices (le corporatisme d'association de La Tour du Pin). Le 26 décembre 1926, le Saint-Siège, inquiet du néo-paganisme en germe dans le maurrassisme et souhaitant renouveler l'invitation des catholiques au ralliement, interdira la lecture de *L'Action française* (1). L'Eglise de France aggravera la condamnation pontificale en refusant la communion aux membres de la ligue, en leur interdisant mariages et enterrements religieux. Cruel déchirement pour les nombreuses familles dont la fidélité à l'Eglise est inséparable de la fidélité au prétendant ! Retrouvant des accents gallicans, certains catholiques refuseront de se soumettre, d'autres — tel Maritain — se détacheront du mouvement.

(1) Interdiction levée en juillet 1939.

« Toute notre vie est à refaire », soupire Bernanos. Reniée par l'Eglise catholique, débordée par de nouvelles ligues qui lui reprochent son embourgeoisement et son intellectualisme, l'Action française sera désavouée en 1937 par le prétendant lui-même. Le comte de Paris souhaitera en effet dissocier le royalisme du nationalisme et revenir à des positions plus modérées. Plus qu'aucune autre formation, le mouvement d'Action française aura joué entre les deux guerres le rôle d'une société de pensée, formant à son école toute une génération intellectuelle, et dont le rayonnement diffus débordera largement le cadre de la ligue et de son journal.

5. Le reclassement des forces politiques. — L'agitation nationaliste du début du siècle cache mal la défaite des droites dans le pays qui ne peuvent s'opposer aux mesures anticléricales consécutives à la séparation de l'Eglise et de l'Etat. Avec le discours de Guillaume II à Tanger (1905) et surtout le « coup d'Agadir » (1911) la menace allemande provoque une nouvelle ligne de partage des forces politiques.

On assiste en effet dans l'opinion à une renaissance du patriotisme et du nationalisme de sentiment. D'anciens dreyfusards rejoignent alors les positions de droite. C'est l'époque où Péguy, rompant avec le socialisme humanitaire, célèbre Jeanne d'Arc et le culte de la revanche *(Notre Patrie)*, où Psichari, petit-fils de Renan, écrit *L'appel des armes*. Toute une jeunesse intellectuelle retrouve par antigermanisme les valeurs nationales, comme en témoigne l'enquête d'Agathon (pseudonyme collectif de Henri Massis et Alfred de Tarde) : *Les jeunes gens d'aujourd'hui* (1912). Ce renouveau national va de pair avec un retour au spiritualisme, en réaction contre le scientisme, le rationalisme, le positivisme de la génération précédente. La pensée de Bergson, de Boutroux, de Blondel, de William James, de Kipling, de Barrès est comme un vent qui souffle du large, après des années d'étroitesse desséchante. Une génération nouvelle est conduite par des voies diverses à redécouvrir le catholicisme à travers les excès de l'anticléricalisme. Maritain, Psichari se convertissent.

La réaction politique ne tarde pas. Le pacifiste Caillaux, attaqué par la droite et une fraction des radicaux derrière Clemenceau, est renversé pour avoir proposé à Guillaume II de lui céder une partie du Congo en échange de sa neutralité au Maroc (janvier 1912). A partir de cette époque, le nationalisme d'expansion coloniale et le nationalisme continental se ressoudent dans une même haine du Germain. Poincaré, républicain lorrain, patriote intransigeant, succède à Caillaux. Il a le soutien des progressistes de droite. C'est la fin du bloc des gauches, la mise en place d'une politique de réarmement militaire et diplomatique. En avril 1912, la majorité « nationale » porte à la présidence de la Chambre le progressiste Paul Deschanel et, en janvier 1913, assure la victoire de Poincaré à la Présidence de la République au détriment du candidat des gauches. Ce climat nouveau inquiète socialistes et radicaux qui se rapprochent, font campagne contre la loi militaire de trois ans et pour l'impôt sur le revenu. Le bloc des gauches reconstitué l'emporte aux élections d'avril-mai 1914. Victoire sans lendemain : six semaines après la constitution du cabinet Viviani, la guerre éclate. De l'Action française aux socialistes se réalise « l'Union sacrée ».

II. — De la victoire à la défaite

1. **Les droites au Parlement.** — La Chambre élue en 1919, dite « bleu horizon » en raison du nombre d'anciens combattants qui la composent, est la plus à droite que le pays ait connue depuis 1871. Associée au centre, la droite forme un « bloc national républicain » qui détient 433 sièges sur 613, bloc qui doit son succès à la popularité de Georges Clemenceau, le « père La Victoire », et qui prolonge en quelque sorte la mystique patriotique de l'Union sacrée, perpétue au Parlement la camaraderie des tranchées.

A) *Le rapprochement des droites.* — Ainsi les partis de droite, individualistes par nature, ont su faire taire leurs divisions et s'unir lors de la première campagne électorale de l'après-guerre. Leur victoire est celle de l'organisation : ils ont formé une véritable « machine électorale », à l'image de celles qui existent aux Etats-Unis, composée d'une hiérarchie de comités locaux que coordonnent des comités nationaux chargés d'arbitrer et d'accorder les investitures (1). Leurs caisses électorales sont financées par des organismes patronaux tels que le Comité républicain du Commerce et de l'Industrie ou l'Union des Intérêts économiques du sénateur Billiet. Idéologiquement, la droite apparaît moins divisée qu'auparavant. Elle se trouve unie au moins sur trois points : le patriotisme, les questions financières et l'anticommunisme.

Du chauvinisme triomphant au patriotisme conciliant, toutes les nuances du nationalisme de sentiment semblent représentées à la Chambre. Nul à droite ne se réclame de l'idéal démocratique wilsonien, tous se méfient du pacifisme utopique de la Société des Nations. Le problème qui domine tous les autres est celui de l'Allemagne. Nombreux sont ceux qui pensent, comme le maréchal Foch, que le traité de Versailles « n'assure pas la sécurité de la France ». Il paraît « trop faible pour ce qu'il a de dur » (Jacques Bainville). Poincaré et Foch auraient voulu démanteler l'Allemagne. Ils n'ont guère confiance dans les garanties alliées et auraient préféré des avantages concrets. Désarmer l'Allemagne, la contraindre à payer une indemnité de guerre, en prenant au besoin des gages (occupation de la Ruhr), telle est la politique de la droite. Mais, avec le temps, celle-ci finira par préférer le maintien du *statu quo* de Versailles à tout assouplissement.

Sur le plan financier, la droite nationale défend les thèses de la stricte orthodoxie budgétaire. Elle s'accorde à ne vouloir ni augmentation des dépenses publiques ni aggravation de la fiscalité directe. Pour

(1) Cet effort d'unification des droites sera repris avec une moindre ampleur, à partir de 1927, par le Centre de Propagande des Républicains nationaux de Henri de Kérillis.

équilibrer le budget, elle préfère avoir recours à l'emprunt et aux impôts indirects.

Enfin, elle est farouchement anticommuniste. Les grèves révolutionnaires de 1919 ont éveillé de vives inquiétudes dans les régions rurales les plus reculées. Une partie de la campagne électorale s'est faite contre le péril « rouge » (« l'homme au couteau entre les dents »). Devant les progrès des « bolcheviks » en Europe de l'Est et les troubles révolutionnaires qui éclatent un peu partout, elle ressent la nécessité de défendre la civilisation occidentale (mission Weygand en Pologne).

La coalition des diverses droites ne signifie pas que celles-ci aient perdu toute originalité. La difficulté réside désormais dans la diversité des étiquettes, le caractère assez imprécis des groupes parlementaires dont les frontières ne correspondent pas nécessairement à celles des familles idéologiques.

La première constatation qui s'impose est qu'il ne reste presque rien des anciennes formations monarchistes. Les royalistes n'ont que quelques représentants à la Chambre (Léon Daudet par exemple), presque tous inscrits comme indépendants, avec quelques élus bonapartistes ou plébiscitaires. La question du régime ne se pose plus. La république est sortie consolidée de l'épreuve du feu.

Si on laisse de côté les questions de rivalité de personnes et de sous-groupes, on peut répartir les élus du bloc national en deux grandes tendances : « Une bonne moitié d'entre eux vient de la tradition catholique et l'autre moitié de la tradition voltairienne » (Tardieu).

B) *Les traditionalistes*. — La droite traditionaliste se retrouve presque entière à l'Entente républicaine démocratique E.R.D. (U.R.D. en 1924), nouvelle appellation de la Fédération républicaine, qui, en glissant de plus en plus à droite, a abandonné l'héritage orléaniste. Elle représente la civilisation rurale qui, en 1919, est encore largement dominante. Ses élus, dont le plus célèbre est Louis Marin, sont généralement des notables ruraux issus des régions où la pratique religieuse est restée vivace. Cette droite qui a les sympathies de plusieurs chefs militaires (Lyautey, Weygand, de Castelnau...) accepte sans réticence la forme républicaine de gouvernement. Mais elle rejette la société individualiste et centralisée créée par la Révolution française. Hostile à l'étatisme, à la bureaucratie, elle défend la propriété, les libertés publiques, les communautés naturelles (famille, métier, région), au profit desquelles elle souhaite une assez large décentralisation. Comme la droite légitimiste autrefois, elle admet cependant que l'Etat puisse intervenir dans les mécanismes économiques pour venir déjouer les effets néfastes du capitalisme libéral.

La droite traditionaliste est religieuse. De cette époque date le vrai ralliement des catholiques au régime. La guerre, en effet, a contribué à les faire sortir de l'exil dans lequel la gauche laïque entendait les maintenir. Une large fraction de l'opinion n'aurait pas admis qu'ils y retournassent. Les religieux anciens combattants veulent désormais être considérés comme des citoyens à part entière et militent dans ce sens avec le D.R.A.C. du P. Doncœur. Que le climat politique ait changé, il suffit pour s'en persuader de considérer l'élection du Président de la République : c'est en raison de ses idées anticléricales que Clemenceau, pourtant en pleine gloire, est écarté au profit de Paul Deschanel. La République rétablit ses relations diplomatiques avec le Saint-Siège. En 1920, une délégation parlementaire assiste à Rome aux cérémonies de canonisation de Jeanne d'Arc. Mais les traditionalistes veulent aller encore plus loin sur le terrain de l'école libre : ils se battent pour la répartition des fonds scolaires au prorata des effectifs (R.P.S.), sans résultat d'ailleurs.

Ils puisent leur force dans l'appui qu'ils reçoivent de l'Eglise catholique dont ils se veulent les défenseurs naturels. En 1924, la Fédération nationale catholique, ancêtre de l'Action catholique, est placée sous la présidence de l'un des leurs, le général de Castelnau. Mais en quelques années leur position dominante va se dégrader. Bientôt l'Eglise, sous l'impulsion de Pie XI, se démarquera de la droite en encourageant le syndicalisme chrétien et les mouvements de jeunesse d'inspiration démocrate chrétienne. Bientôt le petit parti démocrate populaire cherchera à leur disputer la clientèle catholique. Au grand scandale de la droite, le cardinal Verdier donnera l'absoute à Briand, qui fut rapporteur de la loi de séparation, tandis que des prêtres refuseront les derniers sacrements aux militants d'Action française. Les traditionalistes seront alors contraints à la défensive, à un combat d'arrière-garde contre un monde qui semble les rejeter en bloc (1).

C) *Les libéraux.* — La seconde droite est la droite libérale, héritière des orléanistes et des opportunistes. On la trouve à la Chambre dans des groupes aux consonances républicaines : Indépendants de gauche, Républicains de gauche, Gauche républicaine, car le terme de droite suscite toujours dans les esprits la même répulsion instinctive. L'événement nouveau est que le bloc national réconcilie

(1) L'évolution de l'Eglise vers la gauche ne s'arrêtera qu'en 1936 lorsque Rome prendra conscience du danger marxiste.

les deux fractions des progressistes qui s'étaient séparés en 1899, lors de l'affaire Dreyfus. En 1919, l'Alliance démocratique n'était pas encore totalement passée à droite. Elle se situait plutôt au centre. Mais en 1924 rien ne la sépare plus de la droite. Ainsi, à nouveau, une ancienne formation de gauche franchit la ligne de démarcation et bascule dans le camp opposé où elle vient se fondre dans les éléments les plus proches.

Poincaré, Barthou, Georges Leygues, Pierre-Etienne Flandin, Paul Reynaud sont les représentants de cette droite à la fois libérale et conservatrice. Ces hommes n'ont pas la même opinion que les traditionalistes sur la question scolaire : ils ne veulent pas de la répartition proportionnelle scolaire. Ils ne sont pas anticléricaux — n'ont-ils pas accepté de renouer avec le Vatican ? — mais ils ne sont pas pour autant cléricaux. S'ils sont catholiques, ils ont la nuance discrète du catholicisme libéral qu'apportaient les orléanistes à leur foi. Ils sont surtout attachés à l'individualisme libéral. Représentants de la civilisation industrielle, ils ont de multiples liens avec le monde de l'économie et de la finance, avec les milieux patronaux de la Confédération générale de la Production française.

Le libéralisme conservateur triomphe pendant le gouvernement Poincaré (1926 à 1929). Peut-être atteint-il son apogée au moment de l'Exposition coloniale de 1931 ? Ensuite il décline, se crispe sur des positions de défense, devient de plus en plus régressif et malthusien lorsque la grande crise économique remet en cause le bien-fondé de ses postulats. Ici et là naissent des tentatives de rajeunir les thèmes libéraux : néo-libéralisme (J. Rueff) ou libéralisme organisateur né de l'expérience du *New Deal* et des leçons de Keynes. A ces recherches doctrinales répond sur le plan politique la volonté d'un André Tardieu de moderniser et de simplifier la vie politique française. Il réclame le renforcement du pouvoir exécutif, l'institution d'un véritable parlementarisme équilibré par le *two parties system*. S'inspirant de Disraëli, il rêve d'un « torysme français », d'une sorte d' « orléanisme à l'américaine » répudiant le laisser-faire et le dirigisme.

D) *L'alternance des blocs au pouvoir.* — La victoire de 1918 a fait naître puis s'évanouir l'illusion d'un nouvel âge d'or. La France, qui a récupéré l'Alsace-Lorraine au prix d'un sacrifice immense, se croit redevenue en Europe la « Grande Nation », et Paris, la capitale du monde. Personne ne se rend compte que la guerre de 1914 a marqué la fin de la suprématie européenne dans le monde, le déclin d'une certaine forme de civilisation. Le bilan de l'après-guerre est lourd : le quart du territoire ravagé, des pertes humaines et matérielles considérables, une monnaie fortement dépréciée. La nature des grands problèmes a changé : ils deviennent sociaux, démographiques, économiques, financiers. Mais la classe politique, elle, n'a pas bougé. Méconnaissant complètement la réalité, elle n'a aucune conscience des données nouvelles qui bouleversent l'univers politique. Elle semble en marge des préoccupations de la nation. C'est d'autant plus grave que la politique est devenue la condition essentielle de la vie des Français. Nul ne peut plus dire comme Anatole France autrefois : « La république gouverne mal mais je lui pardonne de gouverner mal parce qu'elle gouverne peu. »

Il résulte de ce déphasage une crise permanente des institutions, une instabilité chronique des gouvernements et des partis. Le faux bipartisme qui semble s'instaurer entre les deux guerres ne saurait faire illusion. En 1919, le bloc des droites est au pouvoir. En 1924, c'est le tour de la gauche, avec le Cartel des gauches. En 1928, la droite y revient grâce à l'Union nationale qui forme autour de Poincaré un nouveau bloc national élargi. Quatre ans plus tard, la gauche l'emporte à nouveau et en 1936 les socialistes prennent les leviers de commande. Mais la victoire de la gauche n'est pas significative, car deux ans après les élections qui la portent au pouvoir elle doit céder la place à des gouvernements du centre ou du centre-droit : en 1926 (Poincaré), en 1934 (Doumergue), en 1938 (Daladier). On s'est interrogé sur les causes qui ont motivé ces singuliers revirements en cours de législature. Faut-il accuser le « mur d'argent » contre lequel viendrait immanquablement se briser l'élan réformateur de la gauche ? Faut-il au contraire y voir la preuve de la totale incompétence financière des partis de gauche, plus habiles à déclencher l'inflation qu'à la maîtriser ? Il est certain que le programme économique du Parti socialiste effraie les possédants et qu'il est de nature à provoquer la fuite des capitaux. Mais il faut surtout considérer la position du groupe charnière que constitue le Parti radical à cette époque. Il se situe de moins en moins à gauche et de plus en plus au centre. Une majorité parlementaire peut difficilement se dégager sans son concours. Les motions de synthèse de ses congrès relèvent plus de l'acrobatie verbale que de la politique. A la vérité, elles cachent mal l'écartèlement du parti entre la « mystique cartelliste » (J. Chastenet) et les dures réalités du pouvoir. Au moment des élections, les radicaux se présentent comme des hommes de gauche et font jouer à plein la « solidarité républicaine ». Ils recherchent l'entente avec les socialistes sur le terrain usé mais toujours fructueux de l'anticléricalisme. Mais lorsqu'il s'agit de gouverner, les radicaux, qui sont des libéraux en matière économique, ne parviennent pas à s'entendre avec les socialistes. La coalition de gauche se dénoue. Les radicaux s'appuient donc sur le centre-droit, ce qui ne saurait durer car ils éprouvent alors la nostalgie du mariage avec les socialistes. Ils décident, comme en 1928, de faire une « cure d'opposition ». Le mouvement de balancier qui les conduit d'une combinaison politique à une autre n'est pas rigoureusement symétrique. Il accentue son amplitude à droite où les radicaux ont tendance à se déporter. En 1938, le gouvernement Daladier a le soutien de tous les modérés.

2. Les ligues et la tentation fasciste. — A) *L'antiparlementarisme.* — A l'alternance des « blocs » au pouvoir répond, dans la rue, soit l'accalmie soit l'agitation nationaliste des ligues et des associations d'anciens combattants. La république, de plus en plus déconsidérée dans l'opinion, est ainsi secouée par trois vagues d'antiparlementarisme : en 1924, 1934 et 1936. Déjà les grèves révolutionnaires de 1919 ont donné naissance à d'éphémères « unions civiques ». Mais c'est principalement après l'arrivée au pouvoir du Cartel des gauches qu'éclate une nouvelle flambée nationaliste. L'Action française atteint son apogée. Le journal tire dans les années 1924-1926 entre 60 et 100 000 exemplaires. La ligue elle-même compte environ 60 000 membres dont 2 000 camelots ou militants de choc dans la région parisienne. Ernest Mercier, le magnat de l'électricité, fonde en 1926 une ligue antiparlementaire aux idées autoritaires et technocratiques, le Redressement français. La vieille Ligue des Patriotes, tombée en léthargie depuis plusieurs années, trouve dans ce climat d'agitation un regain d'activité et porte à sa présidence un catholique conservateur, le général de Castelnau. En 1924, Pierre Taittinger prend la direction des Jeunesses Patriotes (J.P.), qui ne sont au début que la section des jeunes de la Ligue des Patriotes. Mais progressivement le mouvement s'affranchit de cette pesante tutelle et conquiert son autonomie. Il s'organise alors sous la forme de groupes de combat et de commandos paramilitaires qui se heurtent violemment aux communistes. En avril 1925, à la sortie d'une réunion politique rue Damrémont, quatre « J.P. » trouvent la mort dans un affrontement avec leurs adversaires. La nouvelle ligue doit à ces martyrs l'extension considérable de sa popularité et de ses effectifs qui atteindront en 1934 quelques dizaines de milliers de membres.

Qualifiée de fasciste par la gauche, l'organisation de P. Taittinger n'a, en fait, que peu de rapports avec les mouvements fascistes qui font ici et là leur apparition en Europe. A la différence de ceux-ci, elle n'aspire pas au bouleversement des structures sociales, ne met nullement en cause l'ordre économique. Elle comprend même plusieurs députés conservateurs. Son programme politique se situe dans la ligne des organisations nationalistes du début du siècle, dans la tradition ligueuse de la bourgeoisie parisienne : il s'agit de supprimer les effets néfastes du parlementarisme en renforçant l'exécutif. Un élément nouveau cependant : la lutte contre le péril socialiste et la subversion bolchevique qui tient une grande place dans ses préoccupations.

Les Jeunesses patriotes vont être concurrencées par une autre milice de droite, les Croix de Feu.

A l'origine, il s'agit d'un mouvement d'anciens combattants créé par Maurice d'Hartoy et n'ayant aucune attache confessionnelle ou politique, « l'association nationale des combattants de l'avant et des blessés de guerre cités pour action d'éclat » ou « Croix de Feu ». En 1931, sous l'impulsion d'un énergique lieutenant-colonel en retraite, François de La Rocque, ancien membre de l'état-major du maréchal Foch, elle se transforme en mouvement politique antiparlementaire. La nouvelle ligue accueille les enfants des anciens combattants et se double bientôt d'une Ligue des Volontaires nationaux, destinée aux jeunes ainsi qu'aux non-combattants. Elle se dote d'une structure paramilitaire et, pour tenir ses troupes de choc en haleine, organise de vastes rassemblements mobilisant des milliers de militants. En 1933, les Croix de Feu et leurs organisations parallèles comptent environ 60 000 membres qui se sont déjà fait remarquer au cours de plusieurs manifestations, notamment lors d'une réunion de pacifistes au Trocadéro. Sur le plan politique, le colonel de La Rocque reprend les thèmes des autres ligues, mais avec plus de modération : exécutif fort, redressement moral et financier, suppression de la lutte des classes, économie encadrée par l'intervention de l'Etat, antigermanisme. Catholique fervent, il se réclame de la doctrine sociale de l'Eglise, rejette la violence et la haine raciale.

L'antiparlementarisme gagne d'ailleurs, par contagion, une large fraction de la droite conservatrice qui, en période d'accalmie politique et financière, se serait contentée d'une sage république modérée. La presse joue à cet égard un rôle essentiel : le quotidien *L'Echo de Paris*, les hebdomadaires *Candide* et bientôt *Gringoire*, sans parler de la presse d'Action française, soutiennent les ligues. Avec l'ardeur d'un néophyte, un parfumeur corse, immensément riche, François Coty, se lance dans la bataille. Il contrôle *Le Figaro*, *Le Gaulois* et, en 1928, publie un journal bon marché, *L'Ami du Peuple*, dont l'idéologie sommaire et fascisante assimile pêle-mêle dans une même réprobation la bureaucratie inhumaine, la finance apatride, l'internationale juive et pangermaniste.

Les scandales politico-financiers se succèdent (affaire Hanau, krach Oustric) et entretiennent le discrédit dans lequel le régime est plongé. Au début de 1934, un dernier scandale met le feu à la poudrière. On apprend que l'escroc israélite Alexandre Stavisky, qui s'était suicidé le 8 janvier, avait trouvé complaisance et appui auprès de certains parlementaires radicaux. Aussitôt, la presse d'extrême droite se déchaîne et les camelots du roi tiennent le haut du pavé. Daladier (le « taureau du Vaucluse »), qui remplace Chautemps au gouvernement, entend rétablir énergiquement « l'ordre républicain ». Il commet la maladresse de révoquer le préfet de police Chiappe, populaire à droite pour la vigueur avec laquelle il a réprimé les manifestations communistes. Le 6 février, la foule descend dans la rue aux cris de « A bas les voleurs ! », « Les députés à la Seine ! ». Les ligues ainsi que les communistes ont appelé le peuple de Paris à manifester son indignation devant les scandales. La police défend le pont de la Concorde et le Palais-Bourbon. Débordés, les gardes mobiles tirent sur la foule : la fusillade fait 17 morts et plus de 2 300 blessés. Y a-t-il eu complot pour renverser la République ? La rivalité des ligues, leur manque de cohésion dans l'action semblent infirmer cette hypothèse. La question reste ouverte (1). A la vérité, seuls le

(1) Voir Maurice CHAVARDÈS, *Le 6 février 1934. La République en danger*, Paris, Calmann-Lévy, 1966, et Marcel LE CLÈRE, *Le 6 février*, Paris, Hachette, 1967.

colonel de La Rocque et ses Croix de Feu étaient en mesure de tenter le coup de force. Il s'y refusa. Faute de chef, l'émeute tourna court.

Le 7 février, Daladier démissionne. C'est la première fois depuis le 4 septembre 1870 qu'un gouvernement est renversé par une manifestation de rue. Autour du conciliant Gaston Doumergue se constitue un ministère d'Union nationale qui ne résout rien mais apaise les ligues pour un temps.

B) *Vers un fascisme français ?* — L'agitation d'extrême droite ne se réduit pas à la turbulence des ligues nationalistes. Sous l'influence des expériences autoritaires en Europe, on assiste à l'éclosion, en France, d'un nouveau courant politique, le fascisme, qui, comme nous l'avons vu, était en gestation depuis l'affaire Dreyfus. Celui-ci ne se distingue pas toujours nettement du vieux nationalisme avec lequel il a en commun le mépris de la démocratie parlementaire et l'antisémitisme. Sur le plan doctrinal, les inspirations sont cependant différentes. Le nationalisme de doctrine, qui animait autrefois la Ligue des Patriotes, reste profondément conservateur, voire réactionnaire. Le fascisme, en revanche, est un authentique mouvement révolutionnaire, du moins dans son inspiration. Il est, peut-on dire, en Europe, la manifestation politique de la fureur nihiliste d'éléments déclassés, d'aventuriers, de déracinés, de demi-soldes, de chômeurs qu'on trouve après la Grande Guerre. Par son allure, comme par son recrutement, il revêt un aspect prolétarien qu'il serait erroné de négliger. L'image d'un mouvement de petits bourgeois, financé par les barons du grand capital et n'ayant aucune assise populaire, relève de la caricature ou de la passion politique. Le fascisme ne veut ni le maintien de l'ordre bourgeois, ni le retour au passé. Ce n'est pas la restauration d'un régime ancien qu'il appelle de ses vœux mais l'instauration d'un « ordre nouveau » qui serait à la fois nationaliste, impérialiste et socialiste, d'où le double culte que rendront en France les fascistes à Jeanne d'Arc et aux Communards de 1871. Contrairement au nationalisme, le fascisme méprise les traditions, la famille, le pluralisme régional, la décentralisation de l'Etat. Il souhaite unir en un seul faisceau l'ensemble des forces productives du pays, dans une exaltation violente de l'Etat (fascisme italien) ou de la race (nazisme allemand). Le nationalisme ne constitue pour lui qu'un élément au service de l'étatisme ou du racisme, susceptible d'ailleurs de se fondre en un ensemble plus vaste, le « nationalisme européen ».

La première tentative de créer un fascisme à la française date de 1925. Cette année-là, un ancien ouvrier du livre, anarcho-syndicaliste converti au maurrassisme, fonde un parti au titre significatif, le Faisceau, et un journal, *Le Nouveau Siècle*. Georges Valois, qui fut un disciple de Georges Sorel, cherche la voie française du fascisme, en associant les thèmes du syndicalisme révolutionnaire et du nationalisme d'Action française, comme il avait déjà tenté de le faire avant la lettre en 1911, lorsque son Cercle Proudhon unissait en une même haine contre la « république ploutocratique » les fils de chouans et les ouvriers anarchistes. L'expérience échoue. Violemment attaqué par Maurras et les ligues nationalistes, Valois finit par évoluer vers la gauche, dénonçant le fascisme italien comme réactionnaire et réclamant « une république syndicale ».

Le Francisme, fondé le 11 novembre 1933 par un de ses disciples, Marcel Bucard, est une plate copie du fascisme étranger. Ce mouvement n'a pour doctrine que le culte du chef, de l'ordre, de la violence. En politique étrangère, il préconise une entente avec les pays autoritaires, l'Italie et l'Allemagne. Le Francisme connaîtra un certain recrutement prolétarien sans jamais pouvoir dépasser le stade du groupuscule.

Autre microfascisme : la Solidarité française de F. Coty et du commandant Jean-Renaud, qui a le soutien de *L'Ami du Peuple* et qui parodie l'organisation et le rituel des mussoliniens avec ses chemises bleues, son coq gaulois en guise d'emblème et ses groupes de protection. En 1934, un écrivain, J.-P. Maxence, essaiera de donner sans succès une doctrine plus élaborée à cette phalange disciplinée mais vide de toute profonde pensée politique.

Le Comité secret d'action révolutionnaire — la fameuse *Cagoule* — est plus dangereux. Il allie la tradition activiste des ligues au romantisme des sociétés secrètes. Son but est de préparer le putsch militaire qui, comme en Espagne, mettra fin au Front populaire. Il reçoit une aide substantielle de l'Italie. Après une série d'attentats criminels, ses réseaux sont démantelés et ses stocks d'armes saisis.

Le seul parti authentiquement fasciste qui a acquis avant la guerre une audience populaire est le Parti populaire français de Jacques Doriot, enfant terrible du communisme français. Cet ancien dirigeant des Jeunesses communistes, membre influent du bureau politique du parti, en a été exclu en 1934 pour avoir réclamé à contretemps l'unité d'action avec les socialistes contre le péril fasciste. Fort de l'appui de la population ouvrière de Saint-Denis, dont il est maire, il fonde un journal, *L'Emancipation*, et, en 1936, le Parti populaire français (P.P.F.). L'année suivante le mouvement compte, dit-on, 130 000 membres, dont une majorité d'ouvriers et de chômeurs. Ses réunions font salle comble au Vel' d'Hiv. Le P.P.F. évolue assez vite vers le fascisme. Son credo est l'anticapitalisme, le racisme, le nationalisme et surtout l'anticommunisme. Il attire nombre d'intellectuels : B. de Jouvenel, Drieu La Rochelle, Georges Suarez, Fabre-Luce. En mars 1937, Doriot lance le Front de la Liberté et cherche à se rapprocher des ligues d'extrême droite. Le P.P.F. connaît une grave crise au moment de Munich et ses effectifs diminuent.

Son existence démontre en tout cas que la séduction des idées fascistes n'est pas moins grande à gauche qu'à droite. Aucun parti ne semble avoir échappé à sa contagion. Au sein du Parti socialiste, Marcel Déat et Adrien Marquet défendent la thèse d'un socialisme national et autoritaire qui « épouvante » Léon Blum. Ces néo-socialistes seront exclus de la S.F.I.O. Déat deviendra ouvertement fasciste après l'armistice.

C) *L'esprit des années 30*. — A partir des années 1928-1930, la droite littéraire connaît une intense activité de recherche politique. Le maurrassisme, dont se sont nourries des générations d'intellectuels, ne semble plus répondre aux préoccupations du moment : la montée des périls extérieurs, la crise du capitalisme libéral, les succès menaçants du communisme international. Pour beaucoup, l'heure est venue d'explorer de nouvelles voies politiques. Ainsi naissent quantité de petites revues à caractère doctrinal qui témoignent de l'imagination comme du besoin de renouveau des éléments les plus dynamiques de la droite : *Les Cahiers* (J.-P. Maxence), *Réaction* (J. de Fabrègues), *L'Ordre nouveau* (Robert Aron et Arnaud Dandieu), *L'Homme réel* (Dauphin-Meunier), *La Lutte des jeunes* (B. de Jouvenel),

Combat (Thierry Maulnier). Leur objectif est de trouver un système économique à mi-chemin entre le capitalisme et le socialisme, de réconcilier la droite nationale et la gauche sociale dans un nouvel humanisme. Le bouillonnement intellectuel est intense : péguysme, corporatisme, proudhonisme, personnalisme connaissent à cette époque une grande vogue. On remarque une certaine « convergence entre le courant néo-libéral et le courant néo-traditionaliste » dans ce que J. Touchard a appelé « l'esprit des années 30 ». Etant donné la diversité des inspirations, ces efforts n'auront pas tous la même fortune ni le même avenir. Certains courants de pensée inspireront Vichy et la Résistance, par l'intermédiaire de l'Ecole des Cadres d'Uriage, d'autres se tourneront vers le fascisme. Raoul Girardet parle à ce propos d'un « phénomène d'imprégnation fasciste » qui gagne de proche en proche la droite française : ainsi la revue *Je suis partout* glisse-t-elle, après le 6 février, vers un préfascisme puis dans le pur fascisme. Toute une jeunesse intellectuelle, dont Robert Brasillach est sans conteste le représentant le plus brillant, semble atteinte par ce nouveau « mal du siècle ». Elle exalte le romantisme sauvage du « fascisme immense et rouge », les cathédrales de lumière de Nuremberg — ces nouvelles nuits de Walpurgis —, la virilité de l'ordre nouveau, le thème de la jeunesse et de l'amitié retrouvées. Tout cela devait sombrer dans l'effroyable chaos de la guerre.

3. **La division des Français.** — Le Front populaire est une réaction contre la crise économique qui a gagné la France à partir de 1932 et contre le danger fasciste, présenté comme une conséquence de celle-ci. A l'extrême droite, où la crainte du communisme n'a jamais été aussi intense, on assiste alors à une recrudescence inouïe de la violence : campagne de *L'Action française* contre le « juif rabbinique » Léon Blum et son gouvernement « Crétin-Talmud » (L. Daudet), campagnes de

Gringoire contre le ministre Roger Salengro qui finit par se suicider. L'atmosphère rappelle les pires moments de l'affaire Dreyfus. Le 18 juin 1936, le gouvernement de Front populaire riposte par la dissolution des ligues. La plus importante en nombre (500 000 adhérents), le Mouvement social français (ex-Croix de Feu), se transforme en parti politique, le Parti social français, P.S.F. Simple camouflage, dira-t-on. Ce n'est pas certain. Le colonel de La Rocque semble désormais convaincu qu'il peut utiliser le cadre légal des institutions républicaines pour accéder au pouvoir. Il rompt avec la vaine agitation ligueuse, atténue son antiparlementarisme et cherche à élargir son audience auprès des classes populaires. En 1938, avec un million d'adhérents, le P.S.F. représente le mouvement de droite le plus puissant, le mieux structuré. Il n'a encore qu'une faible représentation parlementaire (moins d'une dizaine de députés) mais il prépare activement sa percée électorale. Sur le plan idéologique, il est passé presque insensiblement des idées nationalistes aux thèmes de la droite nationale à laquelle il tend de plus en plus à s'apparenter. Le P.S.F. n'est pas sans rappeler la très conservatrice Ligue de la Patrie française et préfigure par certains côtés ce que sera le R.P.F. du général de Gaulle. Les rapports orageux qu'il entretient avec les autres ligues (procès Pozzo di Borgo) illustrent bien tout ce qui peut séparer la droite classique de l'extrême droite activiste.

La gauche se sent menacée par cette nouvelle force qui organise de vastes rassemblements motorisés dans les forêts de l'Ile-de-France. A Clichy une contre-manifestation se termine dans un bain de sang dont le gouvernement est rendu responsable. Aussi est-il aisé de crier au péril fasciste et d'assimiler sans nuance le colonel de La Rocque à Hitler ou à Mussolini. Les préoccupations extérieures déforment les jugements. A partir de 1935, en effet, la politique étrangère pèse d'un poids accru dans la vie politique du pays.

Lorsque Pierre Laval recherche une alliance militaire à l'Est avec les Soviets pour déjouer la menace allemande, la droite craint qu'on ne fasse le jeu de Staline. Au moment de la crise éthiopienne, elle est hostile aux sanctions que la S.D.N. veut appliquer à l'Italie. Elle n'aime ni l'idéalisme utopique de la S.D.N. ni l'impérialisme hypocrite des Anglo-Saxons. Faut-il réduire l'Angleterre en esclavage ? demande Henri Béraud. Un manifeste « pour la défense de l'Occident et la paix en Europe » recueille plus de 850 signatures, parmi lesquelles celles de nombreux intellectuels. L'idée d'une alliance avec la sœur latine contre « l'Allemagne éternelle » refait surface. Avec la guerre d'Espagne, la droite manifeste sa sympathie à Franco et son hostilité à l'égard des « rouges ». Les lecteurs de *L'Echo de Paris* pensent, comme le vieux général de Castelnau, qu'il s'agit d'un épisode du conflit entre « la barbarie moscovite et la civilisation occidentale ».

Depuis l'affaire Dreyfus, la droite était patriote et nationaliste, la gauche (ou tout au moins une large majorité) inclinait vers le pacifisme et l'antimilitarisme. L'antipathie que cette dernière éprouve à l'encontre des régimes autoritaires, l'appui qu'elle rêve d'apporter aux républicains espagnols tendent à renverser les facteurs. A droite, le pacifisme, à gauche, le bellicisme. Devant la menace hitlérienne, la gauche retrouve les valeurs nationales et militaires. Le 14 juillet 1935, elle acclame l'armée qui défile sur les Champs-Elysées.

Viennent alors la crise tchécoslovaque et la tragique division de l'opinion sur les accords de Munich. Peu nombreux sont à droite les antimunichois partisans de la fermeté : citons Louis Marin, Paul Reynaud, Henri de Kérillis. Mais l'acceptation du démantèlement de la Tchécoslovaquie a rarement pour cause la solidarité avec l'Allemagne hitlérienne qui reste, au moins jusqu'à la défaite, l'ennemie héréditaire. Certains pensent que Hitler est peut-être de bonne foi en proposant la paix. Ceux-là seront désillusionnés quelques mois plus tard par le coup de Prague. D'autres estiment que la France n'est pas prête militairement et que ce serait folie de ne pas profiter du répit offert pour s'armer davantage. Le pacte germano-soviétique réconcilie un moment la droite soulagée de n'avoir plus à choisir entre ses deux ennemis, les totalitarismes bolchevique et hitlérien. Mais combien ont la lucidité de mesurer la menace que cette alliance représente ? A la vérité, la division des Français est telle que le régime sans le savoir est entré en agonie. Le Parlement n'a même pas à se prononcer sur la déclaration de guerre du 3 septembre 1939. Paul Reynaud échoue tristement dans sa tentative de recréer l'Union sacrée. Au lieu de se trouver fortifiée par la lutte comme en 1914, la IIIᵉ République s'effondre. Elle abdique définitivement le 10 juillet 1940, lorsque, par 569 voix contre 80, les parlementaires réunis à Vichy en Assemblée nationale confient tous pouvoirs au maréchal Pétain afin d'établir « une nouvelle Constitution de l'Etat français » garantissant « les droits du travail, de la famille et de la patrie ».

III. — Le régime de Vichy

Par un étrange mouvement récurrent, la France en détresse semble toujours se tourner vers les principes politiques les plus anciens, qui jouent le rôle d'une protection rassurante. De même que la défaite de 1871 a conduit le peuple à retrouver ses élites traditionnelles, légitimistes ou orléanistes, de même le désastre de 1940 provoque-t-il le retour au pouvoir des conservateurs. Ayant perdu confiance en ses maîtres d'hier, le pays traumatisé va naturellement au-devant de ceux qui se sont tenus à l'écart des tragiques événements. Ainsi, en 1940, c'est à nouveau le triomphe des droites, la résurgence soudaine de la contre-révolution, baptisée « révolution nationale ». Le recul est à la mesure de la catastrophe qui le précède. Non seulement les institutions parlementaires de la IIIe République sont abolies, mais on semble effacer cent cinquante ans d'histoire. Tel est bien le sens du mot de Maurras, « la divine surprise ».

1. **Les fondements idéologiques.** — Gardons-nous cependant de voir dans le nouveau régime un système parfaitement cohérent, un bloc monolithique. Comme le constate M. Stanley Hoffmann, Vichy fut essentiellement une « dictature pluraliste », tant par la diversité de ses origines doctrinales que par l'évolution qu'il devait connaître. Il n'est pas excessif de dire qu'en 1940 l'opinion publique dans son ensemble était lasse du régime qui venait de s'effondrer dans la tourmente. Elle n'aspirait plus qu'à l'ordre. Aussi accueillait-elle avec soulagement l'arrivée au pouvoir du maréchal Pétain, vieillard prestigieux qui faisait don de sa personne à la France pour alléger le fardeau de son malheur. « Le Maréchal, a écrit André Siegfried, est comme un aimant qui attire tous les éléments que la IIIe République a combattus, mécontentés, inquiétés ou déçus. » Et ils étaient nombreux. Il n'est pas

étonnant qu'en premier lieu on retrouve autour de lui les nationalistes proches de l'Action française (Raphaël Alibert, du Moulin de Labarthète, Henri Massis...). Le modèle de monarchie élective réalisé par Pétain semble à bien des égards plus conforme à l'idéal de Charles Maurras qu'à celui du prince d'Orléans. Le ralliement de la droite modérée n'a rien d'étonnant non plus. L'orléanisme est par nature une idéologie de ralliement qui s'accommode mal de l'opposition. En revanche, il semble plus surprenant de retrouver à Vichy une partie de la gauche : une fraction du Parti radical, des anciens S.F.I.O., des syndicalistes. En dehors des milieux politiques, il convient de noter également l'appui apporté au nouveau régime par le patronat, les milieux d'affaires, la majorité des cadres de l'armée de terre et de la marine (on ne compte pas les officiers de la Royale qui gravitent autour de l'Hôtel du Parc), le monde rural, la hiérarchie catholique heureuse de prendre sa revanche sur l'anticléricalisme républicain.

Vichy est un syncrétisme des idéologies de ces différents milieux sociaux : le nationalisme d'Action française, le conservatisme de la droite libérale, le courant personnaliste et chrétien que l'on a vu éclore dans les années 30, et enfin un courant de gauche, à la fois national et antimarxiste. Les maîtres à penser du régime seront Maurras, Taine, Péguy et Proudhon. Couronnant cet ensemble hétéroclite, un thème central fait de la défaite (un peu comme en 1871) la juste sanction des fautes nationales et des errements collectifs. Le rachat ne peut se concevoir qu'au prix d'une profonde réforme intellectuelle et morale. Au slogan trinitaire de 1848, *Liberté*, *Egalité*, *Fraternité*, l'Etat français substitue celui plus concret de *Travail*, *Famille*, *Patrie*.

C'est d'ailleurs par une triple réaction que peut s'exprimer la philosophie politique du régime :

1º Réaction contre la démocratie laïque. Le pouvoir, affirme-t-on, vient d'en haut et non d'en bas. Le chef est l'incarnation de la légitimité nationale. Il est entouré de conseils chargés, comme dans la monarchie primitive, de l'éclairer. Mais il décide seul, car en dernier ressort il est l'unique responsable devant la nation, devant l'Histoire et, pour le croyant, devant Dieu. C'est autour du principe d'autorité que doit être organisée la société, ce qui n'exclut nullement l'existence de libertés collectives (familiales, locales ou professionnelles).

2º Réaction contre l'individualisme libéral né de la Révolution française. On veut une société organique et pluraliste faite de corps intermédiaires. Le peuple, aime à dire le Maréchal, est une « hiérarchie de familles, de professions, de communes, de responsabilités administratives, de familles spirituelles ». Ce thème des communautés organiques se trouve surtout développé dans les écrits de Gustave Thibon, qui passe alors pour l'un des penseurs du régime.

3º Réaction contre les excès de la société industrielle. Vichy met les vertus paysannes à l'honneur, prône le « retour à la terre », vante « l'ordre éternel des champs », les bienfaits sécurisants de la civilisation rurale, ceci pour des choix idéologiques mais également pour des raisons d'ordre pratique (la France industrielle se trouve dans la zone occupée).

Incontestablement, l'ensemble de ces idées se rattache au traditionalisme. Elles dégagent comme un parfum d'Ancien Régime et laissent un arrière-goût d'ordre moral.

2. La Révolution nationale. — La mise en application de ces principes ne tarde pas. Les actes constitutionnels du 12 juillet 1940 suppriment la Présidence de la République et confèrent tous les pouvoirs, législatif, exécutif et judiciaire, au maréchal Pétain qui se trouve ainsi avoir presque plus de pouvoirs que Louis XIV. Il y aura autour du vainqueur de Verdun toute une imagerie pieuse et sentimentale faisant de lui un monarque et un père pour tous les Français (la chanson *Maréchal, nous voilà* devient l'hymne populaire du nouveau régime).

Pétain choisit ses collaborateurs parmi les fonctionnaires, les universitaires, les hommes d'affaires, les notables ruraux ou encore les hobereaux plutôt que parmi l'ancien personnel politique. Au sein de l'administration, l'épuration (francs-maçons, israélites) est importante sans être massive, ce qui explique les obstacles divers qui freineront l'œuvre de révolution nationale. Les syndicats professionnels, ouvriers et patronaux, sont dissous. La Charte du Travail du 4 octobre 1941 entend élaborer un nouveau système de rapports sociaux fondé sur la collaboration des classes et l'organisation corporative. A gauche, on qualifiera non sans raison ce système de paternaliste. Par la loi du 16 août 1940, on crée des comités d'organisation par branche d'activité économique, dont l'œuvre, souvent décriée, n'en reste pas moins positive sur le plan de la réorganisation des forces productives, surtout dans une période dominée par la pénurie. Parallèlement, on constitue le 2 décembre 1940 une corporation paysanne.

Pour appuyer cet effort sont formées officiellement des organisations de masse destinées à devenir, dans l'esprit de leurs promoteurs, les piliers du régime : la Légion française des Combattants, le mouvement des Compagnons de France et les Chantiers de Jeunesse. Ces derniers ont pour but inavoué de préparer par un entraînement sportif intense les bases d'une nouvelle armée. Jamais on ne fera tant l'éloge de l'esprit d'équipe, de la santé, de la nature, ce qui donne à Vichy l'aspect d'un scoutisme national, bien-pensant et peu efficace.

A l'égard de l'occupant, le chef de l'Etat entame la « politique de collaboration » après l'entrevue avec Hitler à Montoire (24 octobre 1940), politique dont les limites sont d'abord clairement précisées par l'arrestation de Pierre Laval (13 décembre 1940). La collaboration connaîtra des variations selon l'intensité de la pression allemande et la politique des ministres en place (Flandin, Darlan et à nouveau Laval). Comme l'a bien montré Robert O. Paxton, elle a été délibérément recherchée par les Français, plus que souhaitée par les Allemands qui s'en sont servis en fait pour affirmer leur domination (1).

Rien ne fait mieux apparaître le fossé qui sépare le traditionalisme du fascisme que l'opposition violente manifestée au régime de Vichy par les fascistes de Paris (le P.P.F. de Doriot et son frère ennemi le R.N.P. de Déat) qui lui reprochent son cléricalisme, sa fausse collaboration. Il y avait incompatibilité entre ce que l'on a appelé le « mirage latin » d'une société statique et hiérarchisée, contrôlée par les notables bien-pensants, et le « mirage nordique » d'une société dynamique et révolutionnaire.

3. L'évolution du régime. — Après quelques mois d'illusion, la Révolution nationale ne se fait nullement dans le sens prévu

(1) Robert O. PAXTON, *La France de Vichy, 1940-1944,* Paris, Seuil, 1972.

à l'origine. Les impératifs de l'heure imposent des solutions d'urgence plus que des réformes en profondeur et à long terme. Décentralisateur en principe, le régime se révèle dans les faits extrêmement centralisateur, supprimant les libertés locales, procédant à la nomination autoritaire des maires. Le corporatisme, qui devait régler les problèmes économiques et sociaux en dehors de l'intervention de l'Etat, débouche sur un dirigisme tatillon. La politique de retour à la terre est contrariée par les tendances technocratiques et « synarchiques » s'exerçant en sens contraire.

Le régime évoluera d'ailleurs vite. Le Vichy de Darlan aura peu de ressemblance avec celui de Maxime Weygand. Une nouvelle phase de son histoire s'ouvre le 19 avril 1942 par le retour de Pierre Laval. Désormais, c'en est fait de la Révolution nationale. Le régime se dégrade, s'enfonce dans l'arbitraire. Le S.T.O., la Milice, le développement de l'appareil policier, l'organisation de la propagande, les grandes rafles de Juifs témoignent de la fascisation du régime. La politique de collaboration connaît un autre tournant. « Je souhaite la victoire de l'Allemagne, déclare le nouveau maître du régime, parce que sans elle, demain, le bolchevisme s'installera partout. » Prenant prétexte du débarquement des forces américaines en Afrique du Nord, les Allemands envahissent la zone Sud. Le maréchal Pétain refuse de quitter la France. Cette attitude portera un coup sensible à son prestige. Progressivement, le personnel politique se renouvelle. Pendant l'hiver 1943-1944, Joseph Darnand, Marcel Déat, Philippe Henriot entrent au gouvernement. C'est le dernier acte qui achève de transformer ce régime conservateur et paternaliste en un Etat policier et fasciste. En août, le Maréchal, que le grand âge prive, semble-t-il, de toute clairvoyance, est placé en résidence surveillée au château de Sigmaringen où une poignée d'aventuriers et de collaborateurs rêvent encore, dans leur délire insensé, de bâtir une France nationale-socialiste au sein d'une Europe hitlérienne.

Les conséquences de l'épisode vichyssois seront très importantes pour la droite. Celle-ci ne s'est pas totalement ralliée à Pétain : des libéraux, des maurrassiens, des « cagoulards » ont combattu dans les rangs de la Résistance aux côtés de socialistes et de communistes. Elle n'en sort pas moins totalement déconsidérée par ses compromissions avec l'occupant et assimilée aux fascismes vaincus.

DE LA IVᵉ RÉPUBLIQUE A NOS JOURS

Que reste-t-il de la droite après la Libération ? Ses partis sont moribonds. Sa presse qui était entre les deux guerres un de ses atouts majeurs a disparu, à l'exception d'un quotidien d'information. De nouveaux titres, de nouvelles équipes ont pris la place des disparus. Ses militants sont pourchassés. Fascistes authentiques et fidèles du Maréchal sont traduits pêle-mêle devant des cours spéciales de justice. La vengeance populaire prend le pas sur la légalité. Certains — plusieurs milliers — disparaissent ainsi, exécutés sommairement. Tous n'étaient sans doute pas collaborateurs. La nation tout entière se réclame de l'antifascisme et des différentes formes du socialisme. La droite semble pour toujours rayée de la scène politique. Jamais depuis la Révolution française un renversement de situation n'aura été aussi brutal. Qui eût songé que les droites, annihilées, écrasées dans le sang, allaient connaître en l'espace de quelques années une spectaculaire renaissance ?

I. — La renaissance des droites

1. **La droite libérale.** — Le mythe de la Résistance unie, réconciliant patrons et ouvriers, catholiques et communistes, dure à peine plus que le mythe quarante-huitard. Après le départ du général de Gaulle (janvier 1946), de profondes divergences de vues séparent les trois grands partis de gauche, M.R.P., S.F.I.O. et P.C.F., qui se partagent le pouvoir à la manière des grands féodaux et se surveillent mutuellement. Déjà l'anticommunisme

renaît. La bourgeoisie et les électeurs modérés votent pour le seul parti non marxiste issu de la Résistance, le M.R.P., d'inspiration démocrate-chrétienne. Au référendum du 5 mai 1946 et aux élections de juin et de novembre, celui-ci s'oppose aux communistes. Son slogan est « Bidault sans Thorez ». Les fissures du tripartisme s'élargissent. Elles font craquer l'édifice lors du déclenchement de la guerre froide. Le 5 mai 1947, le socialiste Ramadier chasse les communistes du gouvernement. Ils n'y reviendront plus. Alors le mouvement pendulaire qui rythme notre vie politique reprend. Le balancier entame son retour vers la droite. La participation de Paul Reynaud au gouvernement Marie (juillet 1948) en est le signe annonciateur. Les socialistes, qui jusque-là tiraient prestige d'être au centre de la coalition, flanqués à droite du M.R.P. et à gauche du Parti communiste, se retrouvent être l'aile gauche de la « troisième force ». En 1950, ils quittent le gouvernement Bidault qui s'appuie sur le M.R.P. et les radicaux. C'est le retour au pouvoir de la droite.

Le problème essentiel pour les modérés est de reconstituer un nouveau parti. En octobre 1945, ils ont eu une soixantaine d'élus, dispersés sous des étiquettes diverses. Deux essais de regroupement, l'Union des Forces républicaines nationales et le Parti républicain de la Liberté, se sont traduits par des échecs. La droite libérale a toujours été réfractaire à des formes d'organisation trop structurées. En revanche, la formule souple du Centre national des Indépendants imaginée par Roger Duchet, sénateur de la Côte-d'Or, sera promise à un avenir plus brillant. C'est un parti cadre, composé de notables locaux, qui ne cherche pas l'adhésion des masses. Fédérant des comités et des centres départementaux, le C.N.I. parvient par le jeu des investitures à imposer une certaine discipline, une certaine ligne politique. Ses thèmes sont la lutte contre le communisme, la défense de la civilisation chrétienne, l'affirmation de la nécessaire autorité de l'Etat, de même que l'attachement aux libertés individuelles, à l'exploitation familiale et aux petites et moyennes entreprises ; en bref, un programme de libéralisme conservateur dont l'idéologie est assez largement répandue dans les classes moyennes, les professions libérales, chez les commerçants et les artisans. Bien qu'elle s'adresse à des milieux sociaux variés, aux intérêts parfois opposés (du petit boutiquier de province au P.D.G. de grande société), cette idéologie a conservé, comme au temps de la monarchie de Juillet, sa remarquable cohérence. Sans doute cela tient-il à ce qu'elle vise avant tout à préserver un art social, un cadre de vie, une certaine forme de société satisfaisant les aspirations de la grande comme de la petite bourgeoisie.

Pour la droite, le tournant crucial est l'année 1952 qui voit en mars l'investiture d'Antoine Pinay par les radicaux, le M.R.P. et les modérés. « L'homme au petit chapeau rond » a tout pour plaire aux classes moyennes. Fils d'un petit industriel de la région du Centre, il a un passé irréprochable d'ancien combattant. C'est un notable qui a gravi lentement les échelons du *cursus honorum* traditionnel : conseiller municipal à 37 ans, maire à 38, conseiller général à 43, député à 44, ministre à 57 et président du Conseil à 60 ans. Il a fait partie du Conseil national de Vichy mais n'a pas « collaboré ». Le Français moyen se retrouve en cet homme qui entend gérer l'Etat comme un sage père de famille sa petite entreprise. Le « mythe Pinay » naît de la réussite étonnante de sa politique économique, fondée sur la confiance et le bon sens. Il stabilise les prix, défend le franc, rassure les détenteurs de capitaux et redonne confiance aux industriels. Quelques mois après, un indépendant, Joseph Laniel, devient président du Conseil et, à la fin de 1953, un autre modéré, René Coty, accède à la plus haute charge de l'Etat.

Les indépendants ne sont pas les seuls à faire partie de la droite libérale. A côté d'eux, il faut désormais mentionner les radicaux. C'est une singulière trajectoire qu'a accomplie leur parti en trois quarts de siècle. Venus de l'extrême gauche où ils incarnaient le militarisme anticlérical et le jacobinisme « rouge », ils se situaient au centre à la fin de la III° République. Après la Libération, le radicalisme semble rejeté à droite par la poussée communiste et socialiste et surtout par l'apparition d'un courant démocrate-chrétien aux idées sociales beaucoup plus hardies. Il s'identifie à un passé dont personne ne veut plus, la III° République. Il semble avoir atteint tous ses objectifs avant la première guerre mondiale : réformes démocratiques, libertés individuelles, liberté de la presse, séparation de l'Eglise et de l'Etat. Lorsque le libéralisme conservateur admit la démocratie, rien, hormis la laïcité, ne le séparait plus de lui : économiquement, les radicaux défendent, comme les descendants de Méline, le libéralisme, la propriété privée, l'initiative individuelle. Comme eux ils sont antidirigistes et anticommunistes. La société idéale selon Alain *(Le citoyen contre les pouvoirs)* est-elle fondamentalement différente de celle de M. Pinay ? Reste, il est vrai, la question scolaire. Les indépendants, sans être à proprement parler des cléricaux, réprouvent le combat anticlérical alors que les radicaux ont été de toutes les luttes anticléricales, et chacun sait, comme l'a dit Paul Sérant, qu'il est « plus important en France pour être classé « à gauche » d'être « laïc » que d'être audacieux dans le domaine social ». Or, après 1945, les radicaux sont divisés sur ce terrain. Le parti est travaillé par une tendance néo-radicale (B. Lafay, J.-P. David, A. Morice, R. Mayer, F. Gaillard, E. Faure) qui souhaite l'atténuation du laïcisme. 46 radicaux sur 75 votent la loi Barangé (1951).

On peut dire que sous la IVe République le radicalisme se situe objectivement à droite, en dépit des alliances électorales qu'il peut rechercher à gauche. Rien dans son idéologie ni dans la composition sociologique de son électorat ne le distingue vraiment du libéralisme. La preuve n'en est-elle pas que toutes les tentatives faites pour ramener le Parti radical à gauche se sont soldées par des échecs : la scission des radicaux progressistes en 1946 et surtout le mendésisme à partir de 1954 qui fait éclater le parti et se termine en 1959 par l'exclusion de Pierre Mendès France.

2. La droite autoritaire. — La droite autoritaire, contrairement à la droite libérale, n'apparaît que par intermittence. Ce caractère éphémère vient de ce que la synthèse du nationalisme et de la démocratie, la combinaison de l'appel au peuple et de l'appel au soldat qui en constitue la nature profonde, ne peuvent se réaliser sans la présence d'un chef incontesté, d'un homme « providentiel ». Cent ans après l'élection de Louis-Napoléon Bonaparte, soixante ans après la tentative avortée du général Boulanger, la droite autoritaire connaît un spectaculaire renouveau avec le Rassemblement du Peuple français du général de Gaulle. Les hommes ne se ressemblent pas. Ils n'ont ni le même style, ni la même profondeur historique, ni la même destinée. Mais les phénomènes ont à des degrés divers la même parenté : « Le gaullisme, écrit alors

Raymond Aron, représente bien une espèce de l'opposition de droite ; il appartient à la tradition bonapartiste qui est spécifiquement française. »

Dans l'esprit de son fondateur, le R.P.F. doit être une machine de guerre destinée à faire éclater le « système ». Dès sa création, le 14 avril 1947, le nouveau mouvement connaît un vif succès et recueille un grand nombre d'adhésions. Il n'entend nullement s'identifier aux partis classiques dont il condamne la nocivité. C'est un rassemblement ouvert à tous les Français autour d'une « certaine idée de la France ». Le R.P.F. admet d'ailleurs la double appartenance de ses militants à d'autres partis et à son mouvement. Mais les autres partis, conscients du danger, refuseront ce droit à leurs membres, les radicaux les derniers (mars 1951). Le thème central est la réforme de l'Etat. Il s'agit de constituer, en opposition à la IVe République, une démocratie forte, fondée sur de nouvelles bases, de restaurer la dignité et l'autorité de l'Etat. Anti-parlementaire, le R.P.F. pourrait faire sien le slo-gan boulangiste : Dissolution, Révision, Consti-tuante. De la droite autoritaire il hérite également un nationalisme d'autant plus exacerbé qu'on se trouve alors au plus fort de la tension Est-Ouest. Une troisième guerre mondiale est redoutée. Entre 1947 et 1953 des rixes éclatent au Quartier latin entre jeunes gaullistes et militants communistes. Le géné-ral, voyant en ces derniers des agents de l'étranger qui par leurs idées se sont retranchés de la commu-nauté nationale, les appelle « séparatistes ». Au danger stalinien s'ajoute la dénonciation du mili-tarisme germanique. De Gaulle critique en des termes sévères la politique de rapprochement avec l'Allemagne, allant jusqu'à déclarer que par ce moyen le régime prépare la formation du IVe Reich.

Pour cette raison, il est systématiquement hostile à la construction européenne, à la C.E.C.A. (1) et surtout à la C.E.D. (2) dont le projet prévoyait la formation d'un commandement militaire européen intégré. Pour torpiller les tentatives d'Europe supranationale, d' « Europe allemande », le R.P.F. sera conduit par revirement tactique à se rapprocher de ses ennemis « séparatistes » qui pour d'autres raisons critiquent la politique européenne de Robert Schuman.

Comme l'a écrit F. Goguel, le mouvement gaulliste « est loin d'être toute la droite et il est autre chose qu'elle ». Aux élections municipales d'octobre 1947 il connaît un éclatant succès, y compris dans des villes de tradition socialiste comme Marseille et Lille. Il recueille environ 40 % des suffrages exprimés dans les communes de plus de 9 000 habitants. Un véritable raz de marée. Aux législatives du 17 juin 1951, malgré une loi électorale compliquée conçue contre lui et le Parti communiste, il conquiert 117 sièges à l'Assemblée nationale. Il a obtenu de nombreuses voix dans les banlieues urbaines et dans les arrondissements à prédominance ouvrière. Comme le boulangisme autrefois, le R.P.F. a coalisé sous son nom une partie de la droite et une fraction non négligeable d'électeurs de gauche. Son électorat comprend même davantage d'ouvriers que celui de la S.F.I.O. Il le doit sans doute plus à la personnalité du général de Gaulle qu'à son programme social d'association capital-travail, déjà développé avant lui par le P.S.F. du colonel de La Rocque. Fort de ses succès, le mouvement s'enferme dans une tactique intransigeante et un splendide isolement qui, loin de parvenir à la décomposition

(1) Communauté européenne du Charbon et de l'Acier.
(2) Communauté européenne de Défense.

du régime, sont une des causes de son propre éclatement. Le R.P.F. regroupe des éléments hétérogènes, en particulier des membres de la droite conservatrice qui aspirent à entrer dans le jeu parlementaire, c'est-à-dire, pour le général, à « aller à la soupe ». En mars 1952, 27 députés R.P.F. votent l'investiture d'Antoine Pinay, rompent avec le gaullisme et forment un groupe d'Action républicaine et sociale, apparenté au Centre national des Indépendants. L'année suivante, des députés R.P.F. deviennent ministres dans le gouvernement Laniel. Au lieu d'attirer les indépendants dans l'opposition, ce sont ces derniers qui ont brisé l'élan gaulliste. Les élections municipales d'avril 1953 marquent le reflux de la marée R.P.F. Celui-ci ne totalise que 10,6 % des sièges. Le général abandonne ses élus et en 1955 se retire de la vie politique. Aux élections législatives, les derniers gaullistes, militant cette fois en leur nom propre, n'ont qu'une vingtaine d'élus, dont un tiers derrière M. Chaban-Delmas et sous la bannière du Front républicain.

3. **L'extrême droite.** — Plus durement touchée après la Libération, parce que plus sévèrement compromise, l'extrême droite sera plus longue à refaire surface. Autour de petites revues les chapelles se reconstituent : l'école d'Action française avec *Aspects de la France* et une fraction plus moderne du maurrassisme avec *La Nation française* (Pierre Boutang), les nostalgiques de Vichy avec *Questions actuelles, Ecrits de Paris, Rivarol, Réalisme, Paroles françaises*, les fascistes avec *Défense de l'Occident* animée par le beau-frère de Robert Brasillach, Maurice Bardèche. Dans les années 50, on voit renaître une extrême droite littéraire dont l'anticonformisme et l'impertinence ne sont pas sans rap-

peler la thématique de la jeune droite littéraire des années 30 : le groupe de *La Parisienne* (avec Roger Nimier, Jacques Laurent, Antoine Blondin). Peu à peu, les militants se renouvellent. Les étudiants, renouant avec la tradition d'avant-guerre, remplacent les rescapés de la collaboration. A partir de 1954 (défaite de Dien-Bien-Phu, conférence de Genève, début de la guerre d'Algérie), étudiants et « anciens d'Indo » se retrouvent au sein du mouvement Jeune Nation dont l'emblème, la croix celtique, est peint sur les murs de la capitale. Cette nouvelle ligue, xénophobe, antibolchevique et anti-américaine, se propose de construire un « Etat nationaliste, autoritaire, populaire et hiérarchisé ».

Beaucoup plus important est le phénomène poujadiste. Au départ il s'agit d'une protestation spontanée de boutiquiers et d'artisans contre la fiscalité écrasante. Le mouvement naît d'une manifestation à Saint-Céré le 23 juillet 1953, sous l'impulsion d'un papetier, Pierre Poujade, fils d'un militant d'Action française. Il s'intitule bientôt U.D.C.A. (Union de Défense des Commerçants et Artisans). Dans les premiers mois de 1954, le nouveau syndicat, qui met en cause les monopoles, les féodalités financières, les trusts capitalistes, bénéficie de l'appui communiste. La rupture avec la gauche est consommée l'année suivante. Poujade se rapproche de l'extrême droite, noue des contacts avec Dorgères, ancien responsable de la Corporation paysanne sous Vichy, qui s'était illustré entre les deux guerres par ses commandos de « chouans », les *chemises vertes*. Le poujadisme est à son apogée. L'U.D.C.A. compte plusieurs dizaines de milliers d'adhérents, dispose d'une presse importante *(L'Union, Fraternité française)*. Des unions parallèles sont créées pour élargir le mouvement à l'ensemble des classes moyennes. Le programme politique est simple : la convocation des Etats généraux doit résoudre tous les problèmes. Le poujadisme est plus à l'aise pour dénoncer les tares du « système » que pour proposer des solutions constructives. Aux élections du 2 janvier 1956, lançant le slogan « Pour en sortir, sortez les sortants », il obtient un succès inattendu qui surprend tous les experts politiques : 2,5 millions de voix et 52 élus. L'extrême droite fait une entrée fracassante au Parlement. La presse de gauche crie au fascisme. On surnomme le papetier de Saint-Céré « Poujadolf ». Le dégoût du parlementarisme, l'antisémitisme diffus, la nostalgie corporative, le besoin de nouveauté et d'ordre exprimés par le poujadisme rappellent les thèmes de *L'Ami du Peuple* de F. Coty. Dans une certaine mesure, le mouvement illustre, comme l'ont dit certains, la conception politique d'Alain, celle du « citoyen contre les pouvoirs ».

Que le poujadisme ait été un nationalisme semblable à celui des ligues d'avant-guerre, l'évolution du mouvement pendant la guerre d'Algérie le prouve amplement. Il ne se confond ni avec le fascisme ni avec la droite autoritaire. Le R.P.F. a une clientèle urbaine, surtout implantée au nord de la France. Le poujadisme a une clientèle rurale, celle de la « France pauvre », à l'ouest d'une ligne allant du Havre à Marseille. Il s'effondrera en 1958, après avoir symbolisé une sorte de jacquerie moderne de groupes sociaux menacés par la société industrielle.

II. — Le gaullisme et la droite

Depuis la crise de Suez (1956), le nationalisme de sentiment a gagné une large fraction de l'opinion, y compris à gauche. Les passions se cristallisent sur le drame algérien. « L'Algérie, c'est la France », déclare François Mitterrand à l'Assemblée nationale. Le 13 mai 1958 n'est pas une sédition militaire, mais, comme l'a dit André Siegfried, « un 6 février qui a réussi », un soulèvement populaire que l'armée est parvenue à encadrer. Cependant la situation est vite bloquée. Entre le maintien du « système » et le coup de force en métropole, l'opinion découvre peu à peu une troisième solution : le retour du général de Gaulle qui seul apparaît en mesure d'empêcher la guerre civile. Lui-même déclare qu'il se tient « prêt à assumer les pouvoirs de la République ». Tous les partis à l'exception des extrêmes se rallient à lui. La Ve République est née.

1. **Nature du gaullisme.** — Le gaullisme est avant tout une idéologie de rassemblement qui récuse la distinction traditionnelle droite-gauche et entend se placer au-dessus des partis et des divisions des Français.

Charles de Gaulle, par ses origines, sa famille, son éducation, sa carrière militaire, est un homme de droite. Issu d'un milieu traditionaliste, il a été marqué politiquement par la génération nationaliste de 1910, celle d'Agathon. Mais lui-même n'est ni dreyfusard, ni antidreyfusard. Son nationalisme ne s'apparente pas à celui de Déroulède, encore moins à celui de l'Action française. C'est un nationalisme ouvert, héroïque, jacobin, centralisateur. L'auteur du *Fil de l'épée* se méfie des idéologies. Il croit à l'esprit des peuples et pense que le Français ou l'Allemand resteront toujours identiques à eux-mêmes. « Les réalités d'aujourd'hui, dit-il, ce sont les nations. » De là son refus de l'intégration européenne comme de la subordination aux Etats-Unis.

De Gaulle croit à certaines évolutions irréversibles, au « sens de l'Histoire » (« Il faut que la France épouse son siècle »). Mais ni le poids de l'Histoire, ni la contrainte du progrès ne doivent dans son esprit détourner un peuple de l'ambition collective. Le gaullisme est un empirisme au service de la grandeur et de l'indépendance nationales.

De Gaulle croit en la démocratie, mais, comme tout homme de la droite autoritaire, réduit celle-ci au suffrage universel, à la démocratie directe. Lui-même prétend incarner la légitimité depuis 1940. Il est le « guide » qui doit exprimer seul les aspirations de la nation dans ses profondeurs. La confiance, il la reçoit directement du peuple par référendum. Aux partis, qu'il critique vivement comme tous les corps intermédiaires, il abandonne le jeu de la politique au jour le jour, mais leur dénie le droit de remettre en cause les grandes options de sa politique.

Enfin, sur le plan social, de Gaulle pense réconcilier les classes grâce à un système d'association capital-travail ou de « participation », troisième voie entre le socialisme et le capitalisme mais dont les contours, hormis quelques mesures limitées, ne sont jamais apparus avec netteté.

L'ensemble forme un mélange d'idées propres à la droite classique (l'équilibre budgétaire, l'attachement à l'étalon or...) et d'idées nouvelles (la planification, la politique des revenus, l'aide aux nations sous-développées, le rapprochement avec le tiers monde...). Le gaullisme, avatar moderne de la droite autoritaire, cherche à concilier, comme autrefois le bonapartisme, l'ordre et le progrès.

Le propre et en même temps l'ambiguïté de cette tradition de droite est de rassembler autour d'elle des hommes de formation politique radicalement opposée. Le gaullisme n'a pas échappé à la règle. Il groupe des doctrinaires jacobins (Michel Debré), des gestionnaires (Georges Pompidou), des réformistes (Chaban-Delmas), des hommes de gauche (Capitant, Vallon) ou d'extrême gauche (d'Astier de

La Vigerie), des intellectuels (Mauriac, Malraux...).

Sans doute est-ce la cause de la multiplicité des aspects du gaullisme. Un peu comme sous le Second Empire où existaient différents bonapartismes, on constate au cours d'une même période la coexistence de plusieurs formes de gaullisme : antiparlementaire, réformiste, social, orléaniste, activiste.

Si l'on passe au niveau électoral, la diversité est plus grande encore. Le gaullisme apparaît bien comme une idéologie de rassemblement. L'électorat gaulliste est sociologiquement plus étendu que l'électorat modéré. Une large fraction de la gauche a voté pour le général, séduite sans doute par l'image du libérateur de la France et la politique étrangère de la Ve République.

Là encore il faudrait distinguer le gaullisme référendaire du gaullisme législatif, l'électorat du président de celui de ses partisans, le premier plus vaste, moins conservateur que le second.

2. **Le gaullisme contre les droites.** — A) *Les activistes.* — L'affaire algérienne met en évidence l'incompatibilité idéologique qui existe entre la droite autoritaire et le nationalisme de doctrine. Certes, tous les partisans de « l'Algérie française » ne se classent pas à l'extrême droite. Il y a parmi eux des nationalistes de sentiment, des socialistes ou des radicaux jacobins. Mais l'extrême droite forme le noyau dur de la résistance à la politique algérienne du général de Gaulle.

Devant la lassitude de l'opinion, il apparaît clairement à partir de 1960 que le maintien de l'Algérie dans la République passe par la répudiation de la démocratie et l'instauration d'un régime de type nouveau. Les ligues activistes, de nombreux militaires en acceptent pleinement les conséquences et appellent de leurs vœux un régime dictatorial. L'idée consiste à faire « basculer l'armée », déchirée entre l'obéissance et la fidélité à la parole donnée aux musulmans. Certains officiers, influencés par les techniques de la guerre révolutionnaire découvertes en Indochine, prônent ouvertement un régime fasciste, autoritaire, populaire et social. D'autres préconisent la Contre-Révolution catholique comme unique moyen de défendre la civilisation occidentale face à l'Islam et au marxisme. Tous sont logiques avec eux-mêmes en soutenant l'insurrection des barricades en janvier 1960, le putsch des généraux en avril 1961, puis la résistance de l'O.A.S. (Organisation de l'Armée secrète). Le gaullisme refuse de suivre les activistes dans cette voie extrême. Il en résulte au sein du mouvement une série de crises (octobre 1959, février 1960) qui s'achève par l'exclusion des nationalistes de l'U.N.R. (Union pour la Nouvelle République).

B) *L'opposition des modérés.* — La droite libérale ralliée au général de Gaulle en 1958 se détache progressivement de lui en raison de sa politique algérienne, de sa politique européenne et atlantique et de l'évolution du régime vers un gouvernement personnel.

En 1958, les modérés remportent un succès éclatant (24 % des suffrages exprimés, 133 élus) qui fait suite à leur percée sous la IVe République. Ils participent au pouvoir avec les gaullistes. Mais, en janvier 1960, Antoine Pinay, en désaccord avec le gouvernement, quitte la rue de Rivoli. A l'automne de 1962, Paul Reynaud prend la tête de l'opposition parlementaire en rejetant avec vigueur le projet d'élection du Président de la République au suffrage universel. « Pour nous, républicains, s'écrie-t-il au Palais-Bourbon, la France est ici et non ailleurs. » Il exprimait ainsi toute la philosophie orléaniste méfiante à l'égard de la démocratie directe et de la souveraineté populaire.

Les frontières de la droite libérale semblent s'étendre. Dans les années 60, on peut constater, en dépit de la permanence des appareils politiques jaloux de leur indépendance, une convergence sur le plan idéologique du libéralisme conservateur, du radicalisme et de la démocratie chrétienne.

Le M.R.P. était en 1945 plus proche des socialistes que les radicaux en raison de son programme économique et social. Mais il était antilaïque. Quinze ans après, la situation est inversée. Le M.R.P. est à droite des radicaux. Dès 1952, on peut percevoir cette évolution : il gouverne sans les socialistes, avec les radicaux et les modérés. Il se trouve alors écartelé entre des militants qui penchent à gauche et des électeurs qui sont de droite. Les pesanteurs sociologiques finissent par l'emporter. Sous la Ve République, le M.R.P. participe aux gouvernements Debré et Pompidou. Mais le 16 mai 1962 les ministres M.R.P. démissionnent à la suite d'une conférence de presse du général de Gaulle dans laquelle il précisait ses conceptions européennes. La rupture définitive avec la gauche sera consommée lorsque le M.R.P., en 1965, fera échouer le projet de grande fédération de la gauche parce qu'elle se réclame du socialisme.

Quant aux radicaux, divisés depuis le mendésisme, ils ont

cherché surtout à refaire leur unité en se réconciliant avec leur aile droite. Si certains penchent sentimentalement à gauche, comme ils le montreront plus tard en suivant F. Mitterrand, l'idéologie radicale, elle, n'est plus qu'une « variante de l'idéologie modérée » (R. Rémond).

Aux élections de novembre 1962, la droite libérale et modérée s'effondre. Les indépendants n'ont qu'une cinquantaine d'élus, le M.R.P. une quarantaine. La droite a voté massivement pour les candidats revêtus du label de la Ve République. Les libéraux n'ont plus le choix qu'entre la disparition ou le ralliement. C'est cette dernière solution qu'adoptent 35 indépendants qui forment derrière Valéry Giscard d'Estaing un groupe parlementaire prêt à collaborer avec les gaullistes, les Républicains indépendants.

3. La fédération des droites. — Dès 1962, il apparaît que la droite française a tendance à constituer un bloc majoritaire animé par les gaullistes. L'opposition européenne et libérale parvient néanmoins à mettre le général de Gaulle en ballottage aux élections présidentielles de décembre 1965, grâce à la candidature de Jean Lecanuet (15,8 % des suffrages exprimés). Mais les bases du Centre démocrate, créé autour du M.R.P. au lendemain de la campagne électorale, sont très étroites. Le « centrisme », composé surtout d'hommes de droite ou de centre-droit, est partagé entre l'anti-gaullisme systématique et le ralliement à une majorité conservatrice. L'unité de candidature imposée par les gaullistes aux élections de mars 1967 anéantit son espoir d'arbitrer la situation en même temps qu'elle accélère le ralliement de la droite au général de Gaulle.

La crise de mai 1968 balaie la thèse selon laquelle les pays industriels installés paresseusement dans leur confort ne peuvent connaître d'affrontement politique violent. Idéologiquement, l'événement majeur est l'apparition à la gauche des communistes d'une nouvelle force politique, l'ultra-gauche, composée d'un ensemble hétéroclite de maoïstes, trotskistes, anarchistes, chrétiens progressistes qui ont arraché au Parti communiste français le flambeau révolutionnaire. Pendant les événements de mai le P.C.F. se trouve paradoxalement rejeté dans le camp des défenseurs de l'ordre. Les élections de juin 1968, en revanche, se déroulent dans le cadre classique d'un affrontement droite-gauche : d'un côté les gaullistes et ses alliés, de l'autre les partis et forces de gauche. Il n'est pas douteux que la peur du communisme et de la révolution sociale a poussé l'électorat flottant vers la coalition de droite. Le gaullisme a ainsi poursuivi son rôle de fédérateur des droites, ne laissant qu'une étroite bande de terrain aux irréductibles de l'extrême droite et du centre. Tixier-Vignancour, Poujade, d'anciens sympathisants de l'O.A.S. se sont ralliés à cette vaste coalition. Le défilé de la Concorde, le 30 mai, scellait en quelque sorte la réconciliation des droites hier encore meurtries et divisées par les nostalgies algériennes.

Le gaullisme a rallié également selon son habitude une large fraction de l'électorat de gauche. Ainsi s'explique sa forte pénétration dans des départements du sud de la France, votant habituellement à gauche. Avec 46 % des votants et près de 300 élus, l'Union des Démocrates pour la République (U.D.R.) dispose de la majorité absolue à l'Assemblée, sans avoir besoin de la soixantaine d'indépendants « giscardiens ».

Le gaullisme n'est cependant pas parvenu à fusionner les anciennes familles de droite. Les modérés sont toujours présents, soit à l'intérieur de la majorité, soit au sein d'une opposition dite « centriste », qui groupe sous la bannière du Centre démocrate des libéraux et le dernier carré des démocrates-chrétiens. Leur principal souci est de renouer le dialogue avec les corps intermédiaires, de mettre un terme, selon l'expression de M. Giscard d'Estaing, à « l'exercice solitaire du pouvoir ».

117

Cette fronde, de Gaulle pense la mater en lui imposant son terrain de bataille préféré : le référendum. L'hostilité de la gauche, la défection d'une partie des indépendants provoquent, le 27 avril 1969, le rejet par le peuple du projet de loi sur la régionalisation et la réforme du Sénat. Sur cet échec se termine la carrière politique de Charles de Gaulle.

III. — L'après-gaullisme

La victoire, le 15 juin 1969, de Georges Pompidou sur Alain Poher confirmait, par-delà l'échec du général, la tendance du gaullisme à rassembler la majorité des droites. Le nouveau président a des conceptions très voisines de celles de son prédécesseur sur l'Etat, la nation, l'Europe ou encore l'Alliance atlantique. Pourtant, le néo-gaullisme de Pompidou n'a pas un caractère aussi tranché que son modèle. Si les grandes options gaullistes subsistent, si les institutions de la Ve République s'enracinent, certains aspects du « système gaulliste » tendent à disparaître ou à s'estomper : l'hostilité aux notables et aux corps intermédiaires, la pratique plébiscitaire (échec du référendum d'avril 1972), la participation... Georges Pompidou se fixe pour objectif de transformer la France, avec prudence et dans la stabilité politique, en un grand pays moderne et industriel. Conservateur éclairé, il cherche à regrouper derrière lui les centristes d'opposition, à réconcilier les droites divisées, à s'appuyer enfin sur « la majorité silencieuse ». Il rêve d'une synthèse entre la droite autoritaire et la droite libérale, entre la tradition gaulliste, jacobine, nationaliste et la droite modérée, parlementaire, européenne, entre la « continuité » et l' « ouverture ».

Les élections de mars 1973, qui apportent la victoire aux candidats de la majorité élus sous l'étiquette d'Union des Républicains de Progrès, témoignent du ralliement massif de l'électorat réformateur à cette politique. Le « centrisme » anti-gaulliste disparaît quasiment. L'unification des droites et des « centres » achève le mouvement de bipolarisation amorcé depuis 1962. Mais par là même le néo-gaullisme pompidolien s'ancre plus profondément à droite, perd l'appui de nombreux gaullistes de gauche et le soutien de milieux populaires acquis par le général de Gaulle (en dépit des thèmes sociaux de la « nouvelle société » de J. Chaban-Delmas et du programme de Provins de P. Messmer).

Les élections présidentielles qui suivent la disparition de

G. Pompidou confirment cette tendance. La courte victoire, le 19 mai 1974, de Valéry Giscard d'Estaing (50,80 % des suffrages exprimés) est celle de toute la droite désormais unie. Jamais peut-être dans toute l'histoire de France la vie politique n'a paru à ce point simplifiée. D'un côté, le bloc des forces de droite, animé non plus par les gaullistes mais par les libéraux ; de l'autre, celui des forces de gauche, partis et syndicats, unis par le programme commun de gouvernement et la personnalité de F. Mitterrand.

Conscient des dangers que présenterait la prolongation de cette brutale coupure en deux camps, le nouveau président entend débloquer cette situation. Plus réformateur que conservateur, il met dès lors en chantier des réformes importantes qui sont loin, d'ailleurs, d'emporter l'entière adhésion de ceux qui l'ont élu. En même temps il cherche à rapprocher le pouvoir du peuple et l'administration de ses usagers. Son ambition est de parvenir à une « société libérale avancée », où les inégalités sociales seraient réduites, sans pour autant supprimer le moteur de l'initiative privée, et où les lois consacreraient l'évolution des mœurs et des mentalités. Son projet de démocratie pluraliste et libérale est exposé dans son livre *Démocratie française* (1976). Mais le « giscardisme », plus qu'une doctrine, est avant tout un style et un discours. Style jeune, moderne, décontracté, allégé des conventions et d'une certaine lourdeur empesée qui avaient été la marque des monarchies gaullienne et pompidolienne. Discours voulant séduire et convaincre, cherchant à désacraliser le pouvoir pour mieux le rapprocher des citoyens.

En 1978, sous l'influence de Valéry Giscard d'Estaing, les mouvements qui soutiennent son action — Parti républicain (anciens Républicains indépendants), clubs Perspectives et Réalités, Centre des démocrates sociaux, Parti radical — se regroupent en une confédération, l'Union pour la Démocratie française (U.D.F.). C'est la preuve que sur le plan idéologique peu de choses séparaient encore la tradition modérée des traditions radicale et démocrate-chrétienne. Les giscardiens rêvent même un moment d'intégrer à l'U.D.F. une partie du courant social-démocrate qui a glissé au centre en raison de l'alliance socialo-communiste.

Quant aux gaullistes, traumatisés par la défaite de J. Chaban-Delmas aux présidentielles de 1974, ils sont repris en main par le Premier ministre Jacques Chirac, qui se fait nommer Secrétaire général de l'U.D.R. le 14 décembre 1974. D'aucuns pensent alors qu'il va « giscardiser » le parti gaulliste. Il n'en est rien. Le divorce entre le président et son Premier ministre (août 1976), qui ne s'entendent ni sur l'action à mener ni sur le style à adopter, n'entraîne pas une rupture entre giscardiens et gaullistes. Le nouveau Premier ministre, économiste réputé, Raymond Barre, passe pour être à la fois gaulliste et libéral. Mais, surtout à partir du 5 décembre 1976, date de création du Rassemblement pour la République (R.P.R.), on assiste à une rivalité entre les deux formations de la majorité, qui tourne parfois à la guerre larvée (affaires de la mairie de Paris, de l'appel de Cochin...). Malgré le dynamisme de son chef, le parti gaulliste ne parvient pas à retrouver sa puissance d'antan. Aux législatives de 1978, il obtient 22,6 % des suffrages exprimés et 148 élus contre 21,4 % et 137 élus à l'U.D.F. Aux élections européennes de 1979, il n'a que 16,3 % des voies contre 27,5 % à la liste giscardienne.

Le système des partis s'en trouve modifié : au lieu d'un système bipolaire on se trouve en présence d'un jeu à quatre : deux partis dans la majorité, deux dans l'opposition.

La guerre des chefs (Giscard-Chirac), le style sans séduction de Raymond Barre, la lassitude devant un pouvoir triste qui a perdu peu à peu le contact avec le peuple sont les principales causes de la désaffection de l'électorat majoritaire aux élections présidentielles de 1981 et de la victoire de F. Mitterrand.

IV. — La droite aujourd'hui

1. **Cohabitation et alternance.** — L'ampleur même de la victoire de la gauche — les socialistes ont à eux seuls la majorité à l'Assemblée — fait croire à celle-ci qu'elle peut « changer la vie » et la société alors qu'en réalité l'opinion ne lui en a pas donné le mandat. Les nationalisations, la socialisation progressive de l'économie, la mainmise du Parti socialiste sur la haute administration et l'audiovisuel, les erreurs, les maladresses du pouvoir heurtent l'opinion. Le 24 juin 1984, une vaste manifestation en faveur de l'école libre rassemble à Paris plus d'un million de personnes : la gauche est tournée sur son terrain traditionnel, celui des libertés. La droite retrouve du tonus et Jacques Chirac, maire de Paris et président du R.P.R., plus que Raymond Barre, en apparaît l'animateur. Malgré le changement de cap en matière

économique et le remplacement de Pierre Mauroy par Laurent Fabius à la tête du gouvernement, la gauche socialiste (qui s'est brouillée avec le Parti communiste) ne parvient pas à conserver le pouvoir. Les élections législatives du 16 mars 1986 ramènent une courte majorité de droite (291 députés sur 577).

Jacques Chirac est appelé à l'hôtel Matignon. S'ouvre alors, dans l'histoire de la Ve République, un nouveau chapitre, celui de la cohabitation entre un Président de gauche, qui ne veut ni se démettre ni se soumettre, et un Premier ministre porteur d'un projet politique tout différent. Au bout de deux ans, à son tour Jacques Chirac subit l'usure du pouvoir, d'autant que sa marge de manœuvre était restée étroite entre l'Élysée, l'opposition de gauche et d'extrême droite et la critique des « barristes ». L'élection présidentielle (24 avril-8 mai 1988) sanctionne l'incapacité du gouvernement à faire valoir les acquis de sa politique mais surtout la division des chefs (au premier tour, J. Chirac obtient 19,9 % des suffrages, à peine mieux qu'en 1981, et R. Barre seulement 16,5 %). François Mitterrand l'emporte aisément au second tour (54 %) alors que, dans le pays, la droite et l'extrême droite sont majoritaires. Aux législatives de juin, les candidatures uniques de l'U.D.F. et du R.P.R. parviennent à limiter la poussée de gauche : le P.S. n'a la majorité qu'avec le Parti communiste. Le gouvernement de Michel Rocard ne parvient pas à réaliser l'ouverture au centre, à laquelle renoncent ses successeurs Mme Edith Cresson et Pierre Bérégovoy. Usé par le pouvoir, secoué par le scandale de multiples « affaires », le Parti socialiste a connu parallèlement une crise et une mutation idéologiques considérables, passant en quelques années du « Programme commun » avec le Parti communiste, fondé sur la « rupture avec le capitalisme », aux thèmes de la libre entreprise, de l'économie de marché, de la privatisation des entreprises publiques et du franc fort, autant de thèmes appartenant jusque-là à la droite. Les élections législatives de mars 1993 consacrent la défaite des socialistes déconsidérés et la victoire des droites, amplifiée par le scrutin majoritaire et l'homogénéisation de la carte électorale. Avec 44 % des voix au premier tour, elles obtiennent à l'issue du second 484 sièges sur 577. C'est une nouvelle « assemblée introuvable ». Le gouvernement de cohabitation d'Edouard Balladur, associant gaullistes, libéraux et centristes, semble ouvrir une ère de néo-pompidolisme.

2. **L'extrême droite : du déclin au renouveau.** — De la fin de la guerre d'Algérie à l'arrivée de la gauche au pouvoir, l'extrême droite est en déclin. Comme le montrent les échecs aux élections présidentielles de Me Tixier-Vignancour en 1965 (5,3 %) et de J.-M. Le Pen (0,76 %) en 1974, une large partie de ses électeurs est revenue à des positions plus modérées. Les courants qui la composent ne sont plus que de minces filets. Le fascisme ne survit que dans l'esprit de quelques nostalgiques et les petites ligues qui choisissent la violence (Occident, Ordre nouveau) n'échappent pas à la dissolution. Renonçant à cette agitation impuissante, certains optent pour le combat culturel : ce sera la « nouvelle droite » (les revues *Eléments*, *Nouvelle Ecole*, le Groupement de Recherche et d'Etude pour la Civilisation européenne, G.R.E.C.E.). Ce courant, dont M. Alain de Benoist est l'animateur, axe son combat contre la démocratie égalitaire, le nivellement des particularismes, exalte le retour au paganisme contre le christianisme et retrouve les thèmes élitistes et biologiques de la « droite révolutionnaire ». Après avoir connu quel-

ques succès en direction de la droite classique (*Le Figaro-Magazine*, le Club de l'Horloge), il perd ses appuis et entre en léthargie. La situation n'est pas moins confuse chez les traditionalistes où, à côté des diverses chapelles qui se disputent l'orthodoxie maurrassienne, les catholiques intégristes (derrière Mgr Lefebvre ou l'abbé G. de Nantes) mènent un combat d'arrière-garde contre la démocratie. Bref, en mai 1981, l'extrême droite ne compte plus en tant que force politique. Cinq ans plus tard, le Front national fait une entrée spectaculaire au Palais-Bourbon et devient un parti avec lequel les autres doivent désormais compter. Que s'est-il passé ?

Le Front national, créé en octobre 1972, c'est d'abord un homme : Jean-Marie Le Pen, un « baroudeur » et un « activiste » plus qu'un brasseur d'idées, qui a participé à tous les combats de l'extrême droite depuis 1955 : le poujadisme dont il fut l'un des représentants à l'Assemblée nationale, l'Algérie française, la campagne de Me Tixier-Vignancour. Ce que l'on a appelé « l'effet Le Pen » se fait sentir dès les municipales de mars 1983 et s'amplifie à l'automne à Dreux, où la liste conduite par J.-P. Stirbois recueille 16,7 % des suffrages. La consécration est obtenue aux élections européennes de juin 1984 : 11 % des suffrages (2,2 millions de voix) et dix élus. L'adoption de la représentation proportionnelle permet au Front national et à ses alliés de recueillir 2,7 millions de voix aux législatives de mars 1986 (9,65 % des suffrages). Dès lors, celui-ci fait figure de parti politique respectable ayant pignon sur rue, disposant d'un groupe parlementaire de 35 élus, de 135 conseillers régionaux, d'une école de cadres, d'une presse et de plus de 30 000 adhérents. Aux élections présidentielles de 1988, Le Pen regroupe sur son nom 14,4 % des suffrages exprimés. Au premier tour des législatives qui suivent, son mouvement obtient le même résultat qu'en 1986 (9,65 %) mais n'a qu'un élu par suite du changement de mode de scrutin.

Electoralement, le Front national réalise ses meilleures performances dans les départements du sud de la France où la résurgence d'un vote « pied noir » s'est conjuguée aux réactions « sécuritaires » et anti-immigrées des classes moyennes : Bouches-du-Rhône, Alpes-Maritimes, Pyrénées-Orientales, Var... Aux présidentielles de 1988, l'effet Le Pen s'est étendu au Lyonnais, au Dauphiné, à l'Alsace, à la Lorraine. Le « lepénisme » chasse sur les terres de gauche et remporte des succès dans un électorat populaire frappé par le chômage. Aux législatives de mars 1993, le Front national obtient un bon résultat (12,42 %), mais depuis les cantonales de mars 1992, il est isolé, marginalisé car la droite parlementaire a coupé tous les ponts avec lui.

Les thèmes du Front répondent à l'attente de l'électorat de droite attaché à l'ordre : la préférence nationale, la restauration des valeurs morales, la lutte contre l'infiltration marxiste, la réglementation du droit de grève... Fait nouveau à l'extrême droite, le mouvement entend se situer à l'intérieur du jeu démocratique, sans remettre en cause de manière radicale les institutions.

Idéologiquement, le Front se rattache moins à la contre-révolution ou au néo-fascisme qu'au nationalisme populaire, cette vieille droite conservatrice, xénophobe, antisémite, effrayée par les mutations socio-économiques, dont les ligues puis le poujadisme ont été un moment l'expression. Il est vrai cependant que le parti est composite : on y trouve des nostalgiques du pétainisme, des anciens de l'O.A.S., des maurrassiens, des intégristes, des anciens du R.P.R. et du Parti républicain.

Jamais, depuis 1945, l'extrême droite n'avait

connu un tel succès. C'est assurément la conséquence de tensions et d'exaspérations nées de la crise économique : la montée du chômage, la présence d'îlots immigrés dans les grandes agglomérations, la violence, l'insécurité quotidienne. « J'ai dit tout haut ce que les gens pensent tout bas ! » s'exclamera Le Pen. À cela il faut ajouter la crise des valeurs et des mœurs depuis 1968, la crainte pour nombre de Français d'une perte de leur identité nationale et culturelle.

3. **La droite classique : crise et mutation.** — Que reste-t-il du gaullisme aujourd'hui ? Certes, il fait partie de notre histoire, de notre patrimoine commun. Le large consensus qui existe autour de la Constitution donne au général de Gaulle l'image d'un « père fondateur » auquel la classe politique tout entière se sent obligée de rendre hommage. Mais, au fil des années, on ne peut manquer d'être frappé par la lente désagrégation du système mis en place par lui. En tant que mouvement politique, le gaullisme n'a cessé de perdre des soutiens. En 1985, un sondage de la S.O.F.R.E.S. indiquait que seulement 13 % des personnes interrogées se déclaraient gaullistes. Plus grave, ce qui faisait l'originalité de ce courant, qui permettait de rassembler des hommes aussi différents que Jean-Marcel Jeanneney, Edgar Faure, Edgar Pisani, Michel Droit et Michel Debré, n'existe plus. Des cassures suivies de départs se sont produites. Repris en main par Jacques Chirac le mouvement a évolué vers la droite. Si le R.P.R. n'apparaît pas plus conservateur que l'U.D.F., il n'est pas davantage progressiste ou réformiste. En réalité, les enquêtes et les sondages les plus récents montrent l'homogénéité profonde de l'électorat de droite et du centre-droit, que se disputent aujourd'hui les deux partis alliés, le R.P.R. et l'U.D.F.

C'est cette homogénéité électorale, associée à l'union des deux partis, qui explique la large victoire des droites en mars 1993. Il reste que le référendum sur le traité de Maestricht, voté en septembre 1992 à une courte majorité, a mis en relief l'existence au sein du R.P.R. d'un puissant courant hostile à la construction d'une Europe supranationale (Philippe Seguin, Charles Pasqua). Est-ce le prélude à la naissance d'un néo-gaullisme, national et populaire, qui viendrait mordre sur l'électorat du Front national ? Il n'est pas exclu en tout cas que le débat sur l'Europe et l'identité française constitue dans les années à venir un thème sensible pour la majorité de droite.

Que de changements dans la société française et dans le monde en une vingtaine d'années, que de tourbillons : la fin de la civilisation rurale, le développement d'une société individualiste et hédoniste, la crise des valeurs familiales, l'implosion des systèmes communistes, la fin de la guerre froide, la mort du marxisme, la crise de la pensée socialiste, la montée des peurs, l'immigration, l'explosion du chômage, le drame des villes et des banlieues, les problèmes de l'environnement, l'information-spectacle, les dérèglements des systèmes médiatiques... Les enjeux du IIIe millénaire ne sont plus ceux de la société d'après-guerre. Et pourtant, notre système politique fonctionne toujours selon le même mode binaire. Le renouvellement des thèmes et des partis n'exclut nullement la permanence des familles et des traditions politiques. La droite et la gauche ne seront peut-être plus demain ce qu'elles sont aujourd'hui. Mais, sans doute, subsistera-t-il toujours une droite et une gauche, telles deux dimensions antagonistes et complémentaires rythmant les grandes pulsations de notre vie politique.

BIBLIOGRAPHIE

AZEMA Jean-Pierre, *La collaboration 1940-1944*, Paris, P.U.F., 1975.
BLUCHE Frédéric, *Le bonapartisme. Aux origines de la droite autoritaire (1800-1850)*, Paris, N.E.L., 1980.
DREYFUS François-Georges, *De Gaulle et le gaullisme*, Paris, P.U.F., 1982.
GIRARDET Raoul, *Le nationalisme français (1871-1914)*, Paris, Colin, 1970.
GOGUEL François, *La politique des partis sous la IIIe République*, Paris, Seuil, 1958.
HIRSCHMANN Albert O., *Deux siècles de rhétorique réactionnaire*, Paris, Fayard, 1991.
JARDIN André, *Histoire du libéralisme politique, de la crise de l'absolutisme à la Constitution de 1875*, Paris, Hachette, 1985.
LAPONCE A., *Left and Right. The topography of political perceptions*, University of Toronto Press, 1981.
MILZA Pierre, *Fascisme français, passé et présent*, Paris, Flammarion, 1987.
NGUYEN Victor, *Aux origines de l'Action française. Intelligence et politique à l'aube du XXe siècle*, Paris, Fayard, 1991.
OESCHLIN J.-J., *Le mouvement ultra-royaliste sous la Restauration (1814-1830)*, Paris, L.G.D.G., 1960.
PAXTON Robert O., *La France de Vichy (1940-1944)*, Paris, Seuil, 1973.
RÉMOND René, *Les droites en France*, Paris, Aubier-Montaigne, 1982.
RIALS Stéphane, *Révolution et contre-révolution au XIXe siècle*, Paris, D.U.C./Albatros, 1987.
SAINT-VICTOR Jacques de, *La chute des aristocrates (1787-1792). La naissance de la droite*, Paris, Perrin, 1992.
SIRINELLI Jean-François (sous la direction de), *Histoire des droites en France. Politique, cultures, sensibilités*, 3 vol., Paris, Gallimard, 1992.
STERNHELL Zeev, *La droite révolutionnaire (1885-1914). Les origines françaises du fascisme*, Paris, Seuil, 1978.
TOUCHARD Jean, *Le gaullisme, 1940-1969*, Paris, Seuil, 1978.
TULARD Jean (sous la direction de), *La Contre-Révolution. Origines, histoire, postérité*, Paris, Perrin, 1990.
WINOCK Michel, *Nationalisme, antisémitisme et fascisme en France*, Paris, Seuil, 1990.
WINOCK Michel (sous la direction de), *Histoire de l'extrême droite en France*, Paris, Seuil, 1993.
ZELDIN Théodore, *Histoire des passions françaises (1848-1945)*, t. 4, *Colère et politique*, Paris, Seuil, 1981.

TABLE DES MATIÈRES

Imprimé en France
Imprimerie des Presses Universitaires de France
73, avenue Ronsard, 41100 Vendôme
Janvier 1994 — No 39 747